GOOD HOUSEKEEPING
HEALTHY COOKING

GOOD HOUSEKEEPING
HEALTHY COOKING

LIMITED EDITIONS
BOOKTITLES

Editor: Felicity Jackson
Design: Peartree Design Associates
Typeset in England by SX Composing, Rayleigh
Printed and bound in Italy by New Interlitho Italia

CONTENTS

INTRODUCTION

Eating the right food is essential to good health. In order to stay healthy, the body needs a constant supply of nutrients – protein, carbohydrates, fat, vitamins and minerals, as well as fibre – which it can only get from a well-balanced, varied diet.

Adopting a healthy diet doesn't mean that you must give up your favourite foods, but it does mean that you should eat some of them less frequently or in smaller quantities. Moderation in the amount of certain foods we eat is one of the keys to a healthy eating regime. Medical research is increasingly linking certain diseases with the food we eat and it is generally agreed that we in the West eat too much fat, salt and sugar and not enough fibre.

All fats are made up of compounds called fatty acids and these are either saturated, monounsaturated or polyunsaturated. Saturated fats are found mainly in dairy products and meat, but also in some vegetable oils such as coconut and palm. A diet which is high in fat, particularly saturated fat, causes blood cholesterol to rise and this in turn increases the risk of coronary heart disease.

Polyunsaturated fats which are abundant in fish oils and vegetable oils such as sunflower, corn and safflower, are believed to reduce blood cholesterol levels. Monounsaturated fats, which are present in nuts, olives and olive oil, were considered to have no effect on blood cholesterol levels, but there is growing evidence that they might be beneficial.

To reduce the total amount of fat in your diet, choose skimmed and semi-skimmed milk, low- and medium-fat cheese and lean meat.

A recent Government report (COMA report 'Dietary Sugars and Human Disease' 1989), confirmed that sugar is the most important cause of dental caries in the United Kingdom. Also sugar contains 'empty calories' – that is calories which supply energy but not other nutrients. It is better to obtain energy from other foods such as fruit and vegetables.

Fibre plays an important role in our diets, by ensuring that the digestive system functions properly. A deficiency of fibre in the diet can lead to problems of constipation, diverticular disease and other bowel disorders. Increase your fibre intake by using wholemeal or fibre-enriched bread, pasta and flour, instead of white, and by switching to brown rice. Also by eating more fibrous foods such as fresh fruit, vegetables and pulses.

As far as possible, the ingredients used in the recipes in this book are low in saturated fat, high in fibre and low in salt and sugar.

Remember that eating should always be a pleasure and provided that we strike a healthy balance between different foods, and eat nothing in excess, there is no reason why healthy eating should be less so.

Melon and Prawn Salad

Breakfasts

A healthy, nutritious breakfast gives you a good start to the day, and will help to sustain you through the busiest morning.

In this chapter you will find breakfasts to suit all tastes. Choose home-made Muesli for a quick unsweetened breakfast cereal. It is high in fibre, vitamins and minerals and provides useful amounts of protein when served with milk. Alternatively, try Dried Fruit Compote, which can be prepared the night before and is both quick and refreshing. Apple and Date Porridge is especially good for cold winter mornings when a hot breakfast is needed. Smoked Fish Kedgeree is delicious for weekends or holidays when there is a little more time.

If you prefer a light breakfast try one of the selection of high vitality drinks or bake a batch of Bran Muffins, high in fibre with the delicious flavour of honey. Baked Eggs with Mushrooms are a healthy alternative to fried eggs and can be accompanied by slices of toasted wholemeal bread.

Cocotte Eggs

Fruity Vitality Drink; Vegetable Vitality Drink; Yogurt Vitality Drink

FRUITY VITALITY DRINK

SERVES 1

2 pink grapefruit
1 lemon
1 egg
10 ml (2 tsp) honey, or to taste
5 ml (1 tsp) wheatgerm

/ 1 / Squeeze the juice from the grapefruit and the lemon, and pour it into a blender or food processor.

/ 2 / Add the egg, honey and wheatgerm and blend until well combined. Taste for sweetness and add more honey if liked. Pour into a long glass and serve immediately.

YOGURT VITALITY DRINK

SERVES 1

1 small banana
10 ml (2 tsp) wheatgerm
juice of 1 orange
150 ml (¼ pint) natural low-fat yogurt
1 egg yolk

/ 1 / Peel the banana and slice straight into a blender or food processor.

/ 2 / Add the wheatgerm, orange juice, yogurt and egg yolk and blend to a smooth mixture. Pour into a long glass and serve immediately.

VEGETABLE VITALITY DRINK

SERVES 1

50 g (2 oz) shredded coconut
300 ml (½ pint) boiling water
225 g (8 oz) carrots
juice of ½ lemon
5 ml (1 tsp) wheatgerm oil

/ 1 / Put the coconut in a heatproof jug, pour on the boiling water and stir well to mix. Leave to infuse for 30 minutes.

/ 2 / Meanwhile, scrub the carrots with a stiff vegetable brush to remove any soil from their skins. Grate into a blender or food processor, add the lemon juice and blend until the carrots are broken down to a pulp.

/ 3 / Strain the carrot pulp through a sieve into a jug, then strain in the milk from the coconut. Add the wheatgerm oil and whisk vigorously to combine. Pour the mixture into a long glass and serve immediately.

Muesli

MUESLI

MAKES 14 SERVINGS

250 g (9 oz) porridge oats
75 g (3 oz) wholewheat flakes
50 g (2 oz) bran buds
75 g (3 oz) sunflower seeds
175 g (6 oz) sultanas
175 g (6 oz) dried fruit, such as apricots, pears, figs or peaches, cut into small pieces
semi-skimmed milk, to serve

/ 1 / Mix together the porridge oats, wholewheat flakes, bran buds, sunflower seeds, sultanas and dried fruit.

/ 2 / The dry muesli will keep fresh for several weeks if stored in an airtight container.

/ 3 / Serve in individual bowls with milk.

These healthy breakfast-in-a-glass recipes are full of vitamins and fibre, and you will find they keep you going until lunchtime without any sign of mid-morning hunger pangs.

The original idea for muesli as a breakfast dish came from a Swiss doctor called Max Bircher-Benner, which is why some brands of muesli are called 'Bircher Muesli'. Dr Bircher-Benner had a clinic in Zurich at the beginning of the century where he prescribed muesli for his patients, to be eaten both at breakfast time and supper. The original muesli was based on fresh fruit, with porridge oats (the German word *muesli* means gruel) added. This is why muesli cereal is usually eaten with fruit – in this recipe dried fruit is suggested, but fresh fruit may be used instead.

BRAN MUFFINS

To make scrambled eggs to serve with muffins, lightly whisk together 4 eggs, 60 ml (4 tbsp) milk and seasoning to taste. Melt 40 g (1½ oz) butter or margarine in a heavy-based saucepan, pour in the egg and milk mixture and cook over gentle heat, stirring constantly with a wooden spoon. Cook just for a few minutes until the mixture thickens and looks creamy, then immediately remove from the heat and pile on top of the muffins. Take great care when scrambling eggs that you do not overcook the mixture. Do not leave it in the pan for more than a second or two before serving – even the heat of the pan can make the eggs rubbery.

BRAN MUFFINS

M A K E S   4

75 g (3 oz) plain wholemeal flour
75 g (3 oz) bran
7.5 ml (1½ tsp) baking powder
1 egg, beaten
300 ml (½ pint) semi-skimmed milk
30 ml (2 tbsp) honey
butter or margarine, for spreading

/ 1 / Grease a 4-hole Yorkshire pudding tin. Sift the flour, bran and baking powder together into a bowl. Stir in the bran (from the wholemeal flour) left in the bottom of the sieve.

/ 2 / Make a well in the centre and add the egg. Stir well to mix, then add the milk and honey. Beat to a smooth batter. Divide the batter equally between the prepared tins.

/ 3 / Bake in the oven at 190°C (375°F) mark 5 for 25 minutes until risen. Turn out on to a wire rack and cool for 5 minutes. Serve cut in half and spread with butter or margarine.

DRIED FRUIT COMPOTE

Tip the hazelnuts into a clean tea-towel and rub them while they are still hot to remove the skins.

Chop the hazelnuts roughly, using an automatic chopper or large cook's knife.

DRIED FRUIT COMPOTE

S E R V E S   6

50 g (2 oz) dried apple rings
50 g (2 oz) dried apricots
50 g (2 oz) dried figs
300 ml (½ pint) unsweetened orange juice
25 g (1 oz) hazelnuts

/ 1 / Cut the dried apple rings, apricots and figs into chunky pieces and put in a bowl.

/ 2 / Mix together the unsweetened orange juice and 300 ml (½ pint) water and pour over the fruit in the bowl. Cover and leave to macerate in the refrigerator overnight.

/ 3 / The next day, spread the hazelnuts out in a grill pan and toast under a low to moderate heat, shaking the pan until browned.

/ 4 / Tip the hazelnuts into a clean tea-towel and rub them while hot to remove the skins.

/ 5 / Chop the hazelnuts roughly. Sprinkle them over the compote just before serving.

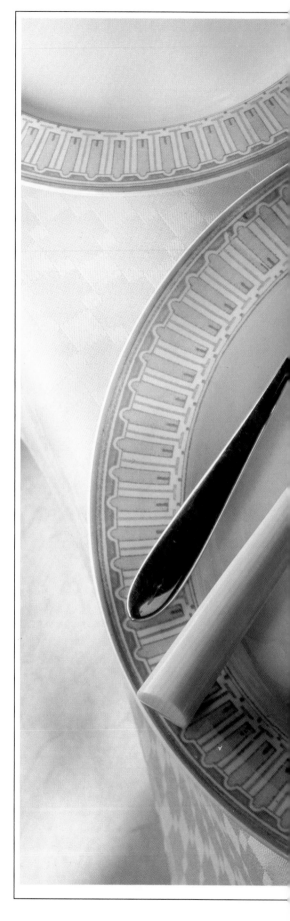

Bran Muffins

APPLE AND DATE PORRIDGE

SERVES 6

Other dried fruits, such as peaches, apple rings or pears, could be used instead of the dried dates used here, and hard cooking pears substituted for the large cooking apple.

100 g (4 oz) dried dates
1 large cooking apple
25 g (1 oz) butter or margarine
25 g (1 oz) bran
15 ml (1 tbsp) light raw cane sugar
175 g (6 oz) porridge oats

/ 1 / Stone and roughly chop the dried dates. Roughly chop, but do not peel, the cooking apple, discarding the core.

/ 2 / Melt the butter or margarine in a large saucepan, stir in the bran and sugar and cook, stirring, for about 2 minutes.

/ 3 / Pour 1.1 litre (2 pints) water into the pan, then sprinkle in the porridge oats. Bring the mixture to the boil, stirring.

/ 4 / Add the dates and apple, then simmer, stirring, for about 5 minutes or until the porridge is desired consistency. Serve hot.

Apple and Date Porridge

14

Baked Eggs with Mushrooms

BAKED EGGS
WITH
MUSHROOMS

S E R V E S 2

25 g (1 oz) butter or margarine

100 g (4 oz) button mushrooms, finely chopped

30 ml (2 tbsp) chopped fresh tarragon or parsley

salt and pepper

2 eggs

/ 1 / Melt three-quarters of the butter or margarine in a frying pan, add the mushrooms and fry until all excess moisture has evaporated. Add the tarragon or parsley and season.

/ 2 / Divide the mushroom mixture between 2 cocotte dishes, ramekins or individual soufflé dishes and, using the back of a dessertspoon, make a well in the centre of the mixture in each dish.

/ 3 / Carefully break an egg into each dish, dot with the remaining butter or margarine and stand the ramekins in a roasting tin. Pour boiling water into the tin to come halfway up the sides of the ramekins (this will prevent the eggs and mushrooms drying out during cooking).

/ 4 / Cover the roasting tin tightly with foil and place in the oven. Bake at 180°C (350°F) mark 4 for 10-12 minutes until the eggs are just set. Serve at once.

Serve the eggs in their dishes with fingers of hot toast and butter or margarine. This recipe makes the perfect snack, supper or lunch dish for 1 person – simply halve the quantities.

A small onion, finely chopped, can be added to the mixture, if wished. Melt a little extra butter or margarine and fry the onion with the mushrooms.

15

Kippers are herrings which are split and gutted, soaked in brine, then smoked. The best kippers are said to come from Loch Fyne in Scotland, although those from the Isle of Man are also considered to be very good. The choice of kippers is quite confusing – at fishmongers they are sold whole, boned, and as fillets, whereas in supermarkets they are available frozen as fillets and in vacuum 'boil-in-the-bag' packs. For this recipe you can use fresh or frozen fillets. Avoid buying those which are a deep, chestnut brown colour as they have probably been dyed.

MARINATED KIPPERS

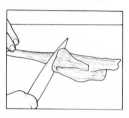

To skin the kipper fillets: place them skin side down on a board, grip each fillet at the tail end and work the flesh away from the skin with a sharp knife, using a sawing motion.

COCOTTE EGGS

As an alternative to the mushrooms in this recipe, you can use fresh tomatoes. At the end of the summer when they are often overripe, they are best used for cooking rather than in salads, and this baked egg dish is a good way to use them up. Skin them first if you have the time as this will make the finished dish more palatable. A quick way to skin a few tomatoes is to pierce them 1 at a time with a fork at the stalk end and then hold in the flame of a gas hob. Turn the tomato until the skin blisters and bursts, leave until cool enough to handle, then peel off the skin with your fingers. To replace the mushrooms, use 4 medium tomatoes, chopped, and substitute basil for the tarragon, if available.

COCOTTE EGGS

SERVES 4

25 g (1 oz) butter or margarine
1 small onion, skinned and finely chopped
4 rashers of lean back bacon, rinded and finely chopped
100 g (4 oz) button mushrooms, finely chopped
10 ml (2 tsp) tomato purée
10 ml (2 tsp) chopped fresh tarragon or 5 ml (1 tsp) dried
salt and pepper
4 eggs, size 2
120 ml (8 tbsp) single cream
chopped fresh tarragon, to garnish

/ 1 / Melt the butter or margarine in a small saucepan, add the onion and fry gently until soft. Add the bacon and fry until beginning to change colour, then add the mushrooms and tomato purée. Continue frying for 2-3 minutes until the juices run, stirring constantly.

/ 2 / Remove from the heat and stir in the tarragon and seasoning to taste. Divide the mixture equally between 4 cocotte dishes, ramekins or individual soufflé dishes. Make a slight indentation in the centre of each one.

/ 3 / Break an egg into each dish, on top of the mushroom and bacon mixture, then slowly pour 30 ml (2 tbsp) cream over each one. Sprinkle with salt and pepper to taste.

/ 4 / Place the cocottes on a baking tray and bake in the oven at 180°C (350°F) mark 4 for 10-12 minutes until the eggs are set.

MARINATED KIPPERS

SERVES 4

4 boneless kipper fillets
150 ml (¼ pint) olive oil
75 ml (5 tbsp) lemon juice
1.25 ml (¼ tsp) mustard powder
1 small onion, skinned and very finely chopped
1-2 garlic cloves, skinned and crushed
pepper
a few raw onion rings, parsley sprigs and paprika, to garnish

/ 1 / Skin the kipper fillets: place them skin side down on a board, grip each one at the tail end and work the flesh away from the skin with a sharp knife, using a sawing motion.

/ 2 / In a jug, whisk together the remaining ingredients, except the garnish, adding pepper to taste.

/ 3 / Put the kippers in a shallow dish and pour over the marinade. Cover and chill in the refrigerator for at least 8 hours. Turn the kippers in the marinade occasionally during this time.

/ 4 / To serve, remove the kippers from the marinade and cut each one in half lengthways. Fold each half over crossways, then place in a single layer in a dish.

/ 5 / Pour the marinade over the kippers and garnish the top with onion rings, parsley sprigs and a sprinkling of paprika.

Marinated Kippers

SMOKED FISH KEDGEREE

SERVES 4

175 g (6 oz) long-grain brown rice
salt and pepper
275 g (10 oz) smoked haddock
25 g (1 oz) butter or margarine
1 egg, hard-boiled and chopped
30 ml (2 tbsp) chopped fresh parsley
juice of ½ lemon

/ 1 / Put the rice in a large saucepan of boiling salted water and cook for about 35 minutes or according to packet instructions until tender.

/ 2 / Meanwhile, place the haddock in a pan, cover with water and poach for about 15 minutes.

/ 3 / Drain the fish well, then flake the flesh, discarding the skin and bones.

/ 4 / Drain the rice well. Melt the butter or margarine in a frying pan, add the rice, haddock, chopped egg and parsley and stir over moderate heat for a few minutes until warmed through. Add the lemon juice and pepper to taste, turn into a warmed serving dish and serve immediately.

Smoked Fish Kedgeree

Starters

Starters set the scene for the rest of the meal. They should be fresh and light and stimulate the appetite. Portions should always be quite small and beautifully presented. A good home-made soup makes a tasty and nutritious starter. Packed with fresh ingredients and no additives in the form of preservatives or colourants, soup is one of the quickest and easiest starters.

Just before serving, add a swirl of yogurt to puréed soup as a healthier alternative to cream, sprinkle with chopped fresh herbs or serve with toasted croûtons, instead of fried. For toasted croûtons, toast slices of brown bread, then cut into dice.

In addition to soups, the choice of starters ranges from pâtés, salads and mousses, to fish, vegetables and fruit. Many of the recipes in this chapter also make nutritious lunch or supper dishes served with wholemeal bread and a salad.

Tomato Ice with Vegetable Julienne

LETTUCE SOUP

This soup has a pretty colour and delicate flavour. It makes a lovely summer starter served with Melba toast.

CHILLED CUCUMBER SOUP

Grate the unpeeled cucumber into a bowl, using the finest side of a conical or box grater.

ICED SWEET PEPPER SOUP

Sieve the cooked vegetables, or purée them in a blender or food processor, then sieve the purée to remove the tomato seeds.

Do not confuse the herb coriander used in Iced Sweet Pepper Soup with the spice of the same name. In this recipe, the fresh herb is used. Looking like frondy parsley, it is available at many supermarkets and also at continental and oriental specialist shops. Its flavour is highly aromatic, much stronger than parsley. The spice coriander is used extensively in Indian cookery; it is available as whole seeds and in ground form. The herb and spice are not interchangeable in recipes, so take care which one you use.

LETTUCE SOUP

SERVES 4

350 g (12 oz) lettuce leaves
100 g (4 oz) spring onions, trimmed
50 g (2 oz) butter or margarine
15 ml (1 tbsp) plain flour
600 ml (1 pint) vegetable or chicken stock
150 ml (¼ pint) semi-skimmed milk
salt and pepper
shredded lettuce or soured cream, to finish (optional)

/ 1 / Chop the lettuce leaves and spring onions roughly. Melt the butter or margarine in a deep saucepan, add the lettuce and spring onions and cook gently for about 10 minutes until both the lettuce and onions are very soft.

/ 2 / Stir in the flour. Cook, stirring, for 1 minute, then add the stock. Bring to the boil, cover and simmer for 45 minutes to 1 hour.

/ 3 / Work the soup to a purée in a blender or food processor, or rub through a sieve. Return to the rinsed-out pan and add the milk with salt and pepper to taste. Reheat to serving temperature. Finish with a garnish of shredded lettuce or a swirl of soured cream, if liked.

CHILLED CUCUMBER SOUP

SERVES 4

1 medium cucumber, trimmed
300 ml (½ pint) natural low-fat yogurt
1 small garlic clove, skinned and crushed
30 ml (2 tbsp) wine vinegar
30 ml (2 tbsp) chopped fresh mint or snipped chives
salt and pepper
300 ml (½ pint) semi-skimmed milk
mint sprigs, to garnish

/ 1 / Grate the unpeeled cucumber into a bowl, using the finest side of a conical or box grater.

/ 2 / Stir in the yogurt, crushed garlic, vinegar and mint or chives. Add seasoning to taste and chill in the refrigerator for 1 hour.

/ 3 / Just before serving, stir in the milk, then taste and adjust seasoning. Spoon into individual soup bowls and garnish with mint.

ICED SWEET PEPPER SOUP

SERVES 4

60 ml (4 tbsp) chopped fresh coriander
225 g (8 oz) sweet red peppers
1 medium onion
225 g (8 oz) ripe tomatoes
900 ml (1½ pints) vegetable or chicken stock
150 ml (¼ pint) semi-skimmed milk
salt and pepper

/ 1 / Make the coriander ice cubes: put the chopped coriander into an ice-cube tray, top up with water and freeze.

/ 2 / Wipe the peppers. Cut the stem end off, scoop out the seeds and slice the flesh. Skin and slice the onion, and slice the tomatoes.

/ 3 / Place the peppers in a large saucepan with the onion, tomatoes and stock. Bring to the boil, then lower the heat, cover and simmer for about 15 minutes or until the vegetables are tender. Drain, reserving the liquid.

/ 4 / Sieve the vegetables, or purée them in a blender or food processor, then sieve the purée to remove the tomato seeds.

/ 5 / Combine the reserved liquid, vegetable purée and milk in a bowl with seasoning to taste. Cool for 30 minutes, then chill in the refrigerator for at least 2 hours before serving. Serve with coriander ice cubes.

Lettuce Soup

Spinach Soup (top); Vegetable Soup (bottom)

SPINACH SOUP

SERVES 4

450 g (1 lb) fresh spinach
900 ml (1½ pints) vegetable or chicken stock
15 ml (1 tbsp) lemon juice
salt and pepper
450 ml (¾ pint) buttermilk
a few drops of Tabasco sauce

/ 1 / Strip the spinach leaves from their stems and wash in several changes of water. Place the spinach, stock, lemon juice and seasoning in a saucepan. Simmer for 10 minutes.

/ 2 / Work the spinach through a sieve, or strain off most of the liquid and reserve, then purée the spinach in a blender or processor.

/ 3 / Reheat the spinach purée gently with the cooking liquid, 300 ml (½ pint) of the buttermilk and Tabasco sauce. Swirl in the remaining buttermilk.

VEGETABLE SOUP

SERVES 4 - 6

350 g (12 oz) carrots
225 g (8 oz) turnips
1 large onion
225 g (8 oz) celery
5 ml (1 tsp) chopped fresh thyme or 2.5 ml (½ tsp) dried
5 ml (1 tsp) chopped fresh basil or 2.5 ml (½ tsp) dried
1 bay leaf
1 garlic clove, skinned and crushed
15 ml (1 tbsp) tomato purée
1.7 litres (3 pints) stock
salt and pepper
125 g (4 oz) macaroni, rigatoni or penne
4 slices of wholemeal bread
50 g (2 oz) Edam cheese, coarsely grated
basil sprigs, to garnish

/ 1 / Cut the carrots, turnips, onion and celery into large dice.

/ 2 / Place the vegetables, thyme, basil, bay leaf and crushed garlic in a large saucepan. Stir over low heat for 2-3 minutes.

/ 3 / Stir in the tomato purée, stock and seasoning to taste. Bring to the boil, then lower the heat and simmer for 25-30 minutes.

/ 4 / Stir in the pasta. Cover and simmer for a further 12-15 minutes or until the pasta is tender. Taste and adjust the seasoning.

/ 5 / Toast the bread lightly on one side. Press a little cheese on to the untoasted side of the bread, dividing it equally between them. Grill until golden. Cut into small triangles.

/ 6 / Pour the soup into a warmed serving bowl. Serve immediately, garnished with the sprigs of basil and toasted cheese triangles.

CARROT AND CARDAMOM SOUP

SERVES 4

200 g (7 oz) carrots, peeled
1 medium onion, skinned
50 g (2 oz) butter or margarine
10 whole green cardamoms
50 g (2 oz) red lentils
1.1 litres (2 pints) vegetable or chicken stock
salt and pepper
parsley sprigs, to garnish

/ 1 / Grate the carrots coarsely. Slice the onion very thinly. Melt the butter or margarine in a large saucepan, add the carrots and onion and cook gently for 4-5 minutes.

/ 2 / Meanwhile, split each cardamom and remove the black seeds. Crush the seeds with a pestle and mortar, or in a bowl with the end of a rolling pin.

/ 3 / Stir the cardamom seeds into the vegetables with the lentils. Cook, stirring, for a further 1-2 minutes.

/ 4 / Add the stock and bring to the boil. Cover and simmer gently for about 20 minutes or until the lentils are just tender. Add salt and pepper to taste before serving and garnish with parsley sprigs.

SPINACH SOUP

For a more substantial dish, serve the Spinach Soup with warm wholemeal rolls or with toasted cheese triangles (see Vegetable Soup).

VEGETABLE SOUP

To turn this into a main meal soup, roughly chop 175 g (6 oz) smoked lean bacon and cook it with the vegetables at the beginning of the recipe and then proceed with the recipe.

CARROT AND CARDAMOM SOUP

To split each cardamom to remove the black seeds: crush the seeds with a pestle and mortar, or with the end of a rolling pin.

Cardamoms go especially well with carrots, and give this soup an exotic Indian flavour. When buying cardamoms, look for the green pods rather than the black. Green cardamoms have a fine flavour, whereas the black ones are coarser and may overpower the delicate sweetness of the carrots in this recipe. Delicatessens and supermarkets sell green cardamoms, but for freshness it is best to buy them from an Indian grocer who has a fast turnover. Buy them loose in small quantities as they quickly go stale and lose both their aroma and flavour. Store them in an airtight jar in a dark cupboard, and do not remove the seeds from the pods until you are ready to use them.

Cut away any green stalks from the cauliflower, then cut it into small florets.

Work the soup mixture to a very smooth purée in a blender or food processor, or rub it through a sieve using a wooden spoon.

While the soup is reheating, melt the remaining butter or margarine in a small frying pan. Add the almonds and parsley and fry until the nuts are golden. Scatter them over the soup before serving.

Serve this creamy, nutritious soup for a quick lunch. Wholemeal baps and a selection of cheeses would go well with it.

CAULIFLOWER BUTTERMILK SOUP

SERVES 6

900 g (2 lb) cauliflower
1 large onion, skinned
50 g (2 oz) butter or margarine
1 garlic clove, skinned and crushed
15 ml (1 tbsp) plain flour
900 ml (1½ pints) semi-skimmed milk
2 eggs, beaten
300 ml (½ pint) buttermilk
pinch of freshly grated nutmeg
salt and pepper
25 g (1 oz) flaked almonds
15 ml (1 tbsp) chopped fresh parsley

/ 1 / Cut away any green stalks from the cauliflower, and separate it into small florets. Roughly chop the onion.

/ 2 / Melt 25 g (1 oz) of the butter or margarine in a saucepan. Add the onion and garlic and fry for 3-4 minutes until golden.

/ 3 / Stir in the flour. Cook, stirring, for 1 minute, then add the milk and cauliflower.

/ 4 / Bring to the boil, cover and simmer for 25-30 minutes or until the cauliflower florets are very soft.

/ 5 / Work the soup to a very smooth purée in a blender or food processor, or rub the mixture through a sieve.

/ 6 / Return to the rinsed-out pan. Beat in the eggs, buttermilk, nutmeg and salt and pepper to taste. Reheat very gently, without boiling.

/ 7 / Melt the remaining butter in a small frying pan. Add the almonds and parsley and fry until the nuts are golden. Scatter over the soup before serving.

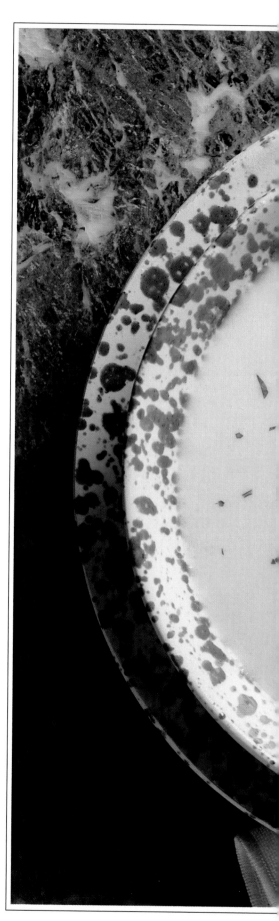

VEGETABLE AND OATMEAL BROTH

SERVES 4 - 6

1 medium onion, skinned
175 g (6 oz) swede, peeled
2 medium carrots, peeled
1 medium leek, trimmed
40 g (1½ oz) butter or margarine
25 g (1 oz) medium oatmeal
1.1 litres (2 pints) vegetable or chicken stock
salt and pepper
150 ml (¼ pint) semi-skimmed milk
chopped fresh parsley, to garnish (optional)

/ 1 / Dice the onion, swede and carrots finely. Slice the leek in 1 cm (½ inch) rings, then wash well under cold running water to remove any grit.

/ 2 / Melt the butter or margarine in a large saucepan, add the vegetables and cook gently without browning for 5 minutes. Add the oatmeal, stir well and cook for a few minutes.

/ 3 / Stir in the stock and salt and pepper to taste and bring to the boil. Lower the heat, cover and simmer for about 45 minutes or until the vegetables are tender.

/ 4 / Add the milk and reheat to serving temperature. Taste and adjust seasoning before serving. Sprinkle the soup with a little chopped parsley, if liked.

SPANISH SUMMER SOUP

SERVES 4

2 very large Marmande or Beefsteak tomatoes
1 medium Spanish onion, skinned
1 green pepper, cored and seeded
450 g (1 lb) can potatoes, drained
4 garlic cloves, skinned
60 ml (4 tbsp) wine vinegar
1 litre (1¾ pints) water
30 ml (2 tbsp) olive oil
2.5 ml (½ tsp) paprika
salt and pepper
a few ice cubes and fresh mint sprigs, to serve

/ 1 / Chop all the vegetables and the garlic roughly and then put half of them in a blender or food processor with the vinegar and about 150 ml (¼ pint) of the measured water. Work to a smooth purée.

/ 2 / Sieve the purée to remove the tomato skins, working it into a large soup tureen or serving bowl.

/ 3 / Repeat the puréeing and sieving with the remaining vegetables and another 150 ml (¼ pint) of the water. Add to the purée in the tureen or bowl.

/ 4 / Pour the remaining water into the soup and add the oil, paprika and seasoning to taste. Stir well to mix, cover and chill in the refrigerator for at least 1 hour before serving.

/ 5 / To serve, taste and adjust the seasoning, then stir in the ice cubes. Float mint sprigs on top of the soup and serve immediately.

GAZPACHO

SERVES 4

100 g (4 oz) green pepper
1 medium cucumber
450 g (1 lb) fully ripened tomatoes
50-100 g (2-4 oz) onions, skinned
1 garlic clove, skinned
45 ml (3 tbsp) vegetable oil
45 ml (3 tbsp) white wine vinegar
425 g (15 oz) can tomato juice
30 ml (2 tbsp) tomato purée
1.25 ml (¼ tsp) salt
green pepper, ice cubes and croûtons, to serve

/ 1 / Remove the core and seeds from the green pepper and chop roughly with the cucumber, tomatoes, onions and garlic.

/ 2 / Mix together with the remaining ingredients in a bowl. Place in a blender or food processor in small portions and blend to form a smooth purée. Pour into a bowl and chill in the refrigerator for 2 hours.

/ 3 / To serve, core and seed the green pepper and dice very finely. Pour purée into a serving bowl and add a few ice cubes. Serve garnished with diced pepper and croûtons.

VEGETABLE AND OATMEAL BROTH

Thick with vegetables and oatmeal, this broth makes a hearty supper. Serve it with crusty wholemeal bread.

With swede and oatmeal, this soup has a definite Scottish flavour. As their name suggests, swedes originally came from Sweden, and were originally called Swedish turnips, although they were also known as Russian turnips and even by the name of rutabaga, from their botanical name. In the eighteenth century, swedes were grown in Scotland and northern England to feed sheep and cattle. It was soon discovered that the sweet flavour and delicate colour of the flesh made them suitable for human consumption, too, and they became a popular vegetable in the nineteenth century. In Scotland, swedes are still called turnips, or neeps for short.

SPANISH SUMMER SOUP

To make croûtons for floating on top of this soup: remove the crusts from 3 slices of stale white bread. Cut the bread into dice, then deep-fry in hot oil until golden brown and crisp. Remove with a slotted spoon and drain on absorbent kitchen paper. For toasted croûtons: toast the crustless bread first, then cut into dice. Croûtons can be successfully frozen.
  For a professional touch, try cutting the bread or toast into different shapes with tiny aspic cutters available from specialist kitchen shops and catering suppliers.

Serve Spanish Summer Soup as a starter for a summer luncheon or barbecue party, with bowls of garnish, such as croûtons (see above), diced red and green pepper, diced cucumber and finely chopped hard-boiled eggs.

Picture opposite: Spanish Summer Soup

TOMATO ICE WITH
VEGETABLE JULIENNE

This tomato ice makes an
unusual starter served with
crisp Melba toast and
butter or margarine.

TOMATO ICE WITH VEGETABLE JULIENNE

SERVES 4 - 6

8 very ripe tomatoes
45 ml (3 tbsp) very hot water
10 ml (2 tsp) gelatine
30 ml (2 tbsp) tomato purée
30 ml (2 tbsp) lemon juice
a few drops of Tabasco sauce
salt and pepper
30 ml (2 tbsp) chopped fresh basil (optional)
1 egg white (optional)
2 small leeks
2 medium carrots, peeled
2 medium courgettes
150 ml (¼ pint) French Dressing (see page 149)
fresh basil leaves, to garnish (optional)

/ 1 / Put the tomatoes in a blender or food processor and work until smooth. Press the tomato pulp through a sieve into a bowl to remove the seeds and skin.

/ 2 / Put the hot water in a small bowl and sprinkle in the gelatine. Stir briskly until dissolved, then leave to cool slightly.

/ 3 / Add the tomato purée to the tomato pulp with the lemon juice, Tabasco and salt and pepper to taste. Mix thoroughly.

/ 4 / Stir in the gelatine and chopped basil, if using. Pour into a chilled shallow freezer container and freeze for about 2 hours until mushy.

/ 5 / Remove the container from the freezer and beat the mixture with a fork to break down any ice crystals. Return to the freezer and freeze for a further 4 hours. (If a creamier texture is desired, whisk the egg white until stiff, fold into the beaten mixture and return to the freezer. Freeze as before.)

/ 6 / Meanwhile, wash the leeks thoroughly and cut into fine julienne strips. Cut the carrots and courgettes into julienne strips of the same size.

/ 7 / Bring a large saucepan of water to the boil and add the leeks. Blanch for 1 minute, then remove with a slotted spoon and drain. Blanch the carrots in the same water for 4 minutes, remove and drain. Blanch the courgettes for 2 minutes and drain.

/ 8 / Put the julienne of vegetables in a bowl, add the French dressing and salt and pepper to taste and toss gently to mix. Cover and chill until required.

/ 9 / To serve, allow the tomato ice to soften in the refrigerator for 30 minutes. Arrange small scoops of tomato ice on chilled individual plates with a nest of julienne vegetables. Garnish with basil leaves, if using.

SMOKED SALMON PÂTÉ

Real aspic jelly is made
from stock, gelatine, wine,
wine vinegar and egg
whites. It is time-consuming
to make because it has to
be boiled time and time
again until the liquid is
clear, then filtered through
a cloth or jelly bag before
setting. Commercial aspic
jelly powder, available in
sachets at good
supermarkets and
delicatessens, makes a
perfectly acceptable
substitute for home-made
aspic. Simply mix the
powder with water until
dissolved, then leave until
on the point of setting
before use. The amount of
water required depends on
the brand of powder used,
so check the instructions
on the sachet before using
it. Aspic is useful for fish
and meat pâtés alike.

Serve Smoked Salmon Pâté
as a dinner party starter
with fingers of wholemeal
or granary toast.

SMOKED SALMON PÂTÉ

SERVES 6

175 g (6 oz) smoked salmon 'off-cuts'
75 g (3 oz) unsalted butter, melted
20 ml (4 tsp) lemon juice
60 ml (4 tbsp) single cream
pepper
cucumber slices, to garnish
150 ml (¼ pint) liquid aspic jelly

/ 1 / Roughly cut up the salmon pieces, reserving a few for garnishing, and place in a blender or food processor.

/ 2 / Add the butter, lemon juice and cream to the blender goblet or food processor.

/ 3 / Blend the mixture until it is smooth. Season to taste with pepper. (Salt is not usually needed as smoked fish is salty enough.)

/ 4 / Spoon into a 300 ml (½ pint) dish to within 1 cm (½ inch) of the rim. Chill in the refrigerator for 1 hour to set.

/ 5 / Garnish with the reserved pieces of smoked salmon and cucumber slices and spoon over the aspic jelly, which should be just on the point of setting. Refrigerate again for 30 minutes to set the aspic (you can leave the pâté in the refrigerator for longer than this, if wished). Leave at room temperature for 30 minutes before serving.

Smoked Salmon Pâté

TARAMASALATA

Taramasalata is a creamy dip with a subtle flavour of smoked fish. From the Greek words *tarama*, meaning dried and salted mullet roe, and *salata* meaning salad, it is eaten all over Greece and Turkey, like Hummus (see page 32), as part of the *mezze* before a meal. Salted mullet roe is not so easy to obtain as it was when the recipe was first made, so these days taramasalata is most often made with smoked cod's roe, which is very similar. Many supermarkets and delicatessens sell taramasalata (sometimes labelled 'smoked cod's roe pâté) by the kg (lb) or ready-packed in cartons. Most brands have artificial colouring added to them which gives them an unnatural bright pink colour; they also taste very strongly of fish.

ARTICHOKE HEARTS À LA GRECQUE

SERVES 4 - 6

75 ml (5 tbsp) olive oil
15 ml (1 tbsp) white wine vinegar
10 ml (2 tsp) tomato purée
1 large garlic clove, skinned and crushed
7.5 ml (1½ tsp) chopped fresh thyme or basil
salt and pepper
175 g (6 oz) button onions, skinned
5 ml (1 tsp) caster sugar
225 g (8 oz) small button mushrooms, wiped
two 400 g (14 oz) cans artichoke hearts

/ 1 / Make the dressing: place 45 ml (3 tbsp) of the oil, the vinegar, tomato purée, garlic, thyme or basil and seasoning to taste in a bowl and whisk together.

/ 2 / Blanch the onions in boiling water for 5 minutes, then drain well. Heat the remaining oil; add the onions and sugar and cook for 2 minutes.

/ 3 / Add the mushrooms and toss over a high heat for a few seconds. Tip the contents of the pan into the dressing. Drain the artichoke hearts, rinse and pat dry. Add the hearts to the dressing and toss together. Cover and chill.

TARAMASALATA

SERVES 8

225 g (8 oz) smoked cod's roe
1 garlic clove, skinned
50 g (2 oz) fresh wholemeal breadcrumbs
1 small onion, skinned and finely chopped
finely grated rind and juice of 1 lemon
150 ml (¼ pint) olive oil
pepper
lemon wedges, to garnish
pitta bread or toast, to serve (optional)

Artichoke Hearts à la Grecque

/ 1 / Skin the smoked cod's roe and break it up into pieces. Place in a blender or food processor with the garlic, breadcrumbs, onion, lemon rind and juice and blend to form a smooth purée.

/ 2 / Gradually add the oil and blend well after each addition until smooth. Blend in 90 ml (6 tbsp) hot water. Season with pepper to taste.

/ 3 / Spoon into a serving dish and chill in the refrigerator for at least 1 hour. To serve, garnish with lemon wedges. Serve with pitta bread or toast, preferably wholemeal, if liked.

KIPPER MOUSSE

SERVES 6

350 g (12 oz) kipper fillets
juice of 1 orange
15 ml (1 tbsp) lemon juice
5 ml (1 tsp) gelatine
100 g (4 oz) cottage or curd cheese
150 ml (¼ pint) natural low-fat yogurt
1 small garlic clove, skinned and crushed
1.25 ml (¼ tsp) ground mace
pepper
lemon or orange slices and herb sprigs, to garnish
wholemeal toast, to serve (optional)

/ 1 / Pour boiling water over the kippers and leave to stand for 1 minute. Drain, pat dry and remove skin. Flake the flesh, discarding any bones; put into a blender or food processor.

/ 2 / In a small heatproof bowl, mix the orange and lemon juices together. Sprinkle on the gelatine and leave to stand for a few minutes until spongy.

/ 3 / Meanwhile, add the cottage or curd cheese, yogurt, garlic and mace to the blender or food processor and blend until smooth.

/ 4 / Place the bowl of gelatine in a saucepan of hot water and heat gently until dissolved. Add to the kipper mixture and blend until evenly mixed. Season with pepper to taste.

/ 5 / Divide the kipper mousse equally between 6 oiled individual ramekin dishes. Chill in the refrigerator for at least 1 hour before serving. Garnish with lemon or orange slices and herb sprigs and serve with wholemeal toast, if liked.

SMOKED TROUT WITH TOMATOES AND MUSHROOMS

SERVES 8

700 g (1½ lb) smoked trout
225 g (8 oz) cucumber, skinned
salt and pepper
175 g (6 oz) mushrooms
45 ml (3 tbsp) creamed horseradish
30 ml (2 tbsp) lemon juice
60 ml (4 tbsp) natural low-fat yogurt
4 very large Continental tomatoes, about 350 g (12 oz) each
spring onion tops, to garnish

/ 1 / Flake the smoked trout flesh, discarding the skin and any bones.

/ 2 / Finely chop the cucumber, sprinkle with salt and leave for 30 minutes to dégorge. Rinse and drain well, then dry thoroughly with absorbent kitchen paper.

/ 3 / Finely chop the mushrooms, combine with the cucumber, horseradish, lemon juice and yogurt. Fold in the trout, then add salt and pepper to taste.

/ 4 / Skin the tomatoes: put them in a bowl, pour over boiling water and leave for 2 minutes. Drain, then plunge into a bowl of cold water. Remove the tomatoes one at a time and peel off the skin with your fingers.

/ 5 / Slice the tomatoes thickly, then sandwich in pairs with the trout mixture.

/ 6 / Arrange the tomato 'sandwiches' in a shallow serving dish. Garnish with snipped spring onion tops and chill in the refrigerator until ready to serve.

KIPPER MOUSSE

Kippers are herrings which have been split and cold-smoked, and they need cooking before eating. Standing them in boiling water for a minute or so is the traditional, and best, method. When buying kippers, check for plump flesh and an oily skin – these are signs of quality. A dark brown colour does not necessarily mean a good kipper, as this is probably an artificial dye. Some of the best kippers are the undyed Manx variety – available from good fishmongers.

Serve tangy Kipper Mousse as part of a light lunch, or as a starter to any main meal, with wholemeal toast.

SMOKED TROUT WITH TOMATOES AND MUSHROOMS

Serve with thin slices of brown bread for a starter before a light main course, or as a light lunch themselves.

HUMMUS

Hummus – or as it is more correctly called, *hummus bi tahini* – is a traditional dip from the Middle East, where it is served as part of the *mezze*. The *mezze* course is similar to the French hors d'oeuvre, a collection of savoury titbits designed to titillate the appetite before the main meal is served. In this country you can serve hummus on its own as a starter.

HUMMUS

SERVES 8

225 g (8 oz) dried chick peas, soaked overnight, or two 400 g (14 oz) cans chick peas

juice of 2 large lemons

150 ml (¼ pint) tahini (paste of finely ground sesame seeds)

1-2 garlic cloves, skinned and crushed

60 ml (4 tbsp) olive oil

salt and pepper

black olives and chopped fresh parsley, to garnish

warm pitta bread, to serve

/ 1 / If using dried chick peas, drain, place in a saucepan and cover with cold water. Bring to the boil and simmer gently for 2 hours or until the peas are tender.

/ 2 / Drain the peas, reserving a little of the liquid. Put them in a blender or food processor, reserving a few for garnish, and gradually add the reserved liquid and the lemon juice, blending well after each addition in order to form a smooth purée.

/ 3 / Add the tahini paste, garlic and all but 10 ml (2 tsp) of the oil. Season with salt and pepper to taste. Blend again until the mixture is completely smooth.

/ 4 / Spoon into a serving dish and sprinkle with the reserved oil. Garnish with the reserved chick peas, the olives and chopped parsley. Serve with warm pitta bread.

AVOCADO RAMEKINS

These Avocado Ramekins are firmer than the Avocado and Garlic Dip and are, therefore, more suitable for serving as individual starters rather than a dip.

BUTTER BEAN PÂTÉ

Serve this creamy dip with fingers of hot wholemeal pitta bread or granary toast for an informal supper party starter.

If you want to make Butter Bean Pâté really quickly, use two 396 g (14 oz) cans butter beans and start the recipe from the beginning of step 3.

BUTTER BEAN PÂTÉ

SERVES 6 - 8

225 g (8 oz) dried butter beans, soaked in cold water overnight

60 ml (4 tbsp) olive oil

juice of 2 lemons

2 garlic cloves, skinned and crushed

30 ml (2 tbsp) chopped fresh coriander

salt and pepper

coriander sprigs and black olives, to garnish

/ 1 / Drain the butter beans into a sieve and rinse thoroughly under cold running water. Put in a saucepan, cover with cold water and bring to the boil.

/ 2 / With a slotted spoon, skim off any scum that rises to the surface. Half cover the pan with a lid and simmer for 1½-2 hours until the beans are very tender.

/ 3 / Drain the beans and rinse under cold running water. Put half of the beans in a blender or food processor with half of the oil, lemon juice, garlic and coriander. Blend to a smooth purée, then transfer to a bowl. Repeat with the remaining beans, oil, lemon juice, garlic and chopped coriander.

/ 4 / Beat the 2 batches of purée together until well mixed, then add seasoning to taste.

/ 5 / Turn the pâté into a serving bowl and rough up the surface with the prongs of a fork. Garnish with coriander sprigs and black olives. Chill in the refrigerator until ready to serve.

AVOCADO RAMEKINS

SERVES 4

1 large ripe avocado

finely grated rind and juice of 1 lemon

100 g (4 oz) curd cheese

60 ml (4 tbsp) natural low-fat yogurt

1 small garlic clove, skinned and crushed

salt and pepper

parsley sprigs, to garnish

fingers of wholemeal toast, to serve

/ 1 / Halve, stone and peel the avocado. Put the flesh in a bowl and mash with a fork, then add the lemon rind and juice, curd cheese, yogurt, garlic and salt and pepper to taste. Blend until smooth.

/ 2 / Spoon the mixture into 4 ramekins and chill in the refrigerator for about 30 minutes.

/ 3 / Garnish each dish with a sprig of parsley and serve immediately with small fingers of wholemeal toast.

AVOCADO AND GARLIC DIP WITH CRUDITÉS

SERVES 4 - 6

2 ripe avocados
juice of 1 lemon
225 g (8 oz) low-fat soft cheese
2 large garlic cloves, skinned and crushed
dash of Tabasco sauce, to taste
salt and pepper
4 medium carrots
4 celery sticks
225 g (8 oz) cauliflower florets
100 g (4 oz) button mushrooms, wiped
8 cherry tomatoes or large radishes

/ 1 / Cut the avocados in half, then twist the halves in opposite directions to separate them. Remove the stones.

/ 2 / With a teaspoon, scoop the avocado flesh from the shells into a bowl.

/ 3 / Mash the avocado flesh with a fork, adding half of the lemon juice to prevent the avocado discolouring.

/ 4 / Whisk in the cheese and garlic until evenly mixed, then add Tabasco and seasoning to taste.

/ 5 / Transfer the dip to a serving bowl. Cover tightly with cling film, then chill in the refrigerator until serving time (but no longer than 2 hours' chilling).

/ 6 / Before serving, prepare the vegetables. Scrape the carrots and cut them into thin sticks. Trim the celery and scrub clean under cold running water, then cut into thin sticks. Wash the cauliflower and separate into bite-sized florets. Toss the mushrooms in the remaining lemon juice.

/ 7 / To serve, uncover the dip and place the bowl in the centre of a large serving platter and surround with the prepared vegetables. Serve immediately or the avocado may discolour.

Serve this garlicky dip for informal nibbles with your drinks before you and your guests sit down to dinner.

Avocado and Garlic Dip with Crudités

HORS D'OEUVRES VARIÉS

SERVES 6

tomato salad with basil (see below)
potato salad (see below)
herbed mushrooms (see below)
marinated green beans (see below)
palm hearts or artichoke hearts
pickled vegetables, such as gherkins, onions or cauliflower
fresh quails' eggs or bottled quails' eggs in the shell
selection of cold cooked meats
selection of fish hors d'oeuvres, such as herring fillets in wine, anchovy fillets and smoked salmon
selection of shellfish, such as smoked oysters, smoked mussels, cockles or winkles

Choose 4-5 dishes from the above, including at least 1 meat and 1 fish dish.

/ 1 / *For the tomato salad:* slice 3 ripe tomatoes thinly, place in a bowl and pour over ½ quantity French dressing (see page 149) mixed with 15 ml (1 tbsp) chopped fresh basil. Chill in the refrigerator for 1 hour.

/ 2 / *For the potato salad:* cook 450 g (1 lb) new potatoes until tender, then drain well. While still hot, toss in ½ quantity French dressing (see page 149) and stir in 4 chopped spring onions. Chill in the refrigerator for at least 2 hours before serving.

/ 3 / *For the herbed mushrooms:* trim 225 g (8 oz) button mushrooms and toss them in a dressing made with 60 ml (4 tbsp) cider vinegar, 15 ml (1 tbsp) polyunsaturated oil, 15 ml (1 tbsp) chopped fresh tarragon or 5 ml (1 tsp) dried, 15 ml (1 tbsp) chopped fresh marjoram or 5 ml (1 tsp) dried, pinch of raw cane sugar and salt and pepper to taste. Chill in the refrigerator for 8-12 hours.

/ 4 / *For the marinated green beans:* trim and boil 450 g (1 lb) green beans until just tender. Drain and toss in a dressing made from 1 medium finely chopped onion, 100 ml (4 fl oz) olive oil, 100 ml (4 fl oz) white wine vinegar, pinch of raw cane sugar and salt and pepper to taste. Chill in the refrigerator for 1 hour.

/ 5 / *For the quails' eggs:* boil the fresh eggs for 3 minutes and plunge immediately into cold water. Leave until completely cold. Serve in their shells.

/ 6 / Serve hors d'oeuvres variés in a series of small dishes; these can be arranged on a large tray lined with lettuce leaves. Serve with French bread.

BUTTERFLY PRAWNS

SERVES 4

900 g (2 lb) medium raw prawns, in their shells
50 g (2 oz) butter or margarine
6 garlic cloves, skinned and crushed
juice of 4 limes or 2 lemons
2.5 cm (1 inch) piece of fresh root ginger, peeled and finely chopped
15 ml (1 tbsp) ground coriander
30 ml (2 tbsp) ground cumin
2.5 ml (½ tsp) ground cardamom
15 ml (1 tbsp) ground turmeric
15 ml (1 tbsp) paprika
2.5 ml (½ tsp) chilli powder
salt
lime wedges, to garnish

/ 1 / Remove the shell from the prawns, leaving the tail shell intact

/ 2 / With kitchen scissors, split each prawn along the inner curve, stopping at the tail shell and cutting deep enough to expose the dark vein running the length of the prawn.

/ 3 / Spread the prawn wide open, remove the dark vein and rinse under cold running water. Dry well on absorbent kitchen paper.

/ 4 / Melt the butter or margarine in a saucepan, then set aside. Put the garlic in a bowl, add the lime or lemon juice, ginger, spices and salt to taste and mix well together. Stir in the melted butter or margarine.

/ 5 / Coat the prawns liberally with this mixture, cover and leave to marinate in the refrigerator for 3-4 hours.

/ 6 / Place the prawns in a grill pan and cook under a hot grill for 2 minutes on each side. Serve immediately, with the juices spooned over, garnished with wedges of lime.

HORS D'OEUVRES VARIÉS

French Hors d'Oeuvres Variés can be anything from a simple choice of grated carrots and tomato salad, to a sumptuous spread of 10 or more dishes. For a family meal, only 1 or 2 dishes are served, whereas for a formal dinner party the choice will obviously be wider. Many French cooks buy hors d'oeuvre from the local *charcuterie.* Far from being inferior, these bought ingredients are beautifully prepared and presented, using only the best ingredients, and French cooks are proud to offer them to their guests.

Serve Hors d'Oeuvres Variés with crusty French bread and a French red or white wine, then follow with any French main course dish and dessert.

Picture opposite:
Hors d'Oeuvres Variés

Mussels with Garlic and Parsley

MUSSELS WITH GARLIC AND PARSLEY

SERVES 4 - 6

2.3 litres (4 pints) or 1.1-1.4 kg (2½-3 lb) mussels in their shells
150 ml (10 tbsp) fresh wholemeal breadcrumbs
150 ml (10 tbsp) chopped fresh parsley
2 garlic cloves, skinned and finely chopped
pepper
100 ml (4 fl oz) olive oil
30 ml (2 tbsp) grated Parmesan cheese
lemon wedges, to garnish
wholemeal French bread, to serve

/ 1 / Put the mussels in the sink and scrub them with a hard brush in several changes of water.

/ 2 / Scrape off any barnacles with a sharp knife. Cut off any protruding hairy tufts.

/ 3 / Leave the mussels to soak in a bowl of cold water for 20 minutes, then discard any that are not tightly closed or do not close on being given a sharp tap.

/ 4 / Drain the mussels and place in a large saucepan. Cover and cook over high heat for 5-10 minutes until the mussels are open, shaking the pan frequently. Discard any unopened mussels and shell the rest, reserving one half of each empty shell.

/ 5 / Strain the mussel liquid through a sieve lined with absorbent kitchen paper. Mix together the breadcrumbs, parsley, garlic and plenty of pepper. Add the oil and 60 ml (4 tbsp) of the mussel liquid. Blend well together.

/ 6 / Place the mussels in their half shells on 2 baking sheets. With your fingers, pick up a good pinch of the breadcrumb mixture and press it down on each mussel, covering it well and filling the shell. Sprinkle with the Parmesan cheese.

/ 7 / Bake in the oven at 230°C (450°F) mark 8 for 10 minutes, swapping the baking sheets over halfway through the cooking time. Garnish the mussels with lemon wedges and serve with French bread.

BLINI

Russian Buckwheat Pancakes

MAKES 24

300 ml (½ pint) semi-skimmed milk
2.5 ml (½ tsp) dried yeast
125 g (4 oz) buckwheat or wholemeal flour
125 g (4 oz) plain white flour
1 egg, separated
15 g (½ oz) butter or margarine, melted
pinch of salt
polyunsaturated oil, for frying
2 eggs, hard-boiled and finely chopped
1 medium onion, skinned and finely chopped
150 ml (¼ pint) smetana or soured cream
caviar or lumpfish roe

/ 1 / Warm the milk to blood temperature (lukewarm). Stir in the dried yeast and leave in a warm place for 15-20 minutes or until beginning to froth.

/ 2 / Mix the flours together in a bowl. Gradually beat in the milk mixture to form a smooth, thick batter. Cover and leave again in a warm place for about 40 minutes until the batter has doubled in size.

/ 3 / Beat the egg yolk, melted butter or margarine and salt into the batter. Whisk the egg white until stiff and fold it into the batter mixture until evenly incorporated.

/ 4 / Lightly oil a non-stick frying pan. Place over moderate heat. Drop tablespoonfuls of batter into the pan. Cook for about 2-3 minutes until bubbles form on the top.

/ 5 / Turn the pancakes over with a palette knife and cook for a further 1 minute until golden brown. Keep warm between layers of greaseproof paper in a low oven until all the batter is cooked.

/ 6 / Serve the blini with chopped hard-boiled egg, chopped onion, spoonfuls of smetana and caviar or lumpfish roe.

BLINI

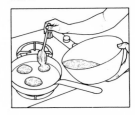

Lightly oil a non-stick frying pan. Place over moderate heat. Drop small spoonfuls of batter into the pan. Cook for about 2-3 minutes until bubbles form.

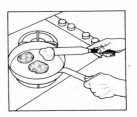

Turn the pancakes over with a palette knife and cook for a further 1 minute until golden brown. Keep warm between layers of greaseproof paper in a low oven until all the batter is cooked.

Serve Blini as part of a Russian-style meal.

MARINATED
MUSHROOMS

These make a light and
refreshing starter before a
substantial main course.
Serve with crusty brown
bread to mop up the juices.

MARINATED
MUSHROOMS

S E R V E S   4

450 g (1 lb) small button mushrooms, wiped

30 ml (2 tbsp) wine vinegar

90 ml (6 tbsp) sunflower oil

pinch of mustard powder

pinch of raw cane sugar

salt and pepper

chopped fresh parsley, to garnish

/ 1 / Trim the mushrooms. Leave small mushrooms whole and cut larger ones in quarters.

/ 2 / Put the vinegar, oil, mustard and sugar in a bowl with seasoning to taste. Whisk together with a fork until well blended.

/ 3 / Add the mushrooms and stir to coat in the marinade. Cover and leave to marinate in the refrigerator for 6-8 hours, stirring occasionally.

/ 4 / Taste and adjust the seasoning of the mushrooms, then divide equally between 4 individual shallow serving dishes. Sprinkle with chopped parsley and serve immediately.

LETTUCE AND
MUSHROOM COCOTTE

Cultivated mushrooms are
commonplace ingredients
today, but in ancient times
mushrooms were called the
'food of the gods' and the
Egyptian Pharaohs believed
that they had magical
powers. These days
mushrooms are valued for
their nutritional value; they
are rich in protein,
containing more than any
other vegetable, and also
extremely rich in vitamins
B1, B2 and B6, plus the
minerals potassium,
phosphorus and copper.
They are the perfect
vegetable to serve for 1 or
2 people because they can
be bought in small
quantities and only take a
few minutes to prepare and
cook. Don't wash cultivated
mushrooms; they are
grown in sterilized
compost and only need
wiping with a damp cloth
to remove any spore dust.

Serve Lettuce and
Mushroom Cocotte with
fingers of wholemeal toast
for a starter, or with a
mixed salad for a light lunch
or supper.

L E T T U C E   A N D
M U S H R O O M
C O C O T T E

S E R V E S   1

15 g (½ oz) butter or margarine

50 g (2 oz) mushrooms, sliced

¼ small lettuce, finely shredded

2.5 ml (½ tsp) grated nutmeg

salt and pepper

1 egg

15 ml (1 tbsp) single cream (optional)

15 ml (1 tbsp) fresh breadcrumbs

/ 1 / Melt the butter or margarine in a saucepan, add the mushrooms and cook gently for 2-3 minutes or until the mushrooms are soft. Stir in the lettuce and cook for 1 minute until the lettuce is wilted. Add the nutmeg and plenty of salt and pepper.

/ 2 / Spoon the lettuce and mushroom mixture into a small, shallow flameproof dish and make a well in the centre.

/ 3 / Crack the egg into the hollow and spoon over the cream, if liked. Sprinkle over the breadcrumbs.

/ 4 / Cook under a preheated moderate grill for about 10 minutes until the egg is just set. Serve immediately.

/ 5 / To serve 2: double the quantity of ingredients and divide the mixture between 2 individual shallow flameproof dishes.

P O T T E D
C H I C K E N   W I T H
T A R R A G O N

S E R V E S   6 - 8

1.4 kg (3 lb) oven-ready chicken

45 ml (3 tbsp) dry sherry

15 ml (1 tbsp) chopped fresh tarragon or 5 ml (1 tsp) dried

50 g (2 oz) butter or margarine

1 medium onion, skinned and chopped

1 medium carrot, peeled and chopped

salt and pepper

fresh tarragon sprigs, to garnish

toast, to serve (optional)

/ 1 / Place the chicken in a flameproof casserole with the sherry, tarragon, butter or margarine, vegetables and salt and pepper to taste. Cover tightly and cook in the oven at 180°C (350°F) mark 4 for 1½ hours.

/ 2 / Lift the chicken out of the casserole, cut off all the flesh, reserving the skin and bones. Coarsely mince the chicken meat in a food processor or mincer.

/ 3 / If necessary, boil the contents of the casserole rapidly until the liquid has reduced to 225 ml (8 fl oz). Strain, reserving the juices.

/ 4 / Mix the minced chicken and juices together, then check the seasoning. Pack into small dishes, cover with cling film and chill in the refrigerator for 4 hours.

/ 5 / Leave at cool room temperature for 30 minutes before serving. Garnish with fresh tarragon sprigs and serve with toast, if liked.

Smoked Mackerel with Apple

SMOKED MACKEREL WITH APPLE

SERVES 6 - 8

100 g (4 oz) celery, washed and trimmed
100 g (4 oz) cucumber
100 g (4 oz) red eating apple, cored
350 g (12 oz) smoked mackerel
150 ml (¼ pint) soured cream
30 ml (2 tbsp) lemon juice
paprika
1 small crisp lettuce
lemon wedges, to serve (optional)

/ 1 / Finely chop the celery, cucumber and apple (skin the cucumber if tough).

/ 2 / Skin the fish, then flake the flesh roughly with a fork. Discard the bones.

/ 3 / Combine the celery, cucumber, apple and mackerel in a bowl. Stir in the soured cream, lemon juice and paprika to taste.

/ 4 / Shred the lettuce on a board with a sharp knife. Place a little lettuce in the bases of 6-8 stemmed glasses. Divide the mackerel equally between them.

/ 5 / Garnish each glass with a lemon wedge if liked, and sprinkle paprika over the top. Serve at room temperature.

There are 2 kinds of smoked mackerel available; hot-smoked and cold-smoked. Hot-smoked mackerel is the one most widely available, and it does not need cooking before eating, whereas cold-smoked mackerel does. When buying mackerel for this recipe, check with the fishmonger or packet instructions.

Aubergines range in colour from white and whitish green through dark green to yellowish purple to red-purple to black. They vary in size, some weighing as much as 450 g (1 lb). When buying aubergines, look for firm, shiny fruit that are free from blemishes.

Avocado and Orange Salad with Citrus Dressing

CHILLED RATATOUILLE

SERVES 6

1 large aubergine, about 350 g (12 oz) in weight
salt and pepper
450 g (1 lb) courgettes
225 g (8 oz) trimmed leeks
450 g (1 lb) tomatoes
1 green pepper
60 ml (4 tbsp) polyunsaturated oil
125 g (4 oz) button mushrooms
150 ml (¼ pint) chicken stock
30 ml (2 tbsp) tomato purée
15 ml (1 tbsp) chopped fresh rosemary or 2.5 ml (½ tsp) dried
French bread, to serve (optional)

/ 1 / Wipe the aubergine, discard the ends and cut the flesh into large bite-sized pieces.

/ 2 / Put the aubergine pieces in a colander, sprinkling each layer lightly with salt. Cover with a plate, place heavy weights on top, then leave to drain for 30 minutes. Rinse under cold running water and pat dry with absorbent kitchen paper.

/ 3 / Wipe the courgettes and slice diagonally into 5 mm (¼ inch) thick pieces.

Cut the aubergines into thin slices. Sprinkle with salt and set aside to drain in a sieve or colander for 30 minutes. Rinse under cold running water and pat dry with absorbent kitchen paper.

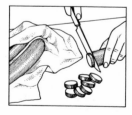

Wash the courgettes and pat dry with absorbent kitchen paper. Top and tail them and then cut into thin slices.

/ 4 / Cut the leeks across into similar sized pieces, discarding the root ends and any tough dark leaves. Wash, pushing the slices apart, and drain well.

/ 5 / Skin and quarter the tomatoes, then push out the pips into a nylon sieve placed over a bowl. Reserve the tomato juice. Halve each tomato quarter lengthwise. Slice the pepper into narrow strips, discarding the seeds.

/ 6 / Heat the oil in a large sauté or frying pan. Add the aubergine and courgettes and fry over high heat for 2-3 minutes, turning frequently. Stir in the remaining vegetables with the chicken stock, tomato purée, reserved tomato juice, rosemary and salt and pepper to taste.

/ 7 / Bring the contents of the pan to the boil, cover and simmer for 8-10 minutes. The vegetables should be just tender with a hint of crispness, not mushy. Adjust the seasoning and pour into a bowl to cool for 30 minutes. Chill in the refrigerator for at least 4 hours.

/ 8 / To serve, turn into a large serving bowl or individual dishes. Serve with French bread, preferably wholemeal, if liked.

AVOCADO AND ORANGE SALAD WITH CITRUS DRESSING

SERVES 6

150 ml (¼ pint) polyunsaturated oil
105 ml (7 tbsp) freshly squeezed grapefruit juice
15 ml (1 tbsp) snipped fresh chives
2.5 ml (½ tsp) raw cane sugar
salt and pepper
3 medium oranges
3 ripe avocados

/ 1 / Put the oil in a screw-top jar with the grapefruit juice, chives, sugar and salt and pepper to taste. Shake well to mix.

/ 2 / Using a serrated knife, remove the rind and white pith from the oranges.

/ 3 / Cut the oranges into segments and place in a shallow dish. Shake the dressing again, then pour over the oranges. Cover the dish with cling film and chill in the refrigerator for at least 1 hour, or for up to 24 hours.

/ 4 / To serve, cut the avocados in half and twist to remove the stones. Peel off the skin, then slice the flesh neatly.

/ 5 / Remove the orange segments from the marinade and arrange on individual plates, alternating with avocado slices. Pour over the marinade and serve immediately.

CARROT AND CELERIAC VINAIGRETTE

SERVES 1

30 ml (2 tbsp) olive or vegetable oil, or 15 ml (1 tbsp) walnut oil and 15 ml (1 tbsp) vegetable oil, mixed
15 ml (1 tbsp) wine or cider vinegar or lemon juice
5 ml (1 tsp) wholegrain mustard
pinch of caster sugar
salt and pepper
50 g (2 oz) celeriac
1 medium carrot
6 walnut halves, chopped
watercress sprigs or lettuce leaves, to garnish

/ 1 / Put the oil, vinegar or lemon juice, mustard and sugar in a small bowl. Whisk together until thick, then add salt and pepper to taste.

/ 2 / Peel the celeriac and grate into the bowl of dressing. Peel the carrot and grate into the celeriac and dressing. Add the chopped walnuts and mix together thoroughly. Cover the bowl tightly with cling film. Chill in the refrigerator for at least 1 hour.

/ 3 / To serve, uncover and mix once more. Pile on to an individual serving plate and garnish with sprigs of watercress or lettuce leaves.

/ 4 / To serve 2: use double the quantity of carrot, celeriac and walnuts, but use 45 ml (3 tbsp) oil and 15 ml (1 tbsp) vinegar and the same amount of sugar and mustard.

MELON AND PRAWN SALAD

SERVES 8

1 small honeydew melon
30 ml (2 tbsp) tomato juice
30 ml (2 tbsp) cider vinegar
30 ml (2 tbsp) clear honey
1 egg yolk
450 g (1 lb) peeled prawns
225 g (8 oz) cucumber, diced
15 ml (1 tbsp) chopped fresh tarragon or 5 ml (1 tsp) dried
salt and pepper
tarragon sprigs and 8 large whole cooked prawns, to garnish

/ 1 / Cut the melon in half and scrape out the pips from the centre with a teaspoon.

/ 2 / Scoop out the melon flesh with a melon baller. Divide the melon balls equally between 8 individual serving dishes.

/ 3 / Make the tomato dressing: put the tomato juice, vinegar, honey and egg yolk in a blender or food processor and blend together.

/ 4 / Toss the prawns, cucumber and chopped tarragon in the tomato dressing. Add salt and pepper to taste. Spoon on top of the melon balls and chill in the refrigerator for at least 1 hour. Garnish with sprigs of tarragon and whole prawns before serving.

The avocado is a very nourishing fruit, high in protein and rich in vegetable oil, vitamins and minerals. Although it is classed as a fruit, it is usually eaten as a vegetable. A ripe avocado always 'gives' slightly when pressed at the pointed end. A hard, under-ripe fruit will ripen in 1-2 days at room temperature, or in about a week in the refrigerator. Ripe avocados can be stored for 3-4 days in the refrigerator.

CARROT AND CELERIAC VINAIGRETTE

Sometimes known as turnip-rooted celery, celeriac is a large, knobbly, swollen root with a pronounced celery flavour. It is a versatile winter vegetable to add to soups, stocks, casseroles and stews, as well as grated raw as an hors d'oeuvre or in salads. Strips or slices may be blanched and served in a salad. Choose bulbs which are firm, heavy and free from blemishes. Avoid very large bulbs, which may be too tough.

SHAMI KEBABS

Spicy Meat and Lentil Patties

SERVES 6

175 g (6 oz) red lentils
450 g (1 lb) fresh lean minced lamb or beef
4 garlic cloves, skinned and crushed
1 medium onion, skinned and finely minced
2.5 cm (1 inch) piece of fresh root ginger, peeled and finely chopped
2 small fresh green chillies, seeded and finely chopped
5 ml (1 tsp) ground cumin
5 ml (1 tsp) ground coriander
salt
8 black peppercorns
45 ml (3 tbsp) chopped fresh mint
50 g (2 oz) butter or margarine, softened
2 eggs, beaten
lemon or lime wedges, to garnish
CUCUMBER RAITA
1 cucumber
salt and pepper
150 ml (¼ pint) natural low-fat yogurt
pinch of chilli powder
pinch of ground cumin

SHAMI KEBABS

In India, kebabs such as these can be bought from street stalls. Although restaurants serve them as starters or main courses, kebabs are really snack foods to be eaten with the fingers, sometimes wrapped in bread.

The Cucumber Raita makes a refreshing contrast to the spicy kebabs.

/ 1 / Put the lentils in a large saucepan with the minced meat, garlic, onion, ginger, chillies, cumin, coriander, salt to taste, peppercorns, half of the mint and 450 ml (¾ pint) water.

/ 2 / Bring to the boil, then lower the heat and simmer, uncovered, for at least 45 minutes or until the lentils are tender and most of the water is absorbed. Stir the mixture frequently during cooking to prevent it sticking. When cooked, turn the mixture into a bowl and cool completely, for at least 2 hours.

/ 3 / Meanwhile, make the raita: coarsely grate the cucumber on to a plate, sprinkle with salt and leave to stand for 30 minutes. Rinse and drain well. Put the yogurt in a small bowl and stir in the chilli powder, cumin and cucumber. Season with pepper, then chill the mixture in the refrigerator.

/ 4 / Put the cold lentil mixture in a blender or food processor with the softened butter or margarine, the remaining mint and eggs. Work until smooth and well amalgamated, then tip out on to a plate or board.

/ 5 / Wetting your hands to prevent the mixture sticking, shape the mixture into 24 small round flat cakes. Place on greaseproof paper and chill in the refrigerator for 30 minutes.

/ 6 / Wipe a heavy frying pan with a little oil and place over a moderate heat until hot. Cook the kebabs for 3 minutes on each side until crisp and golden brown. Do not try to move the kebabs while they are cooking or they will disintegrate.

/ 7 / Serve the kebabs hot, garnished with lemon or lime wedges and accompanied by cucumber raita.

STUFFED CABBAGE

SERVES 4

8-10 large cabbage leaves, trimmed
30 ml (2 tbsp) polyunsaturated oil
2 medium onions, skinned and finely chopped
100 g (4 oz) mushrooms, chopped
50 g (2 oz) long-grain brown rice
450 ml (¾ pint) vegetable or chicken stock
397 g (14 oz) can tomatoes
5 ml (1 tsp) Worcestershire sauce
2.5 ml (½ tsp) dried basil
salt and pepper
50 g (2 oz) hazelnuts, skinned and chopped

STUFFED CABBAGE

Savoy cabbage is particularly good for this recipe. These firm, dark green cabbages are easily recognized by their very crinkly leaves. Look for a cabbage that is a good fresh green colour and heavy for its size.

/ 1 / Blanch the cabbage leaves in boiling water for 3-4 minutes. Drain thoroughly.

/ 2 / Heat 15 ml (1 tbsp) of the oil in a frying pan and fry half the onions with the mushrooms for 5 minutes until browned. Add the rice and stir well.

/ 3 / Add 300 ml (½ pint) of the stock to the rice. Cover and cook for about 40 minutes until the rice is tender and the stock has been completely absorbed.

/ 4 / Meanwhile, make a tomato sauce. Heat the remaining oil in a pan and fry the remaining onion for about 5 minutes until golden. Add the tomatoes, remaining stock, Worcestershire sauce, basil and salt and pepper to taste. Bring to the boil, stirring, and simmer for 8 minutes. Purée in a blender or food processor until smooth.

/ 5 / Stir the hazelnuts into the rice with salt and pepper to taste, then remove from the heat. Divide the rice mixture between the cabbage leaves and roll up to make neat parcels.

/ 6 / Arrange the cabbage parcels in an oven-proof dish. Pour over the tomato sauce. Cover and cook in the oven at 180°C (350°F) mark 4 for about 1 hour until tender.

MOZZARELLA, AVOCADO AND TOMATO SALAD

SERVES 4

2 ripe avocados
120 ml (8 tbsp) French Dressing (see page 149)
175 g (6 oz) Mozzarella cheese, thinly sliced
4 medium tomatoes, thinly sliced
chopped fresh parsley and mint sprigs, to garnish

/ 1 / Halve the avocados lengthways and carefully remove the stones. Peel and cut the avocados into slices.

/ 2 / Pour the dressing over the avocado slices. Stir to coat the slices thoroughly.

/ 3 / Arrange slices of Mozzarella, tomato and avocado on 4 individual serving plates. Spoon over the dressing and garnish with chopped parsley and a sprig of mint.

GREEK SALAD

SERVES 4

½ large cucumber
salt and pepper
450 g (1 lb) firm ripe tomatoes
1 medium red onion
18 black olives
100 g (4 oz) Feta cheese, cut into cubes
60 ml (4 tbsp) olive oil
15 ml (1 tbsp) lemon juice
good pinch of dried oregano
warm pitta bread, to serve

/ 1 / Peel the cucumber and slice thinly. Put into a colander or sieve, sprinkle with a little salt and leave to stand for about 15 minutes.

/ 2 / Slice the tomatoes thinly. Skin the onion and slice into thin rings. Rinse the cucumber under cold running water, drain and pat dry with absorbent kitchen paper.

/ 3 / Arrange the cucumber, tomatoes and onion in a serving dish. Scatter the olives and cubed cheese over the top.

/ 4 / In a bowl, whisk together the oil, lemon juice, oregano and salt and pepper to taste. Spoon the dressing over the salad, cover tightly with cling film and chill in the refrigerator for 2-3 hours or overnight. Allow to come to room temperature for 30 minutes before serving with warm pitta bread.

MOZZARELLA, AVOCADO AND TOMATO SALAD

The Mozzarella cheese used in this salad gives it a lovely Italian flavour. Mozzarella is a pale-coloured Italian cheese. When fresh it is very soft, dripping with buttermilk. Traditionally made from buffalo milk, it is now more often made from cow's milk. It should be eaten fresh, as the cheese ripens quickly and is past its best in a few days.

GREEK SALAD

In Greece, this kind of salad is usually served as a first course with hot pitta bread, or as a side dish to barbecued kebabs.

Mozzarella, Avocado and Tomato Salad

Lunch and Supper Dishes

For quick meals and snacks, many of us rely on convenience foods: either frozen or canned – or even take-away 'junk' food. In this chapter you will find lots of ideas for nutritious quick meals which will make you think twice about opening a can. Burgers, pizzas and pasta dishes are all here, but home-made. They taste fresher and have more flavour – and you know exactly what has gone into them.

Most of the recipes here can be served with a crisp salad, then followed with fresh fruit for a healthy lunch or supper.

Crunchy Baked Potato Skins

CHILLED TROUT WITH YOGURT DRESSING

SERVES 4

4 small smoked trout

finely grated rind and juice of 1 orange

150 ml (¼ pint) natural low-fat yogurt

5 ml (1 tsp) creamed horseradish

salt and pepper

finely shredded lettuce or chicory leaves, to serve

orange segments, to garnish

/ 1 / Carefully remove the skin from the trout, then divide each fish into 2 fillets without breaking them. Discard the bones. Cover the fillets and leave to chill in the refrigerator for 30 minutes.

/ 2 / Meanwhile, mix the orange rind, juice, yogurt and horseradish together. Season with salt and pepper to taste. Chill the dressing in the refrigerator for at least 30 minutes.

/ 3 / Cover 4 small serving plates with shredded lettuce or chicory leaves. Carefully lay 2 fillets on each plate and spoon over the dressing. Garnish each portion with orange segments and serve immediately.

MUSHROOM FLAN

SERVES 4

100 g (4 oz) wholemeal breadcrumbs

300 ml (½ pint) natural low-fat yogurt

salt and pepper

4 eggs

150 ml (¼ pint) semi-skimmed milk

175 g (6 oz) mushrooms, sliced

4 spring onions, trimmed and chopped

75 g (3 oz) low-fat Cheddar type cheese, grated

/ 1 / Mix the breadcrumbs and 150 ml (¼ pint) of the yogurt to a paste. Add salt and pepper.

/ 2 / Use to line a 23 cm (9 inch) flan dish or tin, pressing into shape with the fingers.

/ 3 / Whisk the eggs and milk together with the remaining yogurt and salt and pepper to taste.

/ 4 / Arrange the mushrooms, spring onions and half the cheese on the base of the flan. Pour the egg mixture over the top, then sprinkle with the remaining cheese.

/ 5 / Bake the flan in the oven at 180°C (350°F) mark 4 for about 30 minutes or until brown and set. Serve warm.

CHILLED TROUT WITH YOGURT DRESSING

This makes a lovely light lunch for serving in the garden in the summer time. Serve with slices of lightly buttered brown bread.

MUSHROOM FLAN

This unusual base for a flan is made simply from wholemeal breadcrumbs and yogurt – less fattening than a conventional shortcrust pastry base – and with healthier ingredients.

This cheesy Mushroom Flan is best served with a colourful salad such as a mixture of sweetcorn, green pepper and onion.

Picture opposite:
Chilled Trout with Yogurt Dressing

Mushroom Flan

Fettuccine with Clam Sauce

Chicken Liver Skewers are quick and easy to make for a family lunch or supper, or impromptu entertaining. All you need to accompany them is a quickly cooked colourful vegetable, such as stir-fry mange-tout.

CHICKEN LIVER SKEWERS

SERVES 4

2 small oranges
200 ml (7 fl oz) unsweetened orange juice
5 ml (1 tsp) chopped fresh tarragon or 2.5 ml (½ tsp) dried
450 g (1 lb) whole chicken livers
2 slices of wholemeal bread, crumbed
1 green pepper, about 175 g (6 oz), cored, seeded and roughly chopped
1 medium onion, skinned and roughly chopped
275 g (10 oz) beansprouts
1 small bunch of chives, snipped
salt and pepper

/ 1 / Finely grate the rind of 1 of the oranges. Place in a saucepan with the orange juice and tarragon and simmer for 2-3 minutes until reduced by half.

/ 2 / Cut the tops and bottoms off both oranges, then remove the skin by working around the oranges in a spiral, using a sharp serrated knife and a sawing action.

/ 3 / Divide the oranges into segments by cutting through the membranes on either side of each segment with a sharp knife.

/ 4 / Cut the chicken livers in half and toss lightly in the breadcrumbs. Place in a lightly greased grill pan and grill for 2 minutes on each side or until just firm.

/ 5 / Thread the pepper and onion pieces on to 4 oiled kebab skewers with the livers.

/ 6 / Place the skewers in the grill pan and spoon over a little of the reduced orange juice. Grill for 2-3 minutes on each side, turning and basting occasionally.

/ 7 / Meanwhile, put the beansprouts in a steamer over boiling water for 2-3 minutes until cooked but still slightly crisp. Warm the orange segments in a separate pan with the remaining reduced orange juice.

/ 8 / Mix the beansprouts with the chives and salt and pepper to taste and arrange on a warmed serving dish. Top with the skewers and spoon over the orange segments and juices. Serve immediately.

FETTUCCINE WITH CLAM SAUCE

SERVES 4

15 ml (1 tbsp) olive oil
1 medium onion, skinned and finely chopped
2-3 garlic cloves, skinned and crushed
700 g (1 ½ lb) tomatoes, skinned (see page 57) and roughly chopped, or 397 g (14 oz) and 225 g (8 oz) cans tomatoes
two 200 g (7 oz) cans or jars baby clams in brine, drained
30 ml (2 tbsp) chopped fresh parsley
salt and pepper
400 g (14 oz) fettuccine or other long thin pasta, preferably wholewheat

/ 1 / Make the sauce: heat the oil in a saucepan, add the onion and garlic and fry gently for 5 minutes until soft but not coloured.

/ 2 / Stir in the tomatoes and their juice, bring to the boil and cook for 15-20 minutes until slightly reduced.

/ 3 / Stir the drained clams into the sauce with 15 ml (1 tbsp) parsley and salt and pepper to taste. Remove from the heat.

/ 4 / Cook the fettuccine in a large saucepan of boiling salted water for 8-10 minutes or until just tender.

/ 5 / Reheat the sauce just before the pasta is cooked. Drain the fettuccine well, tip into a warmed serving dish and pour over the clam sauce. Sprinkle with the remaining chopped parsley to garnish.

DRESSED CRAB

SERVES 2 - 3

shell and meat from 1 medium (900 g/2 lb) cooked crab
salt and pepper
15 ml (1 tbsp) lemon juice
30 ml (2 tbsp) fresh wholemeal breadcrumbs
chopped fresh parsley
1 egg, hard-boiled
lettuce or endive, to serve

/ 1 / Using 2 forks, flake all the white meat from the crab, removing any shell or membrane. Season to taste with salt and pepper and add 5 ml (1 tsp) of the lemon juice.

/ 2 / Pound the brown meat and work in the breadcrumbs with the remaining lemon juice and salt and pepper to taste.

/ 3 / Using a small spoon, put the white meat in both ends of the crab's empty shell, making sure that it is well piled up into the shell. Keep the inside edges neat.

/ 4 / Then spoon the brown meat in a neat line down the centre, between the 2 sections of white crab meat.

/ 5 / Hold a blunt knife between the white and brown crab meat and carefully spoon lines of parsley, sieved egg yolk and chopped egg white across the crab, moving the knife as you go to keep a neat edge. Serve the shell on a bed of lettuce or endive, surrounded by the small legs.

PRAWN RISOTTO

SERVES 4

1 medium onion, skinned and thinly sliced
1 garlic clove, skinned and crushed
1 litre (1¾ pints) chicken stock
225 g (8 oz) long-grain brown rice
50 g (2 oz) small button mushrooms
½ sachet saffron threads
salt and pepper
225 g (8 oz) peeled prawns
50 g (2 oz) frozen petits pois
12 whole prawns, to garnish

/ 1 / Put the onion, garlic, stock, rice, mushrooms and saffron in a large saucepan or flameproof casserole. Add salt and pepper to taste. Bring to the boil and simmer, uncovered, for 35 minutes, stirring occasionally.

/ 2 / Stir in the prawns and petits pois. Cook over high heat for about 5 minutes, stirring occasionally, until most of the liquid has been absorbed by the rice.

/ 3 / Turn into a warmed serving dish. Garnish with the whole prawns and serve immediately.

FETTUCCINE WITH CLAM SAUCE

Fresh clams are easy to obtain in Italy, and are preferred for making this delicious sauce. If you are able to get fresh clams, so much the better. For this sauce, you will need about 2.3 litres (4 pints). Scrub them under cold running water with a stiff brush and scrape off any barnacles with a knife. Discard any clams which are not tightly closed, then put the remainder in a colander and leave them under cold running water for 20 minutes. Put the clams in a large saucepan with 300 ml (½ pint) water, cover and bring to the boil. Cook over high heat until all the shells are open (about 10 minutes), shaking the pan occasionally. If some remain closed after this time, discard them. Strain the clams, discarding the cooking liquid. Remove the meat from the shells (reserving a few whole ones to garnish, if liked), then use in step 3 of the recipe as drained canned clams.

Serve Fettuccine with Clam Sauce as either a lunch or supper dish with fresh bread rolls and a bottle of chilled dry white wine, such as Frascati, for an authentic Italian dish.

Pasta, Prawn and Apple Salad

PASTA, PRAWN AND APPLE SALAD

SERVES 6

This makes a delicious light summer lunch dish, and is particularly handy as it can be made in advance. It could also be served as a starter, if wished.

175 g (6 oz) wholemeal pasta shells
salt and pepper
150 ml (¼ pint) unsweetened apple juice
5 ml (1 tsp) chopped fresh mint
5 ml (1 tsp) white wine vinegar
225 g (8 oz) peeled prawns
225 g (8 oz) crisp eating apples
lettuce leaves
paprika, to garnish

/ 1 / Cook the pasta in boiling salted water for 10-15 minutes until tender. Drain well, rinse in cold running water and drain again.

/ 2 / Meanwhile, make the dressing. Whisk together the apple juice, mint, vinegar and salt and pepper to taste.

/ 3 / Dry the prawns with absorbent kitchen paper. Quarter, core and roughly chop the apples. Stir the prawns, apple and cooked pasta into the dressing until well mixed. Cover with cling film and refrigerate for 2-3 hours.

/ 4 / Wash the lettuce leaves, dry and shred finely. Place a little lettuce in 6 individual dishes. Spoon the prawn salad on top and dust lightly with paprika.

SPINACH ROULADE

SERVES 4

900 g (2 lb) fresh spinach, washed and trimmed
4 eggs, size 2, separated
salt and pepper
100 g (4 oz) curd cheese
30 ml (2 tbsp) natural low-fat yogurt

/ 1 / Grease and line a 35.5×25.5 cm (14×10 inch) Swiss roll tin. Set aside.

/ 2 / Chop the spinach coarsely. Place in a saucepan with only the water that clings to the leaves. Simmer for 5 minutes, then drain.

/ 3 / Cool the spinach slightly; beat in the egg yolks and salt and pepper to taste.

/ 4 / Whisk the egg whites until stiff, then fold into the spinach mixture.

/ 5 / Spread the mixture in the tin. Bake at 200°C (400°F) mark 6 for 20 minutes until firm. Beat the cheese and yogurt together.

/ 6 / When the roulade is cooked, turn it out on to a sheet of greaseproof paper, peel off the lining paper and spread immediately and quickly with the cheese mixture.

/ 7 / Roll up the roulade by gently lifting the greaseproof paper. Place, seam side down, on a serving platter. Serve hot or cold.

This makes a good vegetarian lunch or supper dish. Serve it hot with new potatoes or cold with a minted potato salad and a tomato salad.

Spinach Roulade

CHILLI PIZZA FINGERS

SERVES 6

225 g (8 oz) fresh lean minced beef
2.5 ml (½ tsp) chilli powder
1 garlic clove, skinned and crushed
1 medium onion, skinned and chopped
1 small green pepper, cored, seeded and chopped
100 g (4 oz) mushrooms, sliced
225 g (8 oz) tomatoes, skinned (see page 57) and chopped
213 g (7.5 oz) can red kidney beans, drained
150 ml (¼ pint) beef stock
225 g (8 oz) plain wholemeal flour
50 g (2 oz) medium oatmeal
15 ml (1 tbsp) baking powder
salt and pepper
50 g (2 oz) butter or margarine
1 egg, beaten
60 ml (4 tbsp) semi-skimmed milk
15 ml (1 tbsp) tomato purée
175 g (6 oz) Mozzarella cheese, thinly sliced
basil sprigs, to garnish

/ 1 / First prepare the topping: put the minced beef, chilli powder and garlic in a saucepan and dry fry for 3-4 minutes, stirring occasionally. Add the onion, green pepper and mushrooms and fry for a further 1-2 minutes. Stir in the tomatoes, kidney beans and stock. Bring to the boil and simmer for about 15 minutes, stirring the mixture occasionally, until nearly all of the liquid has evaporated.

/ 2 / Meanwhile, combine the flour, oatmeal, baking powder and a pinch of salt in a bowl.

/ 3 / Rub in the butter or margarine until the mixture resembles fine breadcrumbs. Bind to a soft dough with the egg and milk, then turn out on to a floured surface and knead lightly until the dough is smooth.

/ 4 / Roll out the dough to a 25×18 cm (10×7 inch) rectangle. Lift on to a baking sheet, then spread carefully with tomato purée. Pile the beef mixture on top and cover with the sliced Mozzarella cheese.

/ 5 / Bake in the oven at 200°C (400°F) mark 6 for about 30 minutes until golden and bubbling. Cut the pizza into fingers for serving and garnish with basil sprigs.

To make the base: combine the flour, oatmeal, baking powder and a pinch of salt in a bowl. Rub in the butter or margarine until the mixture resembles fine breadcrumbs. Bind to a soft dough with the egg and milk, then turn out on to a floured surface and knead lightly until smooth.

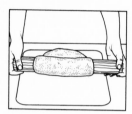

Roll out the dough to a 25 × 18 cm (10 × 7 inch) rectangle. Carefully lift on to a baking sheet using the rolling pin.

Serve these Chilli Pizza Fingers as an easy supper dish accompanied by a salad of thinly sliced or grated courgettes with French Dressing (see page 149) and snipped fresh chives.

Vegetable Terrine

V E G E T A B L E
T E R R I N E

S E R V E S   6 - 8

900 g (2 lb) turnips, peeled and cut into chunks
450 g (1 lb) carrots, peeled and sliced
450 g (1 lb) fresh spinach, trimmed, or 300 g (10.6 oz) packet frozen spinach
50 g (2 oz) butter or margarine
1 medium onion, skinned and thinly sliced
350 g (12 oz) flat mushrooms, sliced
finely grated rind and juice of 1 lemon
4 eggs
salt and white pepper
1.25 ml (¼ tsp) ground coriander
freshly grated nutmeg
30 ml (2 tbsp) chopped fresh parsley
2 ripe tomatoes, skinned
300 ml (½ pint) French Dressing (page 149)

/ 1 / Put the turnips into a medium saucepan, cover with cold water and bring to the boil. Lower the heat and simmer for 10-15 minutes until completely tender.

/ 2 / Meanwhile, put the carrots in a separate saucepan and cover with cold water. Bring to the boil and cook for 10 minutes or until completely tender. Drain both turnips and carrots.

/ 3 / Wash the fresh spinach in several changes of cold water. Place in a saucepan with only the water that clings to the leaves. Cook gently for 5 minutes until wilted, 7-10 minutes if frozen. Drain well.

/ 4 / Melt 40 g (1½ oz) of the butter or margarine in a frying pan, add the onion and fry gently for about 10 minutes until very soft. Add the mushrooms and fry, stirring constantly, for 5 minutes. Stir in the lemon rind and juice.

/ 5 / Put the mushroom mixture in a blender or food processor and work until smooth. Transfer to a small heavy-based pan. Cook over moderate heat, stirring constantly, until all the liquid has evaporated and the purée is dry.

/ 6 / Purée and dry the turnips, carrots and spinach in the same way and place each purée in a separate bowl. Add 1 egg to each purée and mix well. Season each with salt and pepper to taste. Stir the coriander into the carrot purée, the nutmeg into the spinach and the parsley into the mushroom.

/ 7 / Grease a 1.1 litre (2 pint) terrine or loaf tin with the remaining butter or margarine. Put a layer of turnip purée in the bottom, making sure it is quite level. Cover with a layer of carrot, followed by spinach and finally mushroom. Cover the tin tightly with foil.

/ 8 / Place the terrine in a roasting tin and pour in enough hot water to come three-quarters of the way up the sides of the terrine. Bake in the oven at 180°C (350°F) mark 4 for 1 ¼ hours or until firm. Remove and allow to cool slightly before turning out.

/ 9 / Just before serving put the tomatoes and French dressing in a blender or food processor and work until smooth. Do not let the dressing stand or it will separate.

/ 10 / Serve the terrine hot or cold, cut in slices with the tomato vinaigrette.

C R U N C H Y   B A K E D
P O T A T O   S K I N S

S E R V E S   4

4 medium baking potatoes
60 ml (4 tbsp) polyunsaturated oil
salt and pepper
300 ml (½ pint) natural low-fat yogurt
30 ml (2 tbsp) snipped chives

/ 1 / Pierce the potatoes all over with a skewer, then place directly on the oven shelf. Bake in the oven at 200°C (400°F) mark 6 for 1¼ hours until tender.

/ 2 / Cut each potato in half lengthways and scoop out most of the flesh with a sharp-edged teaspoon, taking care not to split the skins.

/ 3 / Stand the potato skins on a lightly oiled baking sheet. Brush them inside and out with the oil and sprinkle with salt and pepper.

/ 4 / Increase the oven temperature to 220°C (425°F) mark 7 and bake for 10 minutes.

/ 5 / Meanwhile, whisk the yogurt and chives together with seasoning to taste. Spoon into a serving bowl or sauceboat.

/ 6 / Serve the potato skins piping hot, with the yogurt dressing handed separately.

VEGETABLE TERRINE

This makes a delicious, light lunch dish served with crusty French bread or granary bread. It can also be served as a dinner party starter, if wished.

Other vegetables may be used when in season, such as cauliflower, fennel, watercress, parsnips and even peas. Try to balance colour and flavour.

CRUNCHY BAKED POTATO SKINS

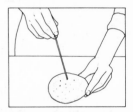

Pierce the potatoes all over with a skewer, then place directly on the oven shelf. Bake in the oven at 200°C (400°F) mark 6 for 1¼ hours until tender.

Cut each potato in half lengthways and scoop out most of the flesh with a sharp-edged teaspoon, taking care not to split the skins.

These crunchy potato skins are an American idea. Put a spoonful of dressing in each potato skin and either eat with the fingers as the Americans do, or with a knife and fork if you prefer. Apart from making a quick and easy lunch, they are also good served as a starter before spareribs or burgers.

These spiced, sweet beans make a lovely vegetarian lunch served with Boiled Rice (see page 146) or hot herb bread. They could also be served as an accompaniment to roast or barbecued pork.

SOUTHERN BAKED BEANS

SERVES 4

275 g (10 oz) dried haricot beans, soaked overnight

15 ml (1 tbsp) polyunsaturated oil

2 medium onions, skinned and chopped

225 g (8 oz) carrots, peeled and chopped

15 ml (1 tbsp) mustard powder

30 ml (2 tbsp) treacle

300 ml (½ pint) tomato juice

45 ml (3 tbsp) tomato purée

300 ml (½ pint) beer

salt and pepper

/ 1 / Drain the beans and place in a saucepan of water. Bring to the boil and simmer for 25 minutes, then drain.

/ 2 / Meanwhile, heat the oil in a flameproof casserole and fry the onions and carrots for 5 minutes until light golden.

/ 3 / Remove from the heat, stir in beans and remaining ingredients except seasoning.

/ 4 / Bring to the boil, cover and cook in the oven at 140°C (275°F) mark 1 for about 5 hours, stirring occasionally, until the beans are tender and the sauce is the consistency of syrup. Season with salt and pepper to taste.

Southern Baked Beans

SPAGHETTI WITH RATATOUILLE SAUCE

SERVES 4

1 aubergine
salt and pepper
1 medium onion, skinned
1 garlic clove, skinned
1 green pepper
1 red pepper
3 medium courgettes
350 g (12 oz) tomatoes
10 ml (2 tsp) chopped fresh basil
400 g (14 oz) wholewheat spaghetti
freshly grated Parmesan cheese, to serve

/ 1 / Dice the aubergine, then spread out on a plate and sprinkle with salt. Dégorge for 30 minutes until the juices flow.

/ 2 / Meanwhile, prepare the remaining vegetables for the ratatouille sauce. Chop the onion finely. Crush the garlic on a board with a little salt and the flat of the blade of a large knife.

/ 3 / Cut the peppers in half, remove the cores and seeds and wash well. Slice the flesh into thin strips.

/ 4 / Top and tail the courgettes, then slice them into very thin strips, leaving the skin on.

/ 5 / Skin the tomatoes. Put them in a heatproof bowl and pour in boiling water to cover. Leave to stand for 2 minutes, then drain and plunge into a bowl of cold water. Remove from the water one at a time, then peel off the skin with your fingers. Chop the flesh finely.

/ 6 / Tip the diced aubergine into a sieve and rinse under cold running water. Put into a large, heavy-based pan with the prepared vegetables, basil and seasoning to taste. Cover and cook over moderate heat for 30 minutes. Shake the pan and stir the vegetables frequently during this time.

/ 7 / Meanwhile, plunge the spaghetti into a separate large saucepan of boiling salted water. Simmer, uncovered, for 12 minutes or according to packet instructions, until *al dente* (tender but firm to the bite).

/ 8 / Drain the spaghetti thoroughly and turn into a warmed serving dish. Taste and adjust the seasoning of the ratatouille sauce, then pour over the spaghetti. Serve immediately, with the Parmesan cheese handed separately.

TOFU BURGERS WITH TOMATO SAUCE

SERVES 4

450 g (1 lb) tomatoes, skinned, or one 397 g (14 oz) can tomatoes, drained
1 garlic clove, skinned and crushed
15 ml (1 tbsp) olive oil
pinch of raw cane sugar
30 ml (2 tbsp) chopped fresh parsley
salt and pepper
225 g (8 oz) firm tofu
100 g (4 oz) fresh wholemeal breadcrumbs
2 medium carrots, grated
1 medium onion, skinned and finely chopped
pinch of dried mixed herbs
15 ml (1 tbsp) Worcestershire sauce
cayenne pepper
1 egg, beaten
polyunsaturated oil, for shallow frying

/ 1 / Make the sauce: put the tomatoes, garlic, oil, sugar, half of the parsley and salt and pepper to taste in a saucepan and simmer, uncovered, for about 10 minutes until reduced and thickened.

/ 2 / Make the burgers: put the tofu, breadcrumbs, carrots and onion in a bowl and mash together. Stir in the remaining parsley, mixed herbs and Worcestershire sauce and season with cayenne pepper and salt and pepper to taste. Bind the mixture together with the egg. Divide into 4 and shape into burgers.

/ 3 / Heat the oil in a large frying pan and shallow fry the burgers for 4-5 minutes on each side until golden brown. Drain on absorbent kitchen paper.

/ 4 / While the burgers are cooking reheat the sauce for 2-3 minutes until hot, stirring occasionally to prevent it burning.

/ 5 / Serve the burgers hot with a little of the sauce poured over and the remainder handed separately in a sauceboat.

SPAGHETTI WITH RATATOUILLE SAUCE

The wholewheat spaghetti and rich vegetable sauce together make this dish a complete meal.

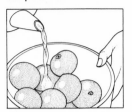

To skin the tomatoes: put them in a heatproof bowl and pour in enough boiling water to cover. Leave to stand for 2 minutes, then drain and plunge into a bowl of cold water. Remove from the water one at a time, then peel off the skin with your fingers.

TOFU BURGERS WITH TOMATO SAUCE

Tofu is also known as soya bean curd. It is off-white in colour and available either in soft blocks or in silken form. Tofu can be bought from Chinese stores, or, in its silken form, in cartons from health food shops.

Tofu provides a first class protein. It has quite low fat and carbohydrate contents and is a good source of calcium, iron and the B vitamins thiamin and riboflavin.

Beef Burgers

BEEF BURGERS

SERVES 4

Home-made burgers taste much better than the commercial varieties – and you know exactly what is in them. Serve these tasty burgers for a quick family supper, or the children's tea, with a colourful mixed salad.

450 g (1 lb) lean beef, such as chuck, shoulder or rump steak, minced
½ small onion, skinned and grated (optional)
salt and pepper
melted butter or polyunsaturated oil, for grilling
4 large soft wholemeal buns
butter or margarine, for spreading
lettuce and onion rings, to serve (optional)

/ 1 / Mix the minced beef well with the onion, if using, and season the mixture with salt and pepper to taste.

/ 2 / Shape the mixture lightly into 4 round, flat patties. Brush sparingly with a little melted butter or oil.

/ 3 / Grill the beef burgers for 8-10 minutes until cooked according to taste, turning once.

/ 4 / Meanwhile, split the buns in half and spread with a little butter or margarine. Put a beef burger inside each bun. Add a lettuce leaf and some onion rings, if liked, and serve the burgers immediately.

VARIATIONS

CHEESE BURGERS
Top the cooked beef burgers with a slice of low-fat Cheddar type cheese and cook under the grill for a further minute or until the cheese has melted.

CHILLI BURGERS
Add 15 ml (1 tbsp) chilli seasoning when mixing burgers.

PEPPERCORN BURGERS
Crush 15 ml (1 tbsp) green peppercorns and add when mixing the beef burgers.

58

SMOKED FISH TIMBALE

SERVES 6

350 g (12 oz) long-grain brown rice
15 ml (1 tbsp) turmeric
salt and pepper
350 g (12 oz) smoked haddock or cod fillet
1 small bunch spring onions, washed
2 eggs, hard-boiled and shelled
watercress sprigs and whole prawns, to garnish

/ 1 / Cook the rice with the turmeric and salt to taste in a saucepan of water for 35-40 minutes. Drain well and cool.

/ 2 / Poach the fish in enough water to just cover for 12-15 minutes. Drain and flake the cooked fish.

/ 3 / Trim the spring onions, then roughly chop them with the hard-boiled eggs. Mix with the cold rice and fish and season with salt and pepper to taste.

/ 4 / Spoon the mixture into an oiled 1.1 litre (2 pint) ring mould. Press down well, cover and chill for 2-3 hours.

/ 5 / To serve, unmould the fish ring on to a plate and garnish with watercress sprigs and the whole prawns.

Turmeric is one spice that is most frequently bought ground. Use it quickly as its flavour deteriorates on keeping. It is widely used in curries and is added to mustards and pickles. Its bright colour makes it useful for colouring rice and sweet Indian dishes.

Smoked Fish Timbale

CYPRUS STUFFED PEPPERS

SERVES 4

8 medium peppers
75 ml (5 tbsp) olive oil
2 medium onions, skinned and chopped
4 garlic cloves, skinned and crushed
350 g (12 oz) tomatoes, skinned (see page 57), seeded and chopped
15 ml (1 tbsp) tomato purée
5 ml (1 tsp) raw cane sugar
salt and pepper
45 ml (3 tbsp) chopped fresh coriander
225 g (8 oz) long-grain brown rice
2.5 ml (½ tsp) ground cinnamon

/ 1 / Cut a slice off the top of each pepper and reserve. Remove the cores, seeds and membranes and discard. Wash and dry the peppers.

/ 2 / Heat 60 ml (4 tbsp) of the oil in a large frying pan, add the peppers and fry gently for 10 minutes, turning them frequently so that they soften on all sides. Remove from the pan with a slotted spoon and drain.

/ 3 / Make the stuffing: drain off all but 30 ml (2 tbsp) of the oil from the pan, then add the onions and garlic and fry very gently for about 15 minutes.

/ 4 / Add the tomatoes and fry gently to soften, stirring constantly. Increase the heat and cook rapidly to drive off the liquid – the mixture should be thick and pulpy.

/ 5 / Lower the heat, add the tomato purée, sugar and salt and pepper to taste and simmer gently for 5 minutes. Remove the pan from the heat and stir in the coriander and rice. Spoon the stuffing into the peppers.

/ 6 / Stand the peppers close together in a heavy-based pan or casserole into which they just fit. Sprinkle with the cinnamon, then the remaining 15 ml (1 tbsp) oil. Put the reserved 'lids' on top.

/ 7 / Pour 150 ml (¼ pint) water into the base of the pan, then bring to the boil. Lower the heat, cover with a plate or saucer which just fits inside the rim of the pan, then place heavy weights on top.

/ 8 / Simmer gently for 1 hour, then remove from the heat and leave to cool. Chill in the refrigerator overnight, still with the weights on top. Serve the peppers chilled.

LENTIL CROQUETTES

SERVES 4

225 g (8 oz) split red lentils
2 celery sticks, trimmed and finely chopped
1 medium onion, skinned and chopped
1-2 garlic cloves, skinned and crushed
10 ml (2 tsp) garam masala
1 egg, beaten
salt and pepper
30 ml (2 tbsp) plain wholemeal flour, to coat
5 ml (1 tsp) paprika
5 ml (1 tsp) ground turmeric
60 ml (4 tbsp) polyunsaturated oil
fresh coriander or parsley and lime wedges, to garnish

/ 1 / Place the lentils in a large saucepan with the celery, onion, garlic, garam masala and 600 ml (1 pint) water. Bring to the boil, stirring with a wooden spoon to mix.

/ 2 / Lower the heat and simmer gently for 30 minutes or until the lentils are tender and have absorbed all the liquid, stirring frequently.

/ 3 / Remove from the heat. Leave to cook for a few minutes, then beat in the egg and seasoning to taste.

/ 4 / Turn the mixture on to a board or flat plate and spread out evenly. Leave until cold, then chill in the refrigerator for 30 minutes to firm the mixture.

/ 5 / With floured hands, form the mixture into 8 triangular croquette shapes. Coat in the flour mixed with the paprika and turmeric. Chill again for 30 minutes.

/ 6 / Heat the oil in a large frying pan, add the croquettes and fry over moderate to high heat for 10 minutes, turning once until crisp and golden on both sides.

/ 7 / Drain on absorbent kitchen paper and serve hot, with a sprinkling of coriander or parsley on top of each and lime wedges.

CYPRUS STUFFED PEPPERS

Cut a slice off the top of each pepper and reserve. Remove the cores, seeds and membranes and discard. Wash the peppers and pat dry with absorbent kitchen paper.

Stand the filled peppers close together in a heavy-based saucepan or casserole into which they just fit. Sprinkle with the cinnamon, then the remaining 15 ml (1 tbsp) oil. Put the reserved 'lids' on top.

When buying peppers for this recipe, look for squat ones which are of uniform size and shape so that they will stand upright for serving. For a pretty effect buy as many different colours as possible.

Sometimes peppers are sold under the name 'capsicum', and the red ones are also called pimientos, but they are all from the same family. The colours differ according to botanical variety and degree of ripeness: green peppers become red when they are fully ripe, yellow and purple peppers were white before they became ripe! If you like peppers to taste sweet, then choose red or purple ones.

Picture opposite:
Cyprus Stuffed Peppers

WHOLEWHEAT MACARONI BAKE

Wholewheat macaroni is widely available in supermarkets and health food shops. It is made from 100 per cent wholewheat flour and therefore has more fibre than white varieties. The flavour of wholewheat macaroni is pleasantly nutty and the texture is quite firm – check with packet instructions for exact cooking times of each brand because many of them tend to be longer than for white pasta. In Italy wholewheat pasta is rarely seen and the shortcut or elbow macaroni that we are used to is not so common.

This supper dish is so substantial that it needs no accompaniment. Follow with a green salad to refresh the palate, then fresh fruit and cheese.

WHOLEWHEAT MACARONI BAKE

SERVES 4 - 6

175 g (6 oz) wholewheat macaroni
salt and pepper
30 ml (2 tbsp) vegetable oil
1 medium onion, skinned and chopped
225 g (8 oz) button mushrooms, wiped
350 g (12 oz) tomatoes, skinned and roughly chopped
300 ml (½ pint) vegetable stock
15 ml (1 tbsp) tomato purée
5 ml (1 tsp) dried mixed herbs
5 ml (1 tsp) dried oregano
30 ml (2 tbsp) plain wholemeal flour
300 ml (½ pint) milk
100 g (4 oz) low-fat soft cheese
1 egg, beaten
5 ml (1 tsp) English mustard powder
30 ml (2 tbsp) wholemeal breadcrumbs
30 ml (2 tbsp) grated Parmesan cheese

/ 1 / Plunge the macaroni into a large saucepan of boiling salted water. Simmer, uncovered, for 10 minutes.

/ 2 / Meanwhile, heat the oil in a separate pan, add the onion and fry gently for 5 minutes until soft but not coloured.

/ 3 / Cut the small mushrooms in half, slice the larger ones. Add to the pan, increase the heat and toss with the onion for 1-2 minutes until the juices run.

/ 4 / Add the tomatoes and stock and bring to the boil, stirring constantly to break up the tomatoes. Lower the heat, add the tomato purée, herbs and seasoning to taste, and simmer gently for 10 minutes.

/ 5 / Drain the macaroni into a colander and leave to stand while making the cheese sauce.

/ 6 / Put the flour and milk in a blender or food processor and blend for 1 minute. Transfer to a heavy-based pan and simmer, stirring constantly, for 5 minutes until thickened. Remove from the heat and beat in the cheese, egg, mustard and seasoning to taste.

/ 7 / Mix the macaroni with the mushrooms in tomato sauce, then pour into a baking dish. Pour the cheese sauce over the top and sprinkle with the breadcrumbs and Parmesan.

/ 8 / Bake in the oven at 190°C (375°F) mark 5 for 20 minutes until golden brown and bubbling. Serve hot, straight from the dish.

LAMB AND AUBERGINE CURRY

SERVES 2

450 g (1 lb) lean boneless lamb, cut into 2.5 cm (1 inch) cubes
15 g (½ oz) plain flour
30 ml (2 tbsp) polyunsaturated oil
1 medium onion, skinned and sliced
1 garlic clove, skinned and crushed
15-30 ml (1-2 tbsp) curry powder
300 ml (½ pint) beef stock or water
30 ml (2 tbsp) tomato purée
pinch of ground cinnamon
pinch of ground cloves
salt and pepper
1 small aubergine
parsley or coriander sprigs, to garnish

/ 1 / Toss the lamb in the flour to coat. Heat the oil in a large frying pan, add the meat a few pieces at a time and brown on all sides, transferring to a bowl as they are browned.

/ 2 / Add the onion, garlic and curry powder to the oil remaining in the pan, and cook over low heat for about 5 minutes, stirring frequently until the onion is soft.

/ 3 / Return the meat to the pan and stir in the stock or water, tomato purée, cinnamon, cloves and salt and pepper to taste. Bring to the boil, then lower the heat, cover and simmer gently for 1 hour, stirring occasionally to prevent sticking.

/ 4 / Meanwhile, trim the aubergine and cut into 2.5 cm (1 inch) chunks. Place in a colander, sprinkling each layer with salt. Cover with a plate, place heavy weights on top and leave to dégorge for 30 minutes.

/ 5 / Rinse the aubergine, pat dry with absorbent kitchen paper and stir into the curry. Add a little more stock or water if necessary, cover and continue cooking for another 30 minutes or until the aubergine is tender. Serve hot, garnished with parsley or coriander sprigs.

Picture opposite:
Lamb and Aubergine Curry

EGG AND SPINACH CROÛTE

SERVES 1

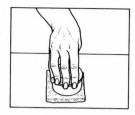

With a 7.5 cm (3 inch) pastry cutter, stamp out a round from the slice of bread.

Toast the bread round on 1 side only. Spread the untoasted side with the remaining butter or margarine mixed with the garlic. Grill again until golden.

Serve Egg and Spinach Croûte on its own for a light and nutritious supper dish.

2.5 cm (1 inch) thick slice of bread
50 g (2 oz) fresh spinach, washed and trimmed
65 g (2½ oz) butter or margarine
15 ml (1 tbsp) plain flour
150 ml (¼ pint) milk
freshly grated nutmeg
salt and pepper
1 garlic clove, skinned and crushed
a few drops of vinegar
1 egg

/ 1 / With a 7.5 cm (3 inch) pastry cutter, stamp out 1 round from the slice of bread. Set aside while preparing the spinach.

/ 2 / Cook the spinach with only the water that clings to the leaves for 3-4 minutes until wilted. Drain well and chop finely.

/ 3 / Melt 15 g (½ oz) of the butter or margarine in a small saucepan, add the flour and cook gently, stirring, for 1-2 minutes. Remove from the heat and gradually blend in the milk. Bring to the boil, stirring constantly, then simmer for 3 minutes until thick and smooth. Stir in the spinach and nutmeg, salt and pepper to taste. Keep hot.

/ 4 / Toast the bread round on 1 side only. Spread the untoasted side with the remaining butter or margarine mixed with the garlic. Grill again until golden. Place the croûte on a warmed serving plate and keep hot.

/ 5 / Half fill a frying pan with water and a few drops of vinegar. Bring the water to the boil, break the egg into a cup, then slip it into the water. Cook gently for 3-4 minutes or until lightly set, then lift the egg out of the water with a slotted spoon.

/ 6 / Top the toasted croûte with the poached egg and spoon over the spinach mixture. Serve immediately.

/ 7 / To serve 2: double the amount of bread, spinach and eggs, but keep the remaining ingredients the same. Follow the recipe above.

TUNA AND PASTA IN SOURED CREAM

SERVES 4

225 g (8 oz) pasta spirals or shells
salt and pepper
5 ml (1 tsp) polyunsaturated oil
198 g (7 oz) can tuna, drained
4 eggs, hard-boiled and shelled
25 g (1 oz) butter or margarine
150 ml (¼ pint) soured cream
5 ml (1 tsp) anchovy essence
30 ml (2 tbsp) malt vinegar
60 ml (4 tbsp) chopped fresh parsley

/ 1 / Cook the pasta in plenty of boiling salted water to which the oil has been added, for about 15 minutes until *al dente* (tender but firm to the bite). Drain well.

/ 2 / Meanwhile, flake the tuna fish with 2 forks. Chop the hard-boiled eggs finely.

/ 3 / Melt the butter or margarine in a deep frying pan and toss in the pasta. Stir in the soured cream, anchovy essence and vinegar.

/ 4 / Add the tuna and egg mixture to the pan with the parsley. Season well and warm through over low heat, stirring occasionally. Serve immediately.

TAGLIATELLE WITH CHEESE AND NUT SAUCE

SERVES 4

400 g (14 oz) wholewheat or green (spinach) tagliatelle
salt and pepper
100 g (4 oz) Gorgonzola cheese
100 g (4 oz) walnuts, chopped
5 ml (1 tsp) chopped fresh sage or 2.5 ml (½ tsp) dried sage
75 ml (5 tbsp) olive oil
15 ml (1 tbsp) chopped fresh parsley, to garnish

/ 1 / Plunge the tagliatelle into a large saucepan of boiling salted water. Simmer, uncovered, for 10 minutes or according to packet instructions, until the pasta is *al dente* (tender but firm to the bite).

/ 2 / Meanwhile, crumble the cheese into a blender or food processor. Add two-thirds of the walnuts and the sage. Blend to combine the ingredients.

/ 3 / Add the oil gradually through the funnel (as when making mayonnaise) and blend until the sauce is evenly incorporated.

/ 4 / Drain the tagliatelle well and return to the pan. Add the nut sauce and fold in gently to mix. Add seasoning to taste.

/ 5 / Transfer the pasta and sauce to a warmed serving bowl and sprinkle with the remaining walnuts. Serve garnished with parsley.

BRUSSELS SPROUTS SOUFFLÉ

SERVES 4

700 g (1½ lb) Brussels sprouts, trimmed weight
salt and pepper
50 g (2 oz) butter or margarine
40 g (1½ oz) plain wholemeal flour
300 ml (½ pint) semi-skimmed milk
pinch of freshly grated nutmeg
3 eggs, separated

/ 1 / Grease a 1.3 litre (2¼ pint) soufflé dish. Cook the Brussels sprouts in boiling salted water for 10-15 minutes until tender. Drain.

/ 2 / Melt the butter or margarine in a saucepan, add the flour and cook gently, stirring, for 1-2 minutes. Remove from the heat and gradually blend in the milk. Bring to the boil, stirring constantly, then simmer for 3 minutes until thick and smooth. Add the nutmeg and remove from the heat.

/ 3 / Chop half of the sprouts. Work the remaining sprouts in a blender or food processor to a purée with the egg yolks and a little of the sauce. Fold into the rest of the sauce with the chopped sprouts. Season with salt and pepper.

/ 4 / Whisk the egg whites until stiff. Gently fold into the Brussels sprout mixture. Turn into the soufflé dish. Bake in the oven at 200°C (400°F) mark 6 for 30-35 minutes until risen. Serve immediately.

TUNA AND PASTA IN SOURED CREAM

The type of pasta you use for this recipe is really a matter of personal taste, although spirals and shells are specified in the ingredients list. As long as the shapes are small (*pasta corta*), the sauce will cling to them and not slide off – Italians serve short-cut pasta with fairly heavy sauces, like this one, which have chunks of fish or meat in them. Long pasta (*pasta lunga*) such as spaghetti and tagliatelle are best served with smoother sauces. Italian pasta in the shape of shells is called *conchiglie*, and there are many different sizes to choose from. *Farfalle* are shaped like small bow-ties; *fusilli* are spirals, so too are *spirale ricciolo; rotelle* are shaped like wheels. There are also many different types of short pasta shaped like macaroni – *penne* are hollow and shaped like quills with angled ends, and *rigatoni* have ridges.

TAGLIATELLE WITH CHEESE AND NUT SAUCE

The Gorgonzola cheese used to make the sauce for this pasta dish must be one of the world's best-known blue cheeses. Real Gorgonzola cheese comes from the town of the same name in Lombardy, northern Italy. Originally it was made in the damp caves there, but nowadays it is mostly made in factories. The unique piquant flavour and creamy paste were produced naturally by the damp atmosphere in the caves, but in factories a similar result is achieved by using bacteria known as *penicillum gorgonzola*.

Picture opposite: Tuna and Pasta in Soured Cream

Drain the potatoes and
transfer to a bowl. Mash
until smooth, then add the
egg, half of the butter or
margarine, the milk and salt
and pepper to taste. Beat
well to mix.

Mark the mashed potato
topping with a fork, then
dot with the remaining
butter or margarine.

If you are living alone,
everyday meals are most
important from a
nutritional point of view.
This dish uses fresh, healthy
ingredients and is perfect
for either lunch or supper.

Serve with a seasonal green
vegetable such as Brussels
sprouts sprinkled with
grated nutmeg, or stir-fried
shredded cabbage.

INDIVIDUAL
COTTAGE PIE

SERVES 1

2 medium carrots, peeled and chopped
salt and pepper
30 ml (2 tbsp) vegetable oil
1 small onion, skinned and finely chopped
100-175 g (4-6 oz) minced beef
275 g (10 oz) old potatoes
225 g (8 oz) can tomatoes
15 ml (1 tbsp) Worcestershire sauce
2.5 ml (½ tsp) dried mixed herbs
1.25 ml (¼ tsp) mustard powder
15 g (½ oz) butter or margarine
30 ml (2 tbsp) milk

/ 1 / Cook the chopped carrots in boiling salted
water for 10 minutes until tender.

/ 2 / Meanwhile, heat the oil in a saucepan,
add the onion and fry gently for about 5
minutes until soft but not coloured. Add the
minced beef and fry over moderate heat, stirring to break up any lumps.

/ 3 / Remove the carrots from the water with a
slotted spoon and set aside. Add the potatoes
and cook for 20 minutes or until tender.

/ 4 / Meanwhile, add the tomatoes with their
juice to the beef, then stir in the Worcestershire sauce, herbs, mustard and salt and pepper
to taste. Simmer for about 20 minutes, stirring
occasionally.

/ 5 / Drain the potatoes and transfer to a bowl.
Mash until smooth, then add half of the butter
or margarine, the milk and salt and pepper to
taste. Beat well to mix.

/ 6 / Add the carrots to the minced beef mixture and heat through. Transfer the mixture to
a gratin dish and spoon the potato on top.

/ 7 / Mark the mashed potato with a fork, then
dot with the remaining butter or margarine.
Put under a preheated hot grill for about 5
minutes until the potato is crisp and golden
brown. Serve hot.

/ 8 / To serve 2: follow the recipe above, increasing the quantity of carrots to 3, the
minced beef to 225-350 g (8-12 oz) and the
potatoes to 450 g (1 lb).

BROWN RICE RISOTTO

Saffron threads are the dried stigmas of the saffron crocus, and saffron is said to be the most expensive spice in the world. The threads will give this dish a subtle colour and delicate flavour. Take care if substituting turmeric; it is more pungent so use it sparingly.

Serve Brown Rice Risotto as a supper dish with a colourful salad such as Crisp Endive with Orange and Croûtons (see page 143).

BROWN RICE RISOTTO

SERVES 4

2 medium onions, skinned

1 green pepper, cored and seeded

45 ml (3 tbsp) polyunsaturated oil

1 garlic clove, skinned and crushed

275 g (10 oz) long-grain brown rice

pinch of saffron or 5 ml (1 tsp) ground turmeric

600 ml (1 pint) vegetable or chicken stock

salt and pepper

chopped fresh parsley, to garnish

freshly grated Parmesan cheese, to serve

/1/ Slice the onions and green pepper finely. Heat the oil in a medium flameproof casserole, add the onions, pepper and garlic and fry gently for about 5 minutes until soft.

/2/ Put the rice in a sieve and wash it thoroughly under cold running water until the water runs clear. Drain well.

/3/ Add the rice with the saffron or turmeric to the pan. Fry gently, stirring, for 1-2 minutes until the rice is coated in oil.

/4/ Stir in the stock, then add salt and pepper to taste. Bring to the boil, then cover the casserole tightly with its lid.

/5/ Cook in the oven at 170°C (325°F) mark 3 for about 1 hour or until the rice is tender and the stock absorbed. Taste and adjust seasoning, then garnish with plenty of parsley. Serve hot, with the grated Parmesan cheese.

CURRIED NUT BURGERS

MAKES 6

90 ml (6 tbsp) vegetable oil

1 medium onion, skinned and finely chopped

15 ml (1 tbsp) Madras curry paste or powder

175 g (6 oz) Edam cheese, diced

175 g (6 oz) chopped mixed nuts

175 g (6 oz) granary breadcrumbs

2 medium carrots, peeled and grated

salt and pepper

2 eggs

30 ml (2 tbsp) plain wholemeal flour, to coat

watercress sprigs, radicchio and cucumber, to serve

Curried Nut Burgers

/ 1 / Heat 30 ml (2 tbsp) of the oil in a small saucepan, add the onion and curry paste or powder and fry gently for 5 minutes until the onion is soft but not coloured.

/ 2 / Put the onion in a bowl with the cheese, 150 g (5 oz) of the nuts and 125 g (4 oz) of the breadcrumbs. Add the carrots and seasoning to taste, and stir well. Bind with one of the eggs.

/ 3 / With floured hands, form the mixture into 6 burger shapes, coating lightly with flour.

/ 4 / Beat the remaining egg in a shallow dish and dip the burgers in it to coat them lightly.

/ 5 / Mix the remaining nuts and breadcrumbs together on a flat plate. Coat the burgers in this mixture, pressing on firmly with your hands. Chill the burgers in the refrigerator for 30 minutes to firm the coating.

/ 6 / Heat the remaining oil in a large frying pan, add the burgers and fry over moderate to high heat for 10 minutes on each side until golden brown and cooked through. Drain on absorbent kitchen paper before serving with the watercress, radicchio and cucumber.

PEPPER AND TOMATO OMELETTE

SERVES 2

30 ml (2 tbsp) olive oil
1 medium onion, skinned and sliced
2 garlic cloves, skinned and crushed
1 green pepper, cored, seeded and sliced
1 red pepper, cored, seeded and sliced
4 tomatoes, skinned and sliced
5 eggs
pinch of dried mixed herbs, or to taste
salt and pepper
50 g (2 oz) low-fat Cheddar type cheese, grated

/ 1 / Heat the oil in a non-stick frying pan. Add the onion and garlic and fry gently for 5 minutes until soft.

/ 2 / Add the pepper slices and the tomatoes and fry for a further 2-3 minutes, stirring frequently to prevent them sticking.

/ 3 / In a jug, beat the eggs lightly with the herbs and seasoning to taste. Pour into the pan, allowing the egg to run to the sides.

/ 4 / Draw in the vegetable mixture with a palette knife so that the mixture runs on to the base of the pan. Cook over moderate heat for 5 minutes until the underside of the omelette is cooked and set.

/ 5 / Sprinkle the top of the omelette with the grated cheese, then put under a pre-heated hot grill for 2-3 minutes until set and browned. Slide on to a serving plate and cut into wedges to serve.

WHOLEWHEAT, APRICOT AND NUT SALAD

SERVES 6 - 8

225 g (8 oz) wholewheat grain
3 celery sticks, washed and trimmed
100 g (4 oz) dried apricots
100 g (4 oz) Brazil nuts, roughly chopped
50 g (2 oz) unsalted peanuts
60 ml (4 tbsp) olive oil
30 ml (2 tbsp) lemon juice
salt and pepper
chopped fresh parsley and cucumber slices, to garnish

/ 1 / Soak the wholewheat grain overnight in plenty of cold water. Drain, then tip into a large saucepan of boiling water. Simmer gently for 25 minutes or until the grains have a little bite left.

/ 2 / Drain the wholewheat into a colander and rinse under cold running water. Tip into a large serving bowl and set aside.

/ 3 / Cut the celery into small diagonal pieces with a sharp knife. Stir into the wholewheat.

/ 4 / Using kitchen scissors, snip the apricots into small pieces over the wholewheat. Add the nuts and stir well to mix.

/ 5 / Mix the oil and lemon juice together with salt and pepper to taste. Pour over the salad and toss well. Chill in the refrigerator for 2 hours, then toss again just before serving. Garnish with parsley and cucumber slices.

CURRIED NUT BURGERS

Serve these burgers hot or cold, with wedges of lemon and lime and a leafy salad. Alternatively, a natural low-fat yogurt, cucumber and mint salad would make a refreshing accompaniment, contrasting well with the spicy richness of the curried nut mixture.

PEPPER AND TOMATO OMELETTE

This type of omelette is different from the classic French kind, which is cooked for a very short time and served folded over. This omelette is more like the Spanish tortilla, a flat omelette which is cooked for a fairly long time so that the eggs become quite set, then browned under a hot grill so that both sides become firm. Some Spanish cooks turn their tortilla several times during cooking, and there is even a special kind of plate used in Spain which is designed to make the turning easier.

Pepper and Tomato Omelette can be served hot, straightaway, but it has far more flavour if left to go cold before serving. In this way it makes the most perfect packed lunch or picnic food.

Drain the soaked mushrooms and squeeze the mushrooms dry. Slice thinly, discarding any hard stalks, then cut into thin matchstick strips.

Look for packets of Chinese dried mushrooms in oriental specialist shops; they are expensive but are only used in small quantities because their flavour is so strong. After opening the packet, store them carefully in an airtight jar in a cool, dark place, where they will keep for many months. Chinese dried mushrooms must always be softened in warm water for 20 minutes or so before use, so be sure not to omit this important part of their preparation.

Oyster sauce, as its name suggests, is made from oysters mixed with soy sauce and brine. Sold in bottles in oriental shops and larger supermarkets, it is very thick and rich, and should be used sparingly. Once opened, store the sauce in the refrigerator.

CHINESE BEEF WITH OYSTER SAUCE

SERVES 2

25 g (1 oz) Chinese dried mushrooms
175-225 g (6-8 oz) rump steak
30 ml (2 tbsp) oyster sauce
30 ml (2 tbsp) dry sherry
salt and pepper
30 ml (2 tbsp) polyunsaturated oil
1 small onion, skinned and thinly sliced
1 garlic clove, skinned and crushed
2.5 cm (1 inch) piece of fresh root ginger, peeled
2 medium carrots, peeled
10 ml (2 tsp) cornflour

/ 1 / Put the dried mushrooms in a bowl, pour in enough boiling water to cover and leave to soak for about 20 minutes.

/ 2 / Meanwhile, cut the steak into thin strips, place in a bowl and add the oyster sauce, sherry and salt and pepper to taste. Stir well to mix, then cover and leave to marinate in a cool place while the mushrooms are soaking.

/ 3 / Heat the oil in a wok or deep, heavy-based frying pan. Add the onion and garlic and fry gently for about 5 minutes until soft but not coloured, stirring occasionally.

/ 4 / Meanwhile, drain the mushrooms and re-serve the soaking liquid. Squeeze the mushrooms dry, then slice thinly, discarding any hard stalks. Cut ginger and carrots into thin matchstick strips.

/ 5 / Add the mushrooms, ginger and carrots to the wok and stir-fry over moderate heat for about 5 minutes until slightly softened. Add the meat and marinade and stir-fry for a few minutes more, until the beef is tender.

/ 6 / Mix the cornflour to a paste with 60 ml (4 tbsp) of the soaking water from the mushrooms. Pour into the wok and stir-fry until the sauce is thickened. Taste and adjust seasoning before serving.

CHEESE AND PINEAPPLE SALAD

SERVES 4

275 g (10 oz) beansprouts

225 g (8 oz) carrots, peeled

225 g (8 oz) Edam cheese

227 g (8 oz) can pineapple slices in natural juice

10 ml (2 tsp) wine vinegar

salt and pepper

/ 1 / Wash the beansprouts. Drain well. Cut the carrots into 2.5 cm (1 inch) matchstick thin strips. Coarsely grate the cheese.

/ 2 / Drain the pineapple, reserving the juice. Cut the pineapple into thin strips.

/ 3 / In a large bowl, mix together the beansprouts, carrots, cheese and pineapple. Cover and chill in the refrigerator until required.

/ 4 / Make the dressing: whisk the pineapple juice and vinegar together with seasoning to taste. Set aside until ready to serve.

/ 5 / Just before serving, pour the dressing over the salad and toss well to mix. Serve at room temperature rather than chilled.

LAMB WITH COURGETTES AND MUSHROOMS

SERVES 1

175 g (6 oz) boneless lamb fillet

30 ml (2 tbsp) polyunsaturated oil

1 small onion, skinned and finely chopped

1 small garlic clove, skinned and crushed

15 ml (1 tbsp) tomato purée

300 ml (½ pint) hot chicken stock

5 ml (1 tsp) chopped fresh rosemary or 2.5 ml (½ tsp) dried

salt and pepper

25 g (1 oz) butter or margarine

2 small courgettes, trimmed and sliced

50-75 g (2-3 oz) button mushrooms, wiped and sliced

rosemary sprig, to garnish (optional)

/ 1 / Cut the lamb into thin slices, discarding all fat and sinew. Heat the oil in a heavy-based frying pan, add the lamb and fry over brisk heat until well browned on all sides. Remove with a slotted spoon and drain on absorbent kitchen paper.

/ 2 / Add the onion and garlic to the pan and fry gently for about 5 minutes until soft but not coloured. Dissolve the tomato purée in the hot stock, then pour into the pan. Return the meat to the pan, then sprinkle in the rosemary and salt and pepper to taste. Simmer, uncovered, for 20 minutes until the lamb is tender.

/ 3 / Melt the butter or margarine in a separate frying pan, add the courgettes and mushrooms and toss over high heat for about 5 minutes.

/ 4 / Add the courgettes and mushrooms to the lamb, increase the heat and stir-fry until most of the liquid has evaporated and the sauce just coats the meat and vegetables. Taste and adjust seasoning before serving. Garnish with a sprig of rosemary, if liked.

/ 5 / To serve 2: follow the recipe above, increasing the lamb to 350 g (12 oz), the stock to 450 ml (¾ pint), the courgettes to 3 and the mushrooms to 100 g (4 oz).

SPINACH PANCAKES

SERVES 4

175 g (6 oz) fresh spinach, washed

100 g (4 oz) plain wholemeal flour

salt and pepper

150 ml (¼ pint) milk

150 ml (¼ pint) water

1 egg, beaten

about 45 ml (3 tbsp) vegetable oil, for frying

225 g (8 oz) cottage cheese with prawns

2.5 ml (½ tsp) paprika

whole prawns and herb sprigs, to garnish

/ 1 / Cut away the thick midribs and stalks from the spinach and put the leaves in a saucepan with only the water that clings to them. Cover and cook gently for 5 minutes until tender.

/ 2 / Drain the spinach in a colander, pressing down with a spoon to extract as much water as possible from the leaves.

Spinach Pancakes

/ 3 / Turn the spinach on to a board and chop very finely with a sharp knife.

/ 4 / Put the flour in a bowl with a pinch of salt. Make a well in the centre, add half of the milk and water and the egg.

/ 5 / Beat vigorously with a whisk, gradually incorporating the flour into the centre. Whisk in the remaining liquid and the spinach.

/ 6 / Heat a little oil in a pancake pan or heavy-based 18 cm (7 inch) frying pan. Pour the batter into a jug and whisk.

/ 7 / Pour one-eighth of the batter into the pan and tip and tilt the pan so that the batter runs all over the base. Cook over moderate heat for about 30 seconds until the underside is golden, then turn pancake over and repeat cooking.

/ 8 / Slide the pancake out on to a sheet of greaseproof paper placed over a plate and keep warm while cooking remaining pancakes.

/ 9 / Season the cottage cheese with the paprika and salt and pepper to taste. Spread a little over each pancake, then roll up or fold into parcels. Garnish and serve.

SPINACH PANCAKES

Serve these healthy pancakes for lunch with a tomato and onion salad.

75

Main Course Dishes

Lean meat, poultry, fish and fresh vegetables all form the basis of a healthy main course. Included in this chapter are low-fat, high-fibre dishes which avoid the use of commercial convenience foods and artificial flavourings and preservatives.

There are dishes for family meals, such as Circassian Chicken which can be accompanied by the traditional two vegetables or a salad. For a change from potatoes, try wholewheat pasta or brown rice. Also included are dishes suitable for vegetarians, such as Vegetable Lasagne, and dishes like Seafood Stir-Fry which are quick and simple to prepare and cook when time is short.

Almond Beef with Celery

Lamb Korma

LAMB KORMA

SERVES 4

2 medium onions, skinned and chopped
2.5 cm (1 inch) piece fresh root ginger, peeled
40 g (1½ oz) blanched almonds
2 garlic cloves, skinned
5 ml (1 tsp) ground cardamom
5 ml (1 tsp) ground cloves
5 ml (1 tsp) ground cinnamon
5 ml (1 tsp) ground cumin
5 ml (1 tsp) ground coriander
1.25 ml (½ tsp) cayenne pepper
900 g (2 lb) lean shoulder or leg of lamb, boned
45 ml (3 tbsp) polyunsaturated oil or ghee
300 ml (½ pint) natural low-fat yogurt
salt and pepper
cucumber and lime slices, to garnish
Boiled Rice (see page 146) and Cucumber Raita (see page 42), to serve

/ 1 / Put the onions, ginger, almonds and garlic in a blender or food processor with 90 ml (6 tbsp) water and blend to a smooth paste. Add the spices and mix well.

/ 2 / Cut the lamb into cubes, trimming off excess fat. Heat the oil or ghee in a heavy-based saucepan and fry the lamb for 5 minutes until browned on all sides.

/ 3 / Add the paste mixture and fry for about 10 minutes, stirring, until the mixture is lightly browned. Stir in the yogurt 15 ml (1 tbsp) at a time and season with salt and pepper to taste.

/ 4 / Cover with a tight-fitting lid, reduce the heat and simmer for 1¼-1½ hours.

/ 5 / Transfer to a warmed serving dish and garnish. Serve with rice and cucumber raita.

MINTED LAMB GRILL

SERVES 4

4 lamb chump chops
30 ml (2 tbsp) chopped fresh mint or 15 ml (1 tbsp) dried
20 ml (4 tbsp) white wine vinegar
30 ml (2 tbsp) clear honey
salt and pepper
mint sprigs, to garnish

/ 1 / Trim the excess fat from the chops using a pair of sharp kitchen scissors. With a knife, slash both sides of the chops to a depth of about 0.5 cm (¼ inch).

/ 2 / Make the marinade: mix together the mint, vinegar, honey and salt and pepper.

/ 3 / Place a sheet of foil in the grill pan and turn up the edges. Place the chops on the foil and spoon over the marinade. Leave in a cool place for about 1 hour, basting occasionally.

/ 4 / Grill under a moderate heat for 5-6 minutes on each side, turning once only. Baste with the marinade. Garnish and serve.

LAMB IN TOMATO SAUCE

SERVES 4

30 ml (2 tbsp) polyunsaturated oil
900 g (2 lb) lean shoulder of lamb, boned, trimmed of fat and cubed
1 medium onion, skinned and sliced
20 ml (4 tsp) plain wholemeal flour
397 g (14 oz) and 227 g (8 oz) cans tomatoes
30 ml (2 tbsp) tomato purée
pinch of raw cane sugar
5 ml (1 tsp) chopped fresh rosemary or 2.5 ml (½ tsp) dried
60 ml (4 tbsp) red wine (optional)
salt and pepper
lamb or beef stock, if necessary
snipped fresh chives, to garnish

/ 1 / Heat the oil in a flameproof casserole, add the lamb and fry over a high heat until browned on all sides. Remove from the casserole with a slotted spoon and set aside.

/ 2 / Add the onion to the pan and fry for 5 minutes until soft. Stir in the flour and cook for 1 minute. Add the tomatoes with their juice, the tomato purée, sugar, rosemary and wine, if using. Bring to the boil, stirring all the time.

/ 3 / Return the meat to the pan and add salt and pepper to taste. Add a little stock, if necessary, to cover the meat. Cover the casserole and cook in the oven at 170°C (325°F) mark 3 for about 2¼ hours until the meat is tender. Sprinkle with snipped fresh chives and serve hot.

LAMB KORMA

Mild in flavour, creamy in texture, the Indian korma is a very special dish, which was originally only served on special occasions such as feast days and holidays. This version is relatively simple compared with some of the korma recipes which were devised for celebrations. These often contained such luxurious ingredients as saffron (the most expensive spice in the world), cashew nuts and double cream. If you want to make a richer korma for a dinner party, then add infused saffron liquid with the ground spices in step 1, and stir in 50 g (2 oz) chopped unsalted cashew nuts just before serving. Substitute double cream for the yogurt and swirl more cream over the top of the korma before garnishing.

Serve Lamb Korma with plain Boiled Rice (see page 146), poppadoms, cucumber and Cucumber Raita (see page 42).

LAMB IN TOMATO SAUCE

Shoulder of lamb is an excellent cut for casseroles such as this one, because it is so economical. It can be fatty so be sure to trim off the excess fat. An alternative cut of lamb which tends to be less fatty is the fillet. This cut comes from the middle neck and scrag; it is lean and tender, yet it does not become dry in casseroles.

NAVARIN D'AGNEAU

This French casserole was originally made with mutton – and so called Navarin de Mouton. These days, mutton is almost impossible to come by, and so lamb is invariably used instead. It is a classic springtime dish, which should be made with freshly picked, young spring vegetables, although frozen peas and beans are often used for convenience at other times of year.

Hot French bread is the traditional accompaniment to Navarin d'Agneau.

NAVARIN D'AGNEAU

Spring Lamb Casserole

SERVES 4

30 ml (2 tbsp) polyunsaturated oil
1 kg (2¼ lb) best end of neck of lamb, divided into cutlets
5 ml (1 tsp) raw cane sugar plus a little extra
15 ml (1 tbsp) plain wholemeal flour
900 ml (1½ pints) lamb or chicken stock
30 ml (2 tbsp) tomato purée
salt and pepper
bouquet garni
225 g (8 oz) button onions, skinned
4 medium carrots, peeled and sliced
1-2 turnips, peeled and quartered
8 small even-sized potatoes, peeled
225 g (8 oz) fresh peas, shelled, or 100 g (4 oz) frozen peas
chopped fresh parsley, to garnish

/ 1 / Heat the oil in a saucepan and fry the cutlets for about 5 minutes on both sides until lightly browned. If there is too much fat at this stage, pour off a little to leave 15-30 ml (1-2 tbsp) in the pan.

/ 2 / Stir in 5 ml (1 tsp) sugar and heat until it browns slightly, then add the flour, stirring all the time until cooked and browned.

/ 3 / Remove from the heat, gradually stir in the stock, then bring to the boil and add the tomato purée, salt and pepper to taste, a pinch of sugar and the bouquet garni. Cover, reduce the heat and simmer for about 1 hour.

/ 4 / Remove the bouquet garni, add the onions, carrots and turnips and continue cooking for 30 minutes. Add the potatoes and cook for 10 minutes more.

/ 5 / Stir in the peas and cook for a further 10 minutes until the lamb cutlets and the potatoes are tender.

/ 6 / To serve, place the meat on a warmed serving dish and surround with the vegetables. Garnish with parsley.

SPICY LAMB KEBABS

SERVES 4

900 g (2 lb) lean leg of lamb, boned
450 g (1 lb) courgettes
8 tomatoes
1 large corn-on-the-cob
salt and pepper
8 shallots
150 ml (¼ pint) natural low-fat yogurt
1 garlic clove, skinned and crushed
2 bay leaves, crumbled
15 ml (1 tbsp) lemon juice
15 ml (1 tbsp) polyunsaturated oil
5 ml (1 tsp) ground allspice
15 ml (1 tbsp) coriander seeds
lemon wedges, to garnish

/ 1 / Using a sharp knife, cut the lamb into 2.5 cm (1 inch) cubes, trimming off any excess fat.

/ 2 / Cut the courgettes into 0.5 cm (¼ inch) slices, discarding the tops and tails. Halve the tomatoes crossways.

/ 3 / Cut the corn cob into 8 slices. Blanch in boiling salted water, drain well and set aside. Blanch the shallots in boiling salted water, skin and set aside.

/ 4 / Make the marinade: pour the yogurt into a shallow dish and stir in the garlic, bay leaves, lemon juice, oil, allspice, coriander seeds and salt and pepper to taste.

/ 5 / Thread the lamb cubes on to 8 skewers with courgettes, tomatoes, corn and shallots. Place in the dish, spoon over the marinade, cover and leave for 2-3 hours, turning once to ensure even coating.

/ 6 / Grill or barbecue the kebabs for about 15-20 minutes, turning and brushing with the marinade occasionally. To serve, spoon the remaining marinade over the kebabs and garnish them with lemon wedges.

Picture opposite:
Spicy Lamb Kebabs

LIVER WITH VERMOUTH

Serve this tangy liver dish on a bed of brown rice or with wholewheat noodles. Stir-fried beansprouts, mushrooms or spinach would make a good vegetable accompaniment.

LIVER WITH VERMOUTH

SERVES 4

450 g (1 lb) lamb's liver, sliced
15 ml (1 tbsp) wholemeal flour
30 ml (2 tbsp) vegetable oil
1 medium onion, skinned and chopped
1 garlic clove, skinned and crushed
finely grated rind and juice of 1 orange
finely grated rind and juice of 1 lemon
60 ml (4 tbsp) sweet vermouth or sherry
30 ml (2 tbsp) chopped fresh parsley
salt and pepper
few orange and lemon slices, to garnish

/ 1 / Cut the liver into thin strips, trimming away all ducts and gristle. Coat in the flour.

/ 2 / Heat the oil in a flameproof casserole, add the onion and garlic to the casserole and fry gently for 5 minutes until the onion is soft but not coloured.

/ 3 / Add the liver strips and cook over high heat until browned on all sides.

/ 4 / Add the orange and lemon rind and juices and the vermouth or sherry and bring to the boil. Stir constantly with a wooden spoon to scrape up any sediment and juices from the base of the casserole, and continue boiling until the sauce reduces.

/ 5 / Lower the heat and add half the parsley and salt and pepper to taste.

/ 6 / Dip the orange and lemon slices in the remaining chopped parsley. Transfer the liver and sauce to a warmed serving dish. Garnish with the orange and lemon slices and serve immediately, while piping hot.

SPICED LAMB WITH SPINACH

Spicy and rich, this Indian dish of lamb and spinach goes well with plain Boiled Rice (see page 146). Serve with mango chutney as well as Cucumber Raita (see page 42), if wished.

SPICED LAMB WITH SPINACH

SERVES 4

900 g (2 lb) leg or shoulder of lamb, boned
90 ml (6 tbsp) natural low-fat yogurt
1 cm (½ inch) piece fresh root ginger, peeled and chopped
2 garlic cloves, skinned and chopped
2 bay leaves
2.5 cm (1 inch) cinnamon stick
2 green cardamoms
4 black peppercorns
3 whole cloves
5 ml (1 tsp) ground cumin
5 ml (1 tsp) garam masala
1.25-2.5 ml (¼-½ tsp) chilli powder
5 ml (1 tsp) ground coriander
salt
450 g (1 lb) fresh or 225 g (8 oz) frozen spinach
mint sprig and lemon slices, to garnish
Boiled Rice (see page 146) and Cucumber Raita (see page 42), to serve

/ 1 / Cut the meat into cubes, trimming off excess fat. Put the cubes in a bowl. In a separate bowl, mix together the yogurt, ginger, garlic, bay leaves, whole and ground spices and salt to taste, stirring well to combine.

/ 2 / Spoon the mixture over the meat and mix thoroughly. Cover and leave to marinate at room temperature for about 4 hours.

/ 3 / Meanwhile, thoroughly wash and chop the fresh spinach. If using frozen spinach, thaw in a saucepan.

/ 4 / Put the marinated meat in a heavy-based saucepan and cook over a low heat for about 1 hour, stirring occasionally, until all the moisture has evaporated and the meat is tender.

/ 5 / Stir in the spinach and cook over low heat for a further 10 minutes. Serve garnished with mint and lemon slices, accompanied by boiled rice and cucumber raita.

MARINATED LAMB KEBABS

SERVES 4

150 ml (¼ pint) natural low-fat yogurt
2.5 cm (1 inch) piece fresh root ginger, peeled and grated
2 garlic cloves, skinned and crushed
30 ml (2 tbsp) chopped fresh mint
10 ml (2 tsp) crushed cumin seeds
5 ml (1 tsp) ground turmeric
5 ml (1 tsp) salt
2.5 ml (½ tsp) chilli powder
700 g (1½ lb) lean lamb shoulder, trimmed of excess fat and cut into cubes
2 medium onions
fresh mint sprigs and lemon wedges, to garnish

/ 1 / Put the yogurt in a large bowl and add the ginger, garlic, mint, cumin, turmeric, salt and chilli powder. Stir well to mix.

/ 2 / Add the cubes of lamb to the bowl and stir to coat in the marinade. Cover and refrigerate for 1-2 days, turning occasionally.

/ 3 / When ready to cook, skin the onions and cut into quarters with a sharp knife.

/ 4 / Thread the lamb and onion quarters alternately on to 4 oiled kebab skewers, pressing the pieces as close together as possible. Reserve any leftover marinade.

/ 5 / Grill the kebabs under moderate heat for 10 minutes until the lamb is browned on the outside and pink in the centre. Turn frequently during grilling and brush with the reserved marinade. Serve hot, garnished with mint and lemon wedges.

The marinating of the lamb in yogurt is an important part of this recipe, so don't be tempted to skimp on the length of marinating time recommended. The yogurt contains a special bacterium which has the effect of tenderising meat and making it more succulent when cooked. The longer the meat is left in the yogurt marinade the more tender it will be. In Middle Eastern cookery, yogurt is frequently used for this purpose, especially with tough, sinewy cuts of meat.

Marinated Lamb Kebabs

Lamb Cutlets with Lemon and Garlic

LAMB AND SPINACH LASAGNE

SERVES 6

450 g (1 lb) fresh spinach, washed, or 225 g (8 oz) frozen chopped spinach, thawed
90 ml (6 tbsp) polyunsaturated oil
1 medium onion, skinned and chopped
450 g (1 lb) fresh lean minced lamb
225 g (8 oz) can tomatoes
1 garlic clove, skinned and crushed
30 ml (2 tbsp) chopped fresh mint
5 ml (1 tsp) ground cinnamon
freshly grated nutmeg
salt and pepper
50 g (2 oz) plain wholemeal flour
900 ml (1½ pints) semi-skimmed milk
150 ml (¼ pint) natural low-fat yogurt
12-15 sheets oven-ready wholemeal lasagne
175 g (6 oz) Feta or low-fat Cheddar type cheese

/ 1 / Put the fresh spinach in a saucepan with only the water that clings to the leaves and cook gently for about 4 minutes. Drain well and chop finely.

/ 2 / Heat 30 ml (2 tbsp) of the oil in a large saucepan, add the onion and fry gently for 5 minutes until softened. Add the lamb and brown well, then drain off all the fat.

/ 3 / Stir in the spinach with the tomatoes and their juice, the garlic, mint and cinnamon. Season with nutmeg, salt and pepper to taste. Bring to the boil and simmer, uncovered, for about 30 minutes. Leave to cool while making the sauce.

/ 4 / Heat the remaining oil in a saucepan, add the flour and cook gently, stirring, for 1-2 minutes. Remove from the heat and gradually blend in the milk. Bring to the boil, stirring constantly, then simmer for 3 minutes until thick and smooth. Add the yogurt and salt and pepper to taste.

/ 5 / Spoon one-third of the meat mixture over the base of a rectangular baking dish.

/ 6 / Cover with 4-5 sheets of lasagne and spread over one-third of the sauce. Repeat these layers twice more, finishing with the sauce, which should completely cover the lasagne. Grate the cheese on top.

/ 7 / Stand the dish on a baking sheet. Bake in the oven at 180°C (350°F) mark 4 for 45-50 minutes or until the top of the lasagne is well browned and bubbling.

LAMB CUTLETS WITH LEMON AND GARLIC

SERVES 4

2 lemons
3 small garlic cloves, skinned and crushed
salt and pepper
8 lamb cutlets
30 ml (2 tbsp) vegetable oil
25 g (1 oz) butter or margarine
1 medium onion, skinned and finely chopped
175 ml (6 fl oz) natural low-fat yogurt
150 ml (¼ pint) chicken stock
5 ml (1 tsp) chopped fresh basil or 2.5 ml (½ tsp) dried
parsley or basil sprigs, to garnish

/ 1 / On the finest side of a conical or box grater, grate the rind of 1½ lemons into a bowl. Add the garlic and pepper to taste and blend together. Set aside.

/ 2 / Place the cutlets on a board and spread the lemon rind and garlic evenly over the meat. Leave for 15 minutes.

/ 3 / Heat the oil and butter or margarine in a pan, add the cutlets and fry for about 3 minutes each side or until tender. Drain and keep warm on a serving dish.

/ 4 / Pour off all but 30 ml (2 tbsp) fat from the pan, add the onion and fry gently for 5 minutes until soft but not coloured. Stir in the yogurt and stock with the squeezed juice of the 1½ lemons and the basil. Bring to the boil and simmer for 2-3 minutes. Season with salt and pepper to taste.

/ 5 / Spoon the juices over the meat and garnish with the parsley or basil sprigs and the remaining ½ lemon, cut into wedges, if liked. Serve immediately.

LAMB AND SPINACH LASAGNE

This dish is rich and filling. Serve it with a tomato salad dressed with oil, lemon juice and raw onion rings, chopped spring onion or snipped fresh chives.

LAMB CUTLETS WITH LEMON AND GARLIC

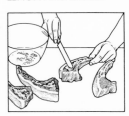

Place the cutlets on a board and spread the lemon rind and garlic evenly over the meat. Leave for 15 minutes.

Serve with French beans topped with grilled almonds and new potatoes in their skins.

STUFFED HEARTS

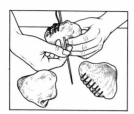

Fill the hearts with the stuffing and sew up neatly. Coat the hearts in flour.

Hearts are inexpensive to buy, yet ideal for casseroling. Their dense, muscular tissue benefits from long, slow cooking, resulting in tender, moist meat which is amazingly lean. Lamb's hearts are the ideal size for stuffing, because 1 heart is just about the right quantity for 1 serving.

Serve with creamed potatoes and a dish of braised red cabbage, onion and apple, which can be cooked in the oven at the same time.

STUFFED HEARTS

SERVES 4

4 lamb's hearts, each weighing about 175 g (6 oz)
45 ml (3 tbsp) polyunsaturated oil
1 small onion, skinned and chopped
50 g (2 oz) fresh wholemeal breadcrumbs
5 ml (1 tsp) grated lemon rind
15 ml (1 tbsp) chopped fresh sage
pinch of freshly grated nutmeg
salt and pepper
1 egg, beaten
30 ml (2 tbsp) plain wholemeal flour
300 ml (½ pint) chicken stock
chopped fresh sage and grated lemon rind, to garnish

/ 1 / Wash the hearts thoroughly under cold running water. Trim each of them and then remove any ducts.

/ 2 / Heat 30 ml (2 tbsp) of the oil in a frying pan and lightly fry the onion for about 5 minutes until softened. Remove from the heat and stir in the breadcrumbs, lemon rind, sage, nutmeg and salt and pepper to taste. Add enough beaten egg to bind and mix well.

/ 3 / Fill the hearts with the stuffing and sew up neatly. Coat the hearts in the flour.

/ 4 / Heat the remaining oil in a flameproof casserole and brown the hearts well. Pour over the stock, add salt and pepper to taste and bring to the boil.

/ 5 / Cover and cook in the oven at 150°C (300°F) mark 2 for about 2 hours or until tender. Serve the hearts whole or sliced and pour the skimmed juices over. Garnish with sage and grated lemon rind.

LAMB WITH ROSEMARY

LAMB WITH ROSEMARY

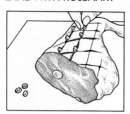

Using a sharp knife, score the surface of the lamb into a diamond pattern to the depth of about 1 cm (½ inch). Cut the cloves of garlic into wafer thin slices. Push the slices into the scored surface of the lamb with your fingers.

LAMB WITH ROSEMARY

S E R V E S 6

2 kg (4½ lb) leg of lamb
2 large garlic cloves, skinned
50 g (2 oz) butter or margarine, softened
15 ml (1 tbsp) chopped fresh rosemary or 5 ml (1 tsp) dried
salt and pepper
30 ml (2 tbsp) plain wholemeal flour
450 ml (¾ pint) lamb or chicken stock
rosemary sprigs, to garnish

/ 1 / Using a sharp knife, score the surface of the lamb into a diamond pattern to a depth of about 1 cm (½ inch).

/ 2 / Cut the cloves of garlic into wafer thin slices. Push the slices into the scored surface of the lamb with your fingers.

/ 3 / Mix the butter or margarine with the chopped rosemary and salt and pepper to taste, then spread all over the lamb. Place the joint in a shallow dish, cover tightly with cling film and refrigerate for at least 12 hours.

/ 4 / Uncover the lamb and transfer it to a medium roasting tin. Cook in the oven at 180°C (350°F) mark 4 for about 2¼ hours, basting occasionally as the fat begins to run. Pierce the joint with a fine skewer; when done the juices should run clear at first, then with a hint of red.

/ 5 / Place the joint on a serving plate, cover loosely and keep warm in a low oven. Pour all excess fat out of the roasting tin, leaving about 45 ml (3 tbsp) fat with the meat juices. Sprinkle the flour into the roasting tin and stir until evenly mixed. Cook over a gentle heat for 2-3 minutes until well browned, stirring all the time to prevent it burning.

/ 6 / Add the stock and salt and pepper to taste and bring to the boil, stirring. Simmer for 3-4 minutes, then adjust the seasoning. To serve, garnish the lamb with rosemary sprigs and hand the gravy separately.

LIVER GOUJONS WITH ORANGE SAUCE

The French word *goujon* is used in cooking to describe small strips or thin slivers of food. Fish is often cut into goujons, then coated in egg and breadcrumbs before deep-frying. In this recipe, goujons of liver are coated in egg and oatmeal, which gives a nutty crunch to the coating, contrasting well with the soft texture of the liver inside.

LIVER GOUJONS WITH ORANGE SAUCE

S E R V E S 4

350 g (12 oz) lamb's liver, sliced
75 ml (5 tbsp) plain wholemeal flour
salt and pepper
1 egg, beaten
125 g (4 oz) medium oatmeal
105 ml (7 tbsp) polyunsaturated oil
1 medium onion, skinned and sliced
300 ml (½ pint) lamb or beef stock
finely grated rind and juice of 1 medium orange
5 ml (1 tsp) dried sage
dash of gravy browning
sage sprigs and orange twists, to garnish

/ 1 / Cut the liver into 5 cm (2 inch) pencil-thin strips. Coat in 45 ml (3 tbsp) of the flour, seasoned with salt and pepper.

/ 2 / Dip the liver in the beaten egg, then roll in the oatmeal to coat. Chill in the refrigerator while preparing the sauce.

/ 3 / Heat 30 ml (2 tbsp) of the oil in a saucepan, add the onion and fry gently until golden brown. Add the remaining flour and cook gently, stirring, for 1-2 minutes.

/ 4 / Gradually blend in the stock, orange rind and juice, sage and salt and pepper to taste. Bring to the boil, stirring constantly, then simmer for 10-15 minutes. Add the gravy browning, then taste and adjust the seasoning.

/ 5 / Heat the remaining oil in a frying pan, add the liver goujons and fry gently for 1-2 minutes until tender.

/ 6 / Arrange the goujons on a warmed serving platter and pour over a little of the sauce. Garnish with sage sprigs and orange twists. Hand the remaining sauce separately.

Liver Goujons with Orange Sauce

KIDNEYS WITH
TOMATOES

Sautéed kidneys are light
but very tasty. Serve in a
ring of brown rice, with
chopped nuts, pimientos or
peppers and sliced olives, if
wished. Hot garlic bread
also makes a good
accompaniment and helps
to mop up the juices.
Follow with a crisp and
crunchy green salad, to
refresh the palate.

It is well worth
encouraging your family to
eat kidneys. They are
inexpensive to buy, yet
extremely rich in iron, and
in vitamins too. Take care
not to exceed the cooking
time given in the recipe;
overcooked kidneys are
tough and rubbery.

KIDNEYS WITH TOMATOES

SERVES 3 - 4

12 lamb's kidneys
45 ml (3 tbsp) plain wholemeal flour
60 ml (4 tbsp) polyunsaturated oil
1 large onion, skinned and sliced
100 g (4 oz) mushrooms, sliced
397g (14 oz) can tomatoes
10 ml (2 tsp) French mustard
salt and pepper
chopped fresh parsley, to garnish

/ 1 / Wash the kidneys, cut them in half
lengthways and, using scissors, remove the
cores. Toss the kidneys in the flour.

/ 2 / Heat the oil in a large flameproof casserole
or frying pan, add the onion and fry for about 5
minutes until golden brown.

/ 3 / Add the kidneys to the pan with any remaining flour and cook for 3-4 minutes, stirring occasionally, until lightly browned. Add
the mushrooms and cook for 2-3 minutes.

/ 4 / Stir in the tomatoes with their juice, mustard and salt and pepper to taste. Bring to the
boil, stirring all the time, then cover and simmer for 15 minutes until tender. Serve hot, garnish with chopped parsley.

PAN-FRIED LIVER AND TOMATO

SERVES 4

450 g (1 lb) lamb's liver, sliced
30 ml (2 tbsp) Marsala or sweet sherry
salt and pepper
225 g (8 oz) tomatoes, skinned (see page 57)
30 ml (2 tbsp) polyunsaturated oil
2 medium onions, skinned and finely sliced
pinch of ground ginger
150 ml (¼ pint) chicken stock
Chinese egg noodles, to serve (optional)

/ 1 / Using a very sharp knife, cut the liver into
wafer-thin strips. Place in a shallow bowl with
the Marsala or sherry. Sprinkle with pepper.
Cover and marinate for several hours.

/ 2 / Cut the tomatoes into quarters and remove the seeds, reserving the juices. Slice the
flesh into strips and set aside.

/ 3 / Heat the oil in a sauté pan or non-stick frying pan. When very hot, add the liver strips, a
few at a time. Shake the pan briskly for about
30 seconds until pearls of blood appear.

/ 4 / Turn the slices and cook for a further 30
seconds only (liver hardens if it is overcooked). Remove from the pan with a slotted
spoon and keep warm.

/ 5 / Add the onions and ginger to the oil remaining in the pan and cook, uncovered, for
about 5 minutes. Add the stock and salt and
pepper to taste, return the liver to the pan and
add the tomatoes and their juice. Bring just to
the boil, then turn into a warmed serving dish
and serve with egg noodles, if liked.

KIDNEYS PROVENCAL

SERVES 4

12-16 lamb's kidneys
30 ml (2 tbsp) olive oil
1 large onion, skinned and chopped
1-2 garlic cloves, skinned and crushed
3 medium courgettes, trimmed and sliced
4 large tomatoes, skinned and roughly chopped
100 ml (4 fl oz) red wine or stock
10 ml (2 tsp) chopped fresh basil or 5 ml (1 tsp) dried
salt and pepper
12 black olives
sprigs of chervil, to garnish

/ 1 / Skin the kidneys, then cut each one in half. Snip out the cores with kitchen scissors. Cut each half into 2.

/ 2 / Heat the oil in a large heavy-based frying pan, add the onion and garlic to the pan and fry gently for 5 minutes until the onion is soft but not coloured.

/ 3 / Add the kidneys and fry over low heat for 3 minutes until they change colour. Shake the pan and toss the kidneys frequently during frying to prevent them sticking.

/ 4 / Add the courgettes, tomatoes and wine or stock and bring to the boil, stirring constantly. Lower the heat and add half the basil with salt and pepper to taste. Simmer gently for 8 minutes until the kidneys are tender.

/ 5 / Add the olives to the pan and heat through for 1-2 minutes. Taste and adjust the seasoning. Sprinkle with the remaining basil and chervil just before serving. Serve very hot.

This strongly flavoured dish needs a contrasting bland accompaniment such as plain Boiled Rice (see page 146). Follow with a simple green salad, cheese and fresh fruit for a complete, well-balanced meal.

Pan-fried Liver and Tomato

This is a complete meal in
itself, with lamb chops,
lentils, potatoes and swede
baked together in one dish.
Serve with a crisp green
salad or a seasonal green
vegetable.

The different kinds of
lentils available can be
confusing, especially in
health food shops where
there is always such a large
selection. The red lentils
used in this recipe are the
most common kind,
sometimes also described
as 'split red lentils' or even
'Egyptian lentils'. They do
not need soaking and are
quick-cooking, but they
tend to lose their shape.
'Continental lentils' are
green, brown or reddish-
brown in colour, and are
whole rather than split.
These varieties keep their
shape and have a nuttier
texture than red lentils, but
take longer to cook.

SPICED LAMB AND LENTIL BAKE

SERVES 4

8 middle neck lamb chops, total weight about 1.1 kg (2½ lb)
45 ml (3 tbsp) polyunsaturated oil
2 medium onions, skinned and thinly sliced
15 ml (1 tbsp) ground turmeric
5 ml (1 tsp) paprika
5 ml (1 tsp) ground cinnamon
75 g (3 oz) red lentils
salt and pepper
450 g (1 lb) potatoes, peeled and thinly sliced
450 g (1 lb) swede, peeled and thinly sliced
300 ml (½ pint) lamb or chicken stock

/ 1 / Trim the excess fat from the chops. Heat
the oil in a large frying pan, add the chops and
brown on both sides. Remove from pan.

/ 2 / Add the onions to the pan with the turmeric, paprika, cinnamon and lentils. Fry for
2-3 minutes. Season and spoon into a shallow
2 litre (3 ½ pint) ovenproof dish.

/ 3 / Place the chops on top of the onion and
lentil mixture. Arrange the vegetable slices on
top of the chops, then pour over the stock.

/ 4 / Cover the dish tightly and cook in the
oven at 180°C (350°F) mark 4 for about 1½
hours or until the chops are tender. Uncover
and cook for a further 30 minutes or until
lightly browned on top. Serve hot.

MINTED LAMB MEATBALLS

SERVES 4

225 g (8 oz) crisp cabbage, trimmed and finely chopped
450 g (1 lb) lean minced lamb
1 medium onion, skinned and finely chopped
2.5 ml (½ tsp) ground allspice
salt and pepper
397 g (14 oz) can tomato juice
1 bay leaf
10 ml (2 tsp) chopped fresh mint or 5 ml (1 tsp) dried
15 ml (1 tbsp) chopped fresh parsley

/ 1 / Steam the chopped cabbage for 2-3
minutes or until it has softened.

/ 2 / Place the lamb and cabbage in a bowl with
the onion, allspice and salt and pepper to taste.
Beat well to combine all the ingredients.

/ 3 / With your hands, shape the mixture into
16-20 small balls. Place the meatballs in a shallow, large ovenproof dish.

/ 4 / Mix the tomato juice with the bay leaf,
mint and parsley. Pour over the meatballs.
Cover and bake in the oven at 180°C (350°F)
mark 4 for 1 hour until meatballs are cooked.

/ 5 / Skim any fat off the tomato sauce before
serving, adjust the seasoning and serve hot.

MINTED LAMB BURGERS WITH CUCUMBER

SERVES 4

450 g (1 lb) fresh lean minced lamb
1 small onion, skinned and chopped
100 g (4 oz) fresh wholemeal breadcrumbs
finely grated rind of ½ lemon
45 ml (3 tbsp) chopped fresh mint
1 egg, beaten
salt and pepper
30 ml (2 tbsp) plain wholemeal flour
30 ml (2 tbsp) polyunsaturated oil
½ cucumber
6 spring onions, trimmed
200 ml (7 fl oz) lamb or chicken stock
15 ml (1 tbsp) sherry

/ 1 / Mix the lamb, onion, breadcrumbs and
lemon rind with 15 ml (1 tbsp) of the chopped
mint, the beaten egg and salt and pepper.

/ 2 / Shape into 12 flat burgers with floured
hands and coat in the remaining flour.

/ 3 / Heat the oil in a large frying pan, add the
burgers and fry until browned, turning once.

/ 4 / Cut the cucumber into 5 cm (2 inch) long
wedges and the spring onions into 1 cm (½
inch) pieces. Add to the pan.

/ 5 / Pour in the stock and sherry, then add the
remaining mint and salt and pepper to taste.
Bring to the boil, cover the pan and simmer
gently for about 20 minutes, or until the meat
is tender. Skim off any excess fat and serve.

The refreshing flavours of
mint and cucumber in this
dish go particularly well
with new potatoes. Cook
them in their skins to retain
nutrients – and add extra
flavour too.

*Picture opposite:
Minted Lamb Burgers
with Cucumber*

ROGAN JOSH

Indian Lamb Curry with Tomatoes and Yogurt

SERVES 4 - 6

900 g (2 lb) lean shoulder or leg of lamb, boned
45 ml (3 tbsp) polyunsaturated oil
1 medium onion, skinned and sliced
3 garlic cloves, skinned and crushed
10 ml (2 tsp) ground ginger
10 ml (2 tsp) paprika
15 ml (1 tbsp) ground coriander
5 ml (1 tsp) ground cumin
5 ml (1 tsp) ground turmeric
2.5 ml (½ tsp) cayenne pepper
large pinch of ground cloves
large pinch of ground cardamom
300 ml (½ pint) natural low-fat yogurt
salt
4 medium tomatoes, skinned and chopped
extra natural low-fat yogurt and lemon wedges, to garnish

Serve this spicy Indian curry with Boiled Rice (see page 146) and poppadoms for an attractive and tasty main course dish for a supper party.

/ 1 / Cut the meat into cubes, trimming of excess fat. Heat the oil in a large saucepan and brown the onion. Add the crushed garlic and spices with the meat and fry gently for 5 minutes.

/ 2 / Stir in the yogurt, salt to taste and the tomatoes. Bring to the boil, cover and simmer, stirring occasionally, for about 1 ½ hours until the meat is tender and the sauce has thickened. If the sauce thickens too much before the meat is cooked add extra water or tomato juice.

/ 3 / Swirl yogurt over the top of the rogan josh and garnish with lemon wedges.

All spices taste better when freshly ground. Peppercorns and allspice can have their own peppermills. Small amounts of spice can be crushed with a pestle and mortar or with a rolling pin. Grind large amounts in an electric or hand grinder. Most spices benefit from being gently dry-fried for a few minutes before being ground. This releases extra flavour, especially with spices such as cumin and coriander.

CRUMB-TOPPED PORK CHOPS

Serve with jacket potatoes (cooked in the oven at the same time) and a vegetable dish with its own juices, such as ratatouille.

CRUMB-TOPPED PORK CHOPS

SERVES 4

4 lean pork loin chops

50 g (2 oz) fresh wholemeal breadcrumbs

15 ml (1 tbsp) chopped fresh parsley or 5 ml (1 tsp) dried

5 ml (1 tsp) chopped fresh mint or 2.5 ml (½ tsp) dried

pinch of dried thyme

finely grated rind of 1 lemon

2.5 ml (½ tsp) coriander seeds, crushed

1 egg, beaten

salt and pepper

/ 1 / Cut the rind off the chops, trim off the excess fat and put them in a baking tin.

/ 2 / Mix the remaining ingredients together with salt and pepper to taste. Spread this mixture evenly over the chops with a palette knife.

/ 3 / Bake in the oven at 200°C (400°F) mark 6 for about 45-50 minutes or until golden. Serve hot, on a warmed dish.

APPLE BAKED CHOPS

SERVES 4

225 g (8 oz) eating apples

1 medium onion, skinned

50 g (2 oz) raisins

200 ml (7 fl oz) unsweetened apple juice

45 ml (3 tbsp) chopped fresh parsley

salt and pepper

4 lean pork loin chops, about 175 g (6 oz) each

3 or 4 green cardamoms, lightly crushed

30 ml (2 tbsp) dry white wine or cider

basil or parsley sprigs, to garnish

/ 1 / Core and finely chop the apples. Finely chop the onion. Place in a saucepan with the raisins and apple juice. Simmer gently, uncovered, for 3-4 minutes until the apple begins to soften slightly.

/ 2 / Remove from the heat, drain off the juices and reserve. Stir the chopped parsley into the apple mixture, season, then leave to cool.

/ 3 / Meanwhile, trim the rind and excess fat from the chops, then make a horizontal cut through the flesh, almost to the bone. Open out to form a pocket for the apple.

/ 4 / Spoon a little of the apple mixture into the pocket of each chop. Place in a shallow flameproof dish. Sprinkle any remaining stuffing around the chops, with the crushed cardamoms. Mix the reserved juices with the wine or cider and pour over the chops.

/ 5 / Cover with foil and bake in the oven at 190°C (375°F) mark 5 for about 1 hour until the chops are tender.

/ 6 / Remove the chops from the dish and place in a grill pan. Grill until browned.

/ 7 / Meanwhile, pour the cooking juices from the chops into a pan and boil rapidly until reduced by half. Arrange the chops on a dish and pour over the juices. Garnish and serve.

RABBIT WITH CIDER AND MUSTARD

SERVES 4

60 ml (4 tbsp) polyunsaturated oil

12-18 small button onions, skinned

1 rabbit, jointed

25 g (1 oz) plain wholemeal flour

salt and pepper

10 ml (2 tsp) French mustard

300 ml (½ pint) dry cider

450 ml (¾ pint) chicken stock

/ 1 / Heat the oil in a frying pan and fry the onions for 5 minutes until lightly browned. Remove to a casserole with a slotted spoon.

/ 2 / Coat the rabbit joints in a little flour seasoned with salt and pepper to taste and fry in the pan for about 8 minutes until golden brown. Arrange in the casserole.

/ 3 / Stir the remaining flour and the French mustard into the pan. Gradually add the cider and stock. Bring to the boil and pour over the rabbit joints in the casserole.

/ 4 / Cover and cook in the oven at 170°C (325°F) mark 3 for about 2 hours or until the rabbit is tender. Serve hot.

RABBIT WITH CIDER AND MUSTARD

A delicious main course dish for a winter dinner party, this casserole tastes good with ribbon noodles tossed in a little butter and chopped fresh parsley.

Apple Baked Chops

SPICED VEAL WITH
PEPPERS

Pie veal is one of the most
economical cuts of veal,
widely available in both
supermarkets and butchers'
shops, and ideal for
everyday meals. The name
'pie veal' comes from the
fact that the meat was
traditionally used in the
making of veal and ham pie,
but nowadays pie veal is
also used in stews and
casseroles.

The actual cut varies
from one butcher to
another and one region to
another, but it is usually
from the shin, leg and neck
of the calf. Pie veal is
usually sold boned and
cubed, which makes it a
most convenient cut, but
always check the meat
before using as some pie
veal can be fatty. For this
recipe you will have to trim
off as much of the fat as
possible, or it will spoil the
yogurt sauce.

BEEF KEBABS WITH
HORSERADISH RELISH

Serve the kebabs on a bed
of rice. Garnish with extra
parsley, if liked.

SPICED VEAL
WITH PEPPERS

SERVES 4

15 ml (1 tbsp) polyunsaturated oil
2 medium onions, skinned and finely sliced
2 small red peppers, cored, seeded and sliced
1 garlic clove, skinned and crushed
2.5 ml (½ tsp) ground ginger
2.5 ml (½ tsp) ground turmeric
2.5 ml (½ tsp) ground cumin
2.5 ml (½ tsp) chilli powder
1.25 ml (¼ tsp) ground cloves
225 g (8 oz) tomatoes, skinned and chopped
300 ml (½ pint) natural low-fat yogurt
550 g (1¼ lb) pie veal, trimmed and cubed
salt and pepper
Boiled Rice (see page 146), to serve

/ 1 / Heat the oil in a large saucepan. Add the
onions, peppers, garlic and spices and fry for 1
minute. Stir in the tomatoes.

/ 2 / Turn the heat to very low and add the
yogurt very gradually, stirring well between
each addition.

/ 3 / Add the veal, with salt and pepper to
taste. Cover the saucepan and simmer the veal
gently for 30 minutes.

/ 4 / Uncover the pan and cook the veal for a
further 30 minutes or until it is tender and the
liquid has reduced. Stir occasionally to prevent
the meat sticking to the bottom of the pan.
Serve with boiled rice.

MEAT LOAF

SERVES 4

30 ml (2 tbsp) polyunsaturated oil
1 medium onion, skinned and finely chopped
5 ml (1 tsp) paprika
450 g (1 lb) fresh lean minced beef
50 g (2 oz) fresh wholemeal breadcrumbs
45 ml (3 tbsp) natural wheatgerm
1 garlic clove, skinned and crushed
15 ml (1 tbsp) chopped fresh herbs or 5 ml (1 tsp) dried mixed herbs
60 ml (4 tbsp) tomato purée
1 egg, beaten
salt and pepper
Tomato Sauce, to serve (see page 154)

/ 1 / Grease and base line a 450 g (1 lb) 900 ml
(1 ½ pint) loaf tin.

/ 2 / Heat the oil in a frying pan, add the onion
and cook until softened. Add the paprika and
cook for 1 minute, stirring, then turn the mixture into a bowl.

/ 3 / Add all the remaining ingredients, except
the sauce, and stir thoroughly until evenly
mixed. Spoon the mixture into the loaf tin,
level the surface and cover tightly with foil.

/ 4 / Stand the loaf tin in a roasting tin and
pour in water to a depth of 2.5 cm (1 inch).
Cook in the oven at 180°C (350°F) mark 4 for
1½ hours. Turn out and serve with the sauce
handed separately.

BEEF KEBABS
WITH
HORSERADISH
RELISH

SERVES 6

700 g (1½ lb) fresh lean minced beef
250 g (9 oz) grated onion
135 ml (9 tbsp) horseradish sauce
45 ml (3 tbsp) chopped fresh thyme
250 g (9 oz) fresh wholemeal breadcrumbs
salt and pepper
1 egg, beaten
plain wholemeal flour, for coating
150 ml (¼ pint) natural low-fat yogurt
120 ml (8 tbsp) finely chopped fresh parsley

/ 1 / Put the minced beef in a large bowl and
mix in the onion, 90 ml (6 tbsp) of the horseradish, the thyme, breadcrumbs and salt and
pepper to taste.

/ 2 / Add enough egg to bind the mixture together and, with well-floured hands, shape
into 18 even-sized sausages.

/ 3 / Thread the kebabs lengthways on to 6
oiled skewers. Place under a preheated grill
and cook for about 20 minutes, turning the
skewers frequently.

/ 4 / Meanwhile, mix the yogurt with the remaining horseradish and the parsley. Serve the
kebabs hot, with the sauce handed separately.

Beef Kebabs with Horseradish Relish

KOFTA CURRY

K O F T A   C U R R Y

S E R V E S   4

450 g (1 lb) fresh lean minced beef
5 ml (1 tsp) garam masala
5 ml (1 tsp) ground cumin
15 ml (1 tbsp) finely chopped fresh coriander
salt and pepper
30 ml (2 tbsp) ghee or polyunsaturated oil
3 medium onions, skinned and chopped
1 garlic clove, skinned and chopped
2.5 cm (1 inch) piece fresh root ginger, peeled and chopped
1 green chilli, seeded and chopped
3 green cardamoms
4 whole cloves
6 black peppercorns
5 cm (2 inch) cinnamon stick
1 bay leaf
10 ml (2 tsp) ground coriander
2.5 ml (½ tsp) ground turmeric
300 ml (½ pint) natural low-fat yogurt
chopped fresh coriander, to garnish
Boiled Rice (see page 146), to serve

/ 1 / Mix together the beef, garam masala, cumin, the 15 ml (1 tbsp) chopped coriander and salt and pepper to taste. Set aside.

/ 2 / Make the sauce: heat the ghee or oil in a large saucepan and fry the onions, garlic, ginger and chilli for 10 minutes until golden.

/ 3 / Add the cardamoms, cloves, peppercorns, cinnamon and bay leaf and fry over a high heat for 3 minutes. Add the ground coriander, turmeric and salt to taste. Fry for 3 minutes.

/ 4 / Gradually add the yogurt, a tablespoon at a time, stirring thoroughly after each addition, then 150 ml (¼ pint) water. Simmer for 10 minutes or until beginning to thicken.

/ 5 / Meanwhile, shape the meat mixture into 16 small balls. Lower the meatballs into the sauce so that they are completely covered. Cover and simmer gently for 30 minutes or until cooked.

/ 6 / Skim off any excess fat, then transfer to a warmed serving dish and garnish with chopped coriander. Serve with boiled rice.

Kofta Curry

COTTAGE PIE

Shepherd's Pie

SERVES 4

900 g (2 lb) potatoes, peeled

45 ml (3 tbsp) semi-skimmed milk

knob of butter or margarine

salt and pepper

15 ml (1 tbsp) polyunsaturated oil

1 large onion, skinned and chopped

450 g (1 lb) cold cooked beef or lamb, minced

150 ml (¼ pint) beef stock

30 ml (2 tbsp) chopped fresh parsley or 10 ml (2 tsp) dried mixed herbs

/ 1 / Cook the potatoes in boiling salted water for 15-20 minutes, then drain and mash with the milk, butter or margarine and salt and pepper to taste.

/ 2 / Heat the oil in a frying pan, add the onion and fry for about 5 minutes, then stir in the minced meat with the stock, parsley and salt and pepper to taste.

/ 3 / Spoon the meat mixture into an ovenproof dish and cover the top with the mashed potato. Mark the top with a fork and bake in the oven at 190°C (375°F) mark 5 for 25-30 minutes until the surface is crisp and browned.

——— VARIATION ———

Use 450 g (1 lb) fresh minced beef in place of the cooked meat, add it to the softened onion and cook until well browned. Add 30 ml (2 tbsp) plain wholemeal flour and cook for 2 minutes, then add 300 ml (½ pint) beef stock. Bring to the boil and simmer for 30 minutes. Put the meat in an ovenproof dish and proceed as above.

JAPANESE SKEWERED BEEF

SERVES 4

700 g (1½ lb) fillet steak, trimmed of fat

5 cm (2 inch) piece fresh root ginger

2 garlic cloves

100 ml (4 fl oz) sake or dry sherry

60 ml (4 tbsp) soy sauce

30 ml (2 tbsp) sesame or vegetable oil

5 ml (1 tsp) raw cane sugar

carrot and cucumber slices, to garnish

/ 1 / Cut the steak across the grain into slices about 1 cm (½ inch) thick with a sharp knife.

/ 2 / Skin the ginger and garlic. Crush the flesh finely in a mortar and pestle, or on a board with the side of the blade of a large cook's knife.

/ 3 / Put the crushed ginger and garlic in a bowl with the sake or sherry, soy sauce, oil and sugar. Whisk with a fork until well combined, then add the sliced steak and turn to coat in the marinade. Cover and leave to marinate for at least 8 hours, turning occasionally.

/ 4 / When ready to cook, thread the slices of steak on to oiled metal kebab skewers, or wooden skewers that have been soaked for 30 minutes in water. Grill under moderate heat for 5 minutes only, turning frequently to ensure even cooking and basting with the marinade. Serve immediately, garnished with carrot slices and cucumber.

BEEF WITH STOUT

SERVES 4

700 g (1½ lb) lean stewing beef

30 ml (2 tbsp) polyunsaturated oil

2 large onions, skinned and sliced

15 ml (1 tbsp) plain wholemeal flour

275 ml (9.68 fl oz) can stout

200 ml (7 fl oz) beef stock

30 ml (2 tbsp) tomato purée

100 g (4 oz) stoned prunes

225 g (8 oz) carrots, peeled and sliced

salt and pepper

/ 1 / Cut the meat into 4 cm (1½ inch) cubes, trimming off all fat. Heat the oil in a flameproof casserole, add the meat and fry until well browned. Remove with a slotted spoon.

/ 2 / Add the onions to the oil remaining in the pan and fry gently until lightly browned. Stir in the flour and cook for 1 minute. Stir in the stout, stock, tomato purée, prunes and carrots. Bring to the boil and season with salt and pepper to taste.

/ 3 / Replace the meat, cover and cook in the oven at 170°C (325°F) mark 3 for 1½-2 hours until the meat is tender.

JAPANESE SKEWERED BEEF

Cut the steak across the grain into slices about 1 cm (½ inch) thick, using a very sharp knife.

Sake is a wine made from rice. Available in Japanese and other oriental stores, it is used extensively in cooking of the East. It is made by fermenting rice, and is usually 14-18% proof so it tastes rather strong. The Japanese drink it warm in small porcelain bowls called *sakazuki*, and if you eat out in a Japanese restaurant you are sure to be asked to try some. For home cooking, a dry sherry can be used as a substitute in Japanese recipes, although its flavour and bouquet will not be so strong.

BEEF, WALNUT AND ORANGE CASSEROLE

SERVES 4

700 g (1½ lb) lean chuck steak

40 g (1½ oz) seasoned plain wholemeal flour

45 ml (3 tbsp) polyunsaturated oil

1 medium onion, skinned and chopped

4 celery sticks, trimmed and roughly chopped

150 ml (¼ pint) unsweetened orange juice

600 ml (1 pint) beef stock

bouquet garni

2 garlic cloves, skinned and crushed

2 oranges

100 g (4 oz) broken walnuts

salt and pepper

orange shreds, to garnish

/ 1 / Cut the meat into 2.5 cm (1 inch) cubes, trimming off excess fat. Toss the meat cubes in the seasoned flour. Heat the oil in a flameproof casserole and fry the onion and celery for about 5 minutes. Add the meat and fry for 5 minutes until browned. Add the orange juice, stock, bouquet garni and garlic.

/ 2 / Bring to the boil, cover and cook in the oven at 170°C (325°F) mark 3 for 2 hours.

/ 3 / Meanwhile peel the oranges over a plate, removing all the pith. Cut into segments.

/ 4 / Add the walnuts and orange segments to the casserole, together with any juice that may have collected on the plate. Continue to cook for a further 30 minutes until the meat is tender. Taste and adjust the seasoning. Serve garnished with orange shreds.

Beef, Walnut and Orange Casserole

PAPRIKA BEEF

SERVES 4

450 g (1 lb) lean shin of beef

15 ml (1 tbsp) plain wholemeal flour

7.5 ml (1½ tsp) paprika

1.25 ml (¼ tsp) caraway seeds

1.25 ml (¼ tsp) dried marjoram

salt and pepper

2 medium onions, skinned and sliced

225 g (8 oz) carrots, peeled and sliced

200 ml (7 fl oz) beef stock

15 ml (1 tbsp) tomato purée

1 garlic clove, skinned and crushed

1 whole clove

100 g (4 oz) button mushrooms, sliced

chopped fresh parsley, to garnish

/ 1 / Cut the meat into chunky cubes, trimming off excess fat. Mix together the flour, paprika, caraway seeds, marjoram and salt and pepper to taste. Toss the beef in the seasoned flour.

/ 2 / Layer the meat, onions and carrots in a 2 litre (3 ½ pint) flameproof casserole.

/ 3 / Whisk together the stock, tomato purée, crushed garlic and clove. Pour into the casserole. Bring to the boil and simmer, uncovered, for 3-4 minutes.

/ 4 / Cover the casserole and cook in the oven at 180°C (350°F) mark 4 for about 1½ hours, stirring occasionally.

/ 5 / Remove the casserole from the oven and stir in the mushrooms. Cover again and return to the oven for a further 15 minutes or until the meat is tender. Garnish with chopped parsley.

BEEF BEANPOT

SERVES 4 - 6

30 ml (2 tbsp) polyunsaturated oil

225 g (8 oz) small, whole even-sized onions, skinned

900 g (2 lb) rolled silverside

45 ml (3 tbsp) plain wholemeal flour

397 g (14 oz) can tomatoes

450 ml (¾ pint) beef stock

225 g (8 oz) dried haricot beans, soaked overnight

5 ml (1 tsp) dried oregano

salt and pepper

/ 1 / Heat the oil in a flameproof casserole and fry the onions for a few minutes until golden brown. Add the meat and brown all over.

/ 2 / Stir in the flour, then add the tomatoes and stock, stirring to prevent lumps forming.

/ 3 / Drain the beans and add to the casserole with the oregano and pepper to taste. Bring to the boil, cover and simmer for about 2 hours until the meat and beans are tender.

/ 4 / Add salt to taste, with more pepper if wished. Remove the beef from the casserole and carve into slices. Serve with the beans.

ALMOND BEEF WITH CELERY

SERVES 6

900 g (2 lb) lean shin of beef

75 ml (5 tbsp) polyunsaturated oil

15 ml (1 tbsp) plain wholemeal flour

90 ml (6 tbsp) ground almonds

1 garlic clove, skinned and crushed

300 ml (½ pint) beef stock

salt and pepper

4 celery sticks

50 g (2 oz) flaked almonds

/ 1 / Cut the beef into 2.5 cm (1 inch) pieces, trimming off excess fat. Heat 45 ml (3 tbsp) of the oil in a flameproof casserole, add the meat a few pieces at a time and brown well.

/ 2 / Return all the meat to the pan. Stir in the flour, ground almonds and garlic. Stir over the heat for 1 minute, then pour in the beef stock. Bring to the boil and season with salt and pepper to taste.

/ 3 / Cover the casserole and cook in the oven at 180°C (350°F) mark 4 for about 1½ hours or until the meat is tender.

/ 4 / Ten minutes before the end of cooking time, slice the celery. Heat the remaining oil in a large frying pan, add the celery and flaked almonds and sauté for about 6 minutes or until golden brown.

/ 5 / Sprinkle the celery and almond mixture on top of the casserole and serve at once.

PAPRIKA BEEF

Serve this casserole with layered sliced potatoes and onions, moistened with stock and baked in the oven.

ALMOND BEEF WITH CELERY

Serve this unusual casserole with jacket baked potatoes, which can be cooked in the oven at the same time. Carrots tossed in plenty of chopped fresh parsley will help give the meal colour.

The almonds in this casserole help increase its nutritional value – something to bear in mind when preparing everyday meals, especially if there are growing children in the family. Almonds are a good source of protein, B vitamins and unsaturated fats.

SLIMMERS' MOUSSAKA

Serve this delicious moussaka with crusty granary bread and a green salad.

SLIMMERS' MOUSSAKA

SERVES 4

2 medium aubergines
salt and pepper
450 g (1 lb) fresh lean minced beef
2 medium onions, skinned and sliced
1 garlic clove, skinned and finely chopped
397 g (14 oz) can tomatoes
30 ml (2 tbsp) tomato purée
15 ml (1 tbsp) chopped fresh parsley
300 ml (½ pint) natural low-fat yogurt
2 eggs, beaten
pinch of freshly grated nutmeg
15 ml (1 tbsp) grated Parmesan cheese

/ 1 / Thinly slice the aubergines, discarding the tops and tails. Place in a colander, sprinkling each layer with salt. Cover with a plate, weight down and leave to stand for about 30 minutes.

/ 2 / Drain the aubergine slices, then rinse and dry well by patting with absorbent kitchen paper or a clean tea-towel.

/ 3 / Dry fry the aubergine slices on both sides in a non-stick frying pan over high heat until brown, pressing them with the back of a spatula to release the moisture. Remove from the pan and set aside.

/ 4 / In the same pan, cook the meat for 5 minutes until browned, stirring and pressing with a wooden spoon to break up any lumps. Stir in the onions and cook for a further 5 minutes until lightly browned.

/ 5 / Add the garlic, tomatoes with their juice, the tomato purée, parsley and salt and pepper to taste. Bring to the boil, stirring, then lower the heat and simmer for 20 minutes until the meat is cooked.

/ 6 / Arrange a layer of aubergines in the bottom of an ovenproof dish. Spoon over the meat mixture and finish with a layer of aubergines.

/ 7 / Beat the yogurt and eggs together with the nutmeg and salt and pepper to taste. Pour over the dish and sprinkle with the grated Parmesan cheese.

/ 8 / Bake in the oven at 180°C (350°F) mark 4 for about 45 minutes until golden. Serve hot.

CHILLI CON CARNE

If you find this dish hot, serve it with natural low-fat yogurt and sliced cucumber to cool the palate.

If you forget to soak the red beans overnight, there is still no reason why it shouldn't be made on the day. Make the casserole without the beans then, 10 minutes before serving, simply stir in a can of ready-cooked red kidney beans (drained and rinsed) and heat through.

CHILLI CON CARNE

SERVES 6

900 g (2 lb) lean chuck steak
225 g (8 oz) dried red kidney beans, soaked overnight
30 ml (2 tbsp) polyunsaturated oil
2 medium onions, skinned and chopped
1 large garlic clove, skinned and crushed
1 bay leaf
1 green chilli, seeded and chopped
5 cm (2 inch) cinnamon stick
4 whole cloves
2.5 ml (½ tsp) dried oregano or marjoram
2.5 ml (½ tsp) cayenne pepper
1.25 ml (¼ tsp) sesame seeds
salt and pepper
30-45 ml (2-3 tbsp) chilli seasoning or 2.5 ml (½ tsp) chilli powder
30 ml (2 tbsp) tomato purée
793 g (28 oz) can tomatoes
pinch of raw cane sugar
5 ml (1 tsp) malt vinegar
2 coriander sprigs
Boiled Rice (see page 146), to serve

/ 1 / Trim the meat of excess fat and cut into cubes. Drain the beans and place in a saucepan of cold water. Bring to the boil, boil fast for 10 minutes, then drain.

/ 2 / Meanwhile, heat the oil in a flameproof casserole and fry the onions for 5 minutes until softened. Add the meat and cook for about 8 minutes until browned.

/ 3 / Add the next 10 ingredients to the meat and continue to fry for 2 minutes, stirring constantly. Add the tomato purée, tomatoes with their juice, sugar, vinegar, coriander and the boiled and drained beans.

/ 4 / Bring to the boil, cover and cook in the oven at 170°C (325°F) mark 3 for about 2¼ hours until the meat is tender. Serve with plain boiled rice.

Slimmers' Moussaka

TANDOORI CHICKEN

SERVES 4

4 chicken quarters, skinned
30 ml (2 tbsp) lemon juice
1 garlic clove, skinned
2.5 cm (1 inch) piece fresh root ginger, peeled and chopped
1 green chilli, seeded
60 ml (4 tbsp) natural low-fat yogurt
5 ml (1 tsp) ground cumin
5 ml (1 tsp) garam masala
15 ml (1 tbsp) paprika
salt
30 ml (2 tbsp) melted ghee or polyunsaturated oil
shredded lettuce, lemon wedges and onion rings, to serve

/ 1 / Using a sharp knife or skewer, pierce the flesh of the chicken pieces all over.

/ 2 / Put the chicken in an ovenproof dish and add the lemon juice. Rub this into the flesh. Cover and leave for 30 minutes.

/ 3 / Make the marinade: put the garlic, ginger and green chilli and 15 ml (1 tbsp) water in a blender or food processor and grind to a smooth paste.

/ 4 / Add the paste to the yogurt, ground cumin, garam masala, paprika, salt to taste and the melted ghee or oil. Mix all the ingredients together, then pour them slowly over the chicken pieces.

/ 5 / Coat the pieces liberally with the yogurt marinade. Cover and leave to marinate at room temperature for 5 hours. Turn once or twice during this time.

/ 6 / Roast the chicken pieces, uncovered, at 170°C (325°F) mark 3 for about 1 hour, basting frequently and turning once, until they are tender and most of the marinade has evaporated. Alternatively, grill the chicken or barbecue, or roast it in a chicken brick. Serve the chicken hot, with shredded lettuce, lemon wedges and onion rings.

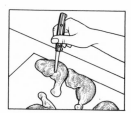

Using a sharp knife or skewer, pierce all the flesh of the chicken pieces.

The Indian *tandoor* is a clay oven which is usually about 1 metre (3 feet) high, although some are as much as twice this height. At the base of the oven is a charcoal or wood fire which burns extremely fiercely so that searing temperatures are reached – small whole chickens can cook in a few minutes.

To achieve exactly the same flavour as food cooked in a tandoor is virtually impossible in a conventional oven, but the tandoori marinade is almost as important as the cooking method, so with the correct marinade you are nearly halfway there.

While the food is cooking the yogurt marinade will form a thick crust which helps seal in the meat's natural juices. Take care not to puncture the crust during cooking or the juices will run out, resulting in dry, flavourless meat.

ITALIAN CHICKEN WITH ROSEMARY

Using 2 slotted spoons, turn the chicken frequently during cooking until the skin is brown and crisp and the juices run clear when the flesh is pierced with a fork.

ITALIAN CHICKEN WITH ROSEMARY

SERVES 4

30 ml (2 tbsp) white wine vinegar
7.5 cm (3 inch) rosemary sprig, chopped
salt and pepper
4 chicken leg joints, cut in half
30 ml (2 tbsp) olive oil
lemon wedges and rosemary sprigs, to garnish

/ 1 / Put the vinegar into a glass, add 15 ml (1 tbsp) water, the rosemary and salt and pepper to taste. Stir well, then leave to infuse.

/ 2 / Season the chicken pieces with salt and pepper to taste. Heat the oil in a large frying pan and, when hot, add the chicken pieces and fry for 5 minutes until they are just golden brown on all sides. Lower the heat and cook, uncovered, for about 35 minutes until tender.

/ 3 / Using 2 slotted spoons, turn the chicken frequently during cooking until the skin is brown and crisp and the juices run clear when the flesh is pierced with a fork.

/ 4 / Remove the pan from the heat. When the fat has stopped sizzling, pour over the wine vinegar infusion.

/ 5 / Return to the heat, boil rapidly for about 5 minutes to reduce the liquid. Garnish with lemon and rosemary sprigs and serve.

TANDOORI CHICKEN KEBABS

Grill or barbecue the chicken for about 15 minutes, turning frequently and brushing with the ghee or the oil.

TANDOORI CHICKEN KEBABS

SERVES 4

4 boneless chicken breasts
150 ml (¼ pint) natural low-fat yogurt
2.5 cm (1 inch) piece of fresh root ginger, peeled and crushed
4 garlic cloves, skinned and crushed
½ small onion, skinned and grated
15 ml (1 tbsp) wine vinegar
5 ml (1 tsp) chilli powder
salt
50 ml (2 fl oz) melted ghee or polyunsaturated oil
lemon wedges and Nan bread, to serve

/ 1 / Cut the chicken into bite-sized chunks, removing all skin. Place in a bowl.

/ 2 / Put the yogurt in a blender or food processor with the remaining ingredients except the ghee or oil and lemon. Work to a paste.

/ 3 / Pour the marinade over the chicken pieces and stir well to mix. Cover the bowl and marinate in the refrigerator for 24 hours.

/ 4 / When ready to cook, thread the chicken pieces on to 4 oiled flat kebab skewers. Place on a barbecue or grill rack and brush with some of the ghee or oil.

/ 5 / Barbecue or grill the chicken for about 15 minutes or until cooked to your liking, turning the skewers frequently and brushing with more of the ghee or oil. Serve hot, with lemon wedges and Nan bread.

HINDLE WAKES

SERVES 4 - 6

1.6 kg (3½ lb) boiling chicken with giblets, trussed
salt and pepper
30 ml (2 tbsp) polyunsaturated oil
450 g (1 lb) leeks, sliced and washed
6 medium carrots, peeled and thickly sliced
225 g (8 oz) prunes, soaked overnight and stoned
25 g (1 oz) butter or margarine
25 g (1 oz) plain wholemeal flour

/ 1 / Place the giblets in a saucepan with 600 ml (1 pint) water and salt to taste. Bring to the boil, then cover and simmer for 30 minutes.

/ 2 / Meanwhile, melt the oil in a large flame-proof casserole and fry the chicken for about 8 minutes until browned all over. Remove from the casserole.

/ 3 / Fry the leeks and carrots for 3 minutes. Return the chicken and add the drained prunes. Strain in the giblet stock and season to taste with pepper.

/ 4 / Cover and cook in the oven at 170°C (325°F) mark 3 for about 2-2½ hours or until tender.

/ 5 / Arrange the chicken, vegetables and prunes on a large warmed platter. Keep hot.

/ 6 / Skim any fat off the sauce. Blend together the butter or margarine and the flour to form a paste. Add to the sauce, a little at a time, and stir over a gentle heat until thickened; do not boil. Serve separately.

Serve this old English dish with jacket baked potatoes or creamed potatoes and a green vegetable.

Hindle Wakes

CHICKEN DHANSAK

Serve this hot Indian curry with Boiled Rice (see page 146) and Cucumber Raita (see page 42). Indian bread such as Parathas (see page 203) can also be served with it.

Ghee or clarified butter is used frequently in Asian cookery. To make it: simmer melted butter in a heavy pan until a thick froth forms on top. Lower the heat and continue simmering until the froth starts to separate and sediment settles at the bottom. Cool slightly, then strain through a metal sieve lined with muslin or a clean tea-towel. Discard the sediment. Store ghee in the refrigerator.

CHICKEN DHANSAK

SERVES 4

40 g (1½ oz) ghee or polyunsaturated oil
1 medium onion, skinned and chopped
2.5 cm (1 inch) piece fresh root ginger, skinned and crushed
1-2 garlic cloves, skinned and crushed
4 chicken portions
5 ml (1 tsp) ground coriander
2.5 ml (½ tsp) chilli powder
2.5 ml (½ tsp) ground turmeric
1.25 cm (¼ tsp) ground cinnamon
salt
225 g (8 oz) red lentils, rinsed and drained
juice of 1 lime or lemon
fresh lime slices and coriander leaves, to garnish

/ 1 / Heat the ghee or oil in a flameproof casserole, add the onion, ginger and garlic and fry gently for 5 minutes until the onion is soft but not coloured.

/ 2 / Add the chicken portions and spices and fry for a few minutes more, turning the chicken constantly so that the pieces become coloured on all sides.

/ 3 / Pour enough water into the casserole to just cover the chicken. Add salt to taste, then the lentils.

/ 4 / Bring slowly to boiling point, stirring, then lower the heat and cover the casserole. Simmer for 40 minutes or until the chicken is tender when pierced with a skewer. During cooking, turn the chicken in the sauce occasionally, and check that the lentils have not absorbed all the water and become too dry – add more water if necessary.

/ 5 / Remove the chicken from the casserole and leave until cool enough to handle. Take the meat off the bones, discarding the skin. Cut the meat into bite-sized pieces, return to the casserole and heat through thoroughly. Stir in the lime or lemon juice. Garnish with fresh lime slices and coriander leaves, then serve immediately.

CIRCASSIAN CHICKEN

SERVES 4 - 6

1.8 kg (4 lb) chicken
1 medium onion, skinned and sliced
2 celery sticks, roughly chopped
1 medium carrot, peeled and roughly chopped
a few parsley sprigs
salt and pepper
100 g (4 oz) shelled walnuts
40 g (1½ oz) butter or margarine
45 ml (3 tbsp) polyunsaturated oil
1.25 ml (¼ tsp) ground cinnamon
1.25 ml (¼ tsp) ground cloves
5 ml (1 tsp) paprika
parsley sprigs and onion rings, to garnish

/ 1 / Put the chicken in a large saucepan with the vegetables, parsley and salt and pepper to taste. Cover the chicken with water and bring to the boil. Lower the heat, half cover the pan with a lid and simmer for 40 minutes.

/ 2 / Remove the chicken from the pan, strain the cooking liquid and set aside. Cut the chicken into 4 or 6 large serving pieces, discarding the skin.

/ 3 / Pound the walnuts with a pestle in a mortar until very fine, or grind them in an electric grinder or food processor.

/ 4 / Melt the butter or margarine with 15 ml (1 tbsp) of the oil in a large frying pan. Add the chicken pieces and fry over moderate heat for 3-4 minutes until well coloured.

/ 5 / Add 450 ml (¾ pint) of the cooking liquid, the walnuts, cinnamon and cloves. Stir well to mix, then simmer, uncovered, for about 20 minutes or until the chicken is tender and the sauce coats it thickly. Stir the chicken and sauce frequently during this time.

/ 6 / Just before serving, heat the remaining oil in a separate small pan. Sprinkle in the paprika, stirring to combine with the oil.

/ 7 / Arrange the chicken and sauce on a warmed serving platter and drizzle with the paprika oil. Garnish with parsley sprigs and onion rings. Serve at once.

Circassian Chicken

GOLDEN BAKED CHICKEN

SERVES 4

4 chicken portions
salt and pepper
1 small onion, skinned and finely chopped
50 g (2 oz) fresh wholemeal breadcrumbs
15 ml (1 tbsp) chopped fresh parsley and thyme or 5 ml (1 tsp) dried mixed herbs
60 ml (4 tbsp) polyunsaturated oil

/ 1 / Season the chicken portions with salt and pepper to taste. Mix the onion with the breadcrumbs and herbs.

/ 2 / Brush the oil all over the chicken joints. Toss them in the herbed breadcrumbs and place in a greased ovenproof dish.

/ 3 / Bake in the oven at 190°C (375°F) mark 5 for about 1 hour or until golden. Baste occasionally during cooking. Serve hot, straight from the dish.

111

INDIAN SPICED ROAST CHICKEN

This dish is known as Chirga in India. It is spicy but dry, so serve with a juicy vegetable dish.

CHICKEN WITH GARLIC

The French name for this popular recipe is Poulet aux Quarantes Gousses d'Ail. It is surprising how such a large number of garlic cloves taste so mild. Any garlic residue can be used spread on slices of French bread. This garlic-spread bread can then be offered as an accompaniment to the chicken dish, and is considered a great delicacy by the French.

INDIAN SPICED ROAST CHICKEN

SERVES 4

2 kg (4 lb) oven-ready chicken, giblets removed and trussed
juice of 1 lemon
10 ml (2 tsp) coriander seeds, finely crushed
2.5 ml (½ tsp) chilli powder
300 ml (½ pint) natural low-fat yogurt
60 ml (4 tbsp) chopped fresh coriander
60 ml (4 tbsp) chopped fresh mint
5 cm (2 inch) piece of fresh root ginger, peeled and crushed
4 garlic cloves, peeled and crushed
5 ml (1 tsp) paprika
5 ml (1 tsp) ground turmeric
salt
50 ml (2 fl oz) melted ghee or polyunsaturated oil
mint sprigs and lemon wedges, to garnish

/ 1 / Prick the skin of the chicken all over with a fine skewer. Mix together the lemon juice, crushed coriander seeds and chilli powder and brush all over the chicken. Leave to stand for about 30 minutes.

/ 2 / Meanwhile, mix together all the remaining ingredients, except the ghee or oil and the mint and lemon wedges for the garnish.

/ 3 / Stand the chicken, breast side up, in a roasting tin. Brush with one-quarter of the yogurt mixture. Roast in the oven at 200°C (400°F) mark 6 for about 30 minutes, or until the yogurt dries on the skin of the chicken.

/ 4 / Turn the chicken over on its side and brush with another quarter of the yogurt mixture. Return to the oven for a further 30 minutes until the yogurt dries again. Continue turning and brushing with yogurt twice more, until it has been cooking for 2 hours.

/ 5 / Stand the chicken breast side up again and brush with the ghee or oil. Increase the oven temperature to 220°C (425°F) mark 7 and roast the chicken for a further 15 minutes or until the juices run clear when the thickest part of a thigh is pierced with a skewer.

/ 6 / Transfer the chicken to a warmed serving dish and remove the trussing string and skewers. Garnish with mint sprigs and lemon wedges. Serve hot.

CHICKEN WITH GARLIC

SERVES 6

60 ml (4 tbsp) olive or polyunsaturated oil
1.8 kg (4 lb) chicken
1 sprig each of rosemary, thyme, savory and basil or 2.5 ml (½ tsp) dried
1 bay leaf
40 garlic cloves (about 5 bulbs)
salt and pepper
freshly grated nutmeg
300 ml (½ pint) hot water

/ 1 / Heat the oil in a large flameproof casserole and fry the chicken for about 8 minutes until browned on all sides. Remove the chicken from the casserole.

/ 2 / Place the herbs in the base of the casserole. Arrange the garlic, unpeeled, in one layer over them. Place the chicken on top and season with salt, pepper and nutmeg to taste.

/ 3 / Cover and cook over a very low heat for 1¼-1¾ hours until tender, adding a little hot water, if necessary, to prevent the chicken from sticking to the base of the casserole.

/ 4 / When cooked, remove the chicken and place on a warmed serving dish. Set aside and keep hot until required.

/ 5 / Strain the sauce into a bowl, pushing the garlic cloves through the sieve, using the back of a wooden spoon.

/ 6 / Add the hot water to the casserole and stir to lift the sediment. Return the sauce and simmer for 2 minutes or until hot. Transfer to a warm sauceboat and serve with the chicken.

Picture opposite:
Chicken with Garlic

TURKEY ESCALOPES EN PAPILLOTE

This dish is a good choice for a special occasion. Serve with new potatoes and tiny fresh green peas.

TURKEY ESCALOPES EN PAPILLOTE

SERVES 4

4 turkey breast fillets, total weight 550-700 g (1¼-1½ lb), boned
15 ml (1 tbsp) corn oil
1 small red pepper, cored, seeded and thinly sliced
225 g (8 oz) tomatoes, skinned (see page 57) and sliced
30 ml (2 tbsp) chopped fresh parsley
salt and pepper
60 ml (4 tbsp) medium dry sherry
40 g (1½ oz) fresh wholemeal breadcrumbs, toasted

/ 1 / Split each turkey breast fillet through its thickness with a sharp knife, then bat out between 2 sheets of greaseproof paper to make 8 thin escalopes.

/ 2 / Place a large sheet of foil on a baking sheet and brush lightly with the oil. Put half of the turkey escalopes side by side on the foil.

/ 3 / Blanch the pepper slices for 1 minute in boiling water, drain and refresh under cold running water. Thoroughly dry the slices with absorbent kitchen paper.

/ 4 / Layer the pepper and tomato slices on top of the escalopes with half of the parsley and seasoning to taste.

/ 5 / Cover with the remaining escalopes, spoon 15 ml (1 tbsp) sherry over each and close up the foil like a parcel.

/ 6 / Bake in the oven at 180°C (350°F) mark 4 for 35-40 minutes or until the meat is tender when pierced with a fork or skewer.

/ 7 / Arrange the escalopes on a warmed serving dish, cover and keep warm in the oven turned to its lowest setting. Transfer the juices to a pan and reduce to 60 ml (4 tbsp), then spoon over the turkey. Sprinkle with the freshly toasted breadcrumbs and the remaining parsley and serve immediately.

QUICK CHICKEN AND MUSSEL PAELLA

Spain's most famous dish, paella gets its name from the pan in which it is traditionally cooked – *paellera*. The pan is usually made of a heavy metal such as cast iron, with sloping sides and 2 flat handles on either side. The *paellera* is not only the best utensil for cooking paella, it is also the most attractive way to serve it, so if you like to make paella fairly frequently it is well worth investing in one.

QUICK CHICKEN AND MUSSEL PAELLA

SERVES 4 - 6

60 ml (4 tbsp) olive oil
about 450 g (1 lb) boneless chicken meat, skinned and cut into bite-sized cubes
1 medium onion, skinned and chopped
2 garlic cloves, skinned and crushed
1 large red pepper, cored, seeded and sliced into thin strips
3 medium tomatoes, skinned (see page 57) and chopped
400 g (14 oz) long-grain brown rice
1.2 litres (2¼ pints) boiling chicken stock
5 ml (1 tsp) paprika
2.5 ml (½ tsp) saffron powder
salt and pepper
two 150 g (5 oz) jars mussels, drained
lemon wedges and peeled prawns (optional), to garnish

/ 1 / Heat the oil in a paella pan or large, deep frying pan, add the cubes of chicken and fry over moderate heat until golden brown on all sides. Remove from the pan with a slotted spoon and set aside.

/ 2 / Add the onion, garlic and red pepper to the pan and fry gently for 5 minutes until softened. Add the tomatoes and fry for a few more minutes until the juices run, then add the rice and stir to combine with the olive oil and softened vegetables.

/ 3 / Pour in 1 litre (1¾ pints) of the boiling stock (it will bubble furiously), then add half the paprika, the saffron powder and salt and pepper to taste. Stir well, lower the heat and add the chicken.

/ 4 / Simmer, uncovered, for 35 minutes until the chicken is cooked through and the rice is tender, stirring frequently during this time to prevent the rice from sticking. When the mixture becomes dry, stir in a few tablespoons of boiling stock. Repeat as often as necessary to keep the paella moist until the end of the cooking time.

/ 5 / To serve: fold in the mussels and heat through. Garnish with lemon wedges, prawns if liked and a sprinkling of the remaining paprika over the top.

TURKEY IN SPICED YOGURT

SERVES 6

turkey leg on the bone, about 1.1 kg (2½ lb) in weight
7.5 ml (1½ tsp) ground cumin
7.5 ml (1½ tsp) ground coriander
2.5 ml (½ tsp) ground turmeric
2.5 ml (½ tsp) ground ginger
salt and pepper
300 ml (½ pint) natural low-fat yogurt
30 ml (2 tbsp) lemon juice
45 ml (3 tbsp) polyunsaturated oil
2 medium onions, skinned and sliced
45 ml (3 tbsp) desiccated coconut
30 ml (2 tbsp) plain wholemeal flour
150 ml (¼ pint) chicken stock or water
chopped fresh parsley, to garnish

/ 1 / Cut the turkey meat off the bone into large bite-sized pieces, discarding the skin – there should be about 900 g (2 lb) meat.

/ 2 / Make the marinade: in a large bowl mix the spices with salt and pepper to taste, the yogurt and lemon juice. Stir well until evenly blended. Fold through the turkey meat until coated with the yogurt mixture. Cover tightly with cling film and leave to marinate in the refrigerator overnight.

/ 3 / Heat the oil in a flameproof casserole, add the onions and fry for about 5 minutes until lightly browned. Add the desiccated coconut and flour and fry gently, stirring the mixture, for about 1 minute.

/ 4 / Remove from the heat and stir in the turkey with its marinade, and the stock. Return to the heat and bring slowly to the boil, stirring all the time to prevent sticking.

/ 5 / Cover tightly and cook in the oven at 170°C (325°F) mark 3 for 1-1¼ hours or until the turkey is tender when tested with a fork. Serve garnished with chopped parsley.

Plain unsweetened yogurt is used extensively in Indian and Middle Eastern cooking for many reasons. It is often used as a marinade as in this recipe, because it has a tenderising effect on meat – it contains bacteria which help break down tough fibres and sinews, making the meat more succulent and juicy when cooked.

Turkey in Spiced Yogurt

CHICKEN AND SPINACH
PIE WITH MUSHROOMS

Skin the chicken portions
and then remove the meat
from the bones. Cut the
meat into bite-sized pieces.

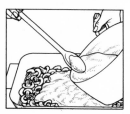

Spread one-third of the
spinach over the bottom of
a lightly greased oven-proof
dish. Arrange half of the
mushrooms on top of the
spinach, then pour over half
the chicken sauce. Repeat
these layers twice more,
then spread over the
remaining spinach.

CHICKEN AND SPINACH PIE WITH MUSHROOMS

SERVES 4

4 cooked chicken portions
900 g (2 lb) fresh spinach or 450 g (1 lb) frozen leaf spinach
1.25 ml (¼ tsp) grated nutmeg
salt and pepper
568 ml (1 pint) milk
45 ml (3 tbsp) wholemeal flour
5 ml (1 tsp) dried tarragon
225 g (8 oz) button mushrooms, wiped and roughly chopped
1 egg, beaten
50 g (2 oz) Gruyère or Edam cheese, grated

/ 1 / Skin the chicken portions, then remove the meat from the bones. Cut the meat into bite-sized pieces.

/ 2 / Trim the fresh spinach, discarding any thick stalks. Wash the leaves thoroughly, then place in a saucepan with only the water that clings to them. Cover the pan and cook for about 5 minutes until tender. Drain and chop roughly. If using frozen spinach, put in a heavy-based saucepan and heat gently for 7-10 minutes until thawed. Season the spinach with the nutmeg and plenty of salt and pepper.

/ 3 / Put the milk and flour in a blender or food processor. Blend until evenly mixed, then pour into a heavy-based saucepan. Bring slowly to boiling point, then simmer for 5 minutes, stirring frequently, until thickened.

/ 4 / Remove the sauce from the heat, reserve one third and stir the chicken, tarragon and salt and pepper into the remaining sauce.

/ 5 / Spread one-third of the spinach over the bottom of a lightly greased ovenproof dish. Arrange half of the mushrooms on top of the spinach then pour over half of the chicken sauce. Repeat these layers once more, then spread over the remaining spinach.

/ 6 / Stir the egg into the reserved sauce, then pour over the spinach. Sprinkle the cheese over the top. Bake in the oven at 190°C (375°F) mark 5 for about 30 minutes or until the topping is bubbling. Serve hot.

MARINATED STIR-FRIED CHICKEN

SERVES 4

4 large boneless chicken breasts
90 ml (6 tbsp) natural low-fat yogurt
juice of 1 lime or lemon
2 garlic cloves, skinned and crushed
2.5 ml (½ tsp) ground turmeric
15 ml (1 tbsp) paprika
seeds of 3 green cardamoms, crushed
salt
60 ml (4 tbsp) ghee or polyunsaturated oil
2.5 ml (½ tsp) garam masala
30 ml (2 tbsp) chopped fresh coriander
lime or lemon wedges, to garnish
Boiled Rice (see page 146), to serve (optional)

/ 1 / Skin the chicken breasts and cut the flesh into strips about 1 cm (½ inch) wide. Put the strips into a bowl with the yogurt, lime or lemon juice, garlic, turmeric, paprika, cardamom seeds and salt to taste. Mix well to coat.

/ 2 / Melt 30 ml (2 tbsp) of the ghee, if using, in a small saucepan. Stir the melted ghee or oil into the chicken mixture, cover and leave to marinate in the refrigerator for at least 2 hours.

/ 3 / Heat the remaining ghee or oil in a heavy frying pan or wok. Add the chicken and marinade and stir-fry for 10 minutes.

/ 4 / Lower the heat and add the garam masala and coriander. Stir-fry for a further 5-10 minutes until the chicken is tender. Transfer to a warmed serving dish, garnish with lime or lemon wedges and serve immediately with boiled rice, if liked.

TURKEY GROUNDNUT STEW

SERVES 4 - 6

30 ml (2 tbsp) polyunsaturated oil
2 medium onions, skinned and chopped
1 garlic clove, skinned and crushed
1 large green pepper, cored, seeded and chopped
900 g (2 lb) boneless turkey, cut into cubes
175 g (6 oz) shelled peanuts
600 ml (1 pint) chicken stock
salt and pepper
60 ml (4 tbsp) crunchy peanut butter
10 ml (2 tsp) tomato purée
225 g (8 oz) tomatoes, skinned and roughly chopped, or 225 g (8 oz) can tomatoes, drained
2.5-5 ml (½-1 tsp) cayenne pepper
a few drops of Tabasco sauce
chopped green pepper, to garnish

/ 1 / Heat the oil in a flameproof casserole, add the onions, garlic and green pepper and fry gently for 5 minutes until soft.

/ 2 / Add the turkey and fry for a few minutes more, turning constantly until well browned on all sides.

/ 3 / Add the peanuts, stock and salt and pepper to taste and bring slowly to boiling point. Lower the heat, cover and simmer for 45 minutes or until the turkey is tender.

/ 4 / Remove the turkey from the cooking liquid with a slotted spoon and set aside. Leave the cooking liquid to cool for about 5 minutes.

/ 5 / Work the cooking liquid and nuts in a blender or food processor, half at a time, until quite smooth. Return to the pan with the remaining ingredients, except the garnish, add the turkey and reheat. Taste and adjust seasoning before serving, adding more cayenne if a hot flavour is liked. Garnish with chopped green pepper.

Groundnut stews are traditionally served in the Caribbean with plain boiled rice and a dish of root vegetables such as turnip, swede or parsnip. If liked, hot pepper sauce can also be offered as an additional accompaniment.

This type of stew originated in West Africa, where groundnuts (or peanuts as we call them) grow in profusion. The cook can buy fresh peanut paste from the market to make groundnut stew, which is a popular Sunday lunch dish – served with ice-cold beer and fried bananas. Due to the slave trade, groundnut stews spread to the West Indies, becoming an integral part of the local cuisine.

Turkey Groundnut Stew

STIR-FRIED CHICKEN
AND CASHEW NUTS

The hoisin sauce used in
this Chinese-style recipe is
just one of the many
bottled and canned sauces
which are used frequently
in Chinese cookery. Look
for them in oriental
specialist shops and some
supermarkets – they will
give an authentic touch to
your oriental dishes.

Chinese cooks use
commercial sauces all the
time. Hoisin sauce is made
from soya bean flour, sugar
and spices.

**MARINATED CHICKEN
WITH PEANUT SAUCE**

Serve these kebabs on a
bed of brown rice or
noodles with a little of the
sauce poured over.

STIR-FRIED CHICKEN AND CASHEW NUTS

SERVES 4

1 bunch spring onions
3 celery sticks
1 green pepper
100 g (4 oz) cauliflower florets
2 medium carrots
175 g (6 oz) button mushrooms
4 boneless chicken breasts
30 ml (2 tbsp) sesame or vegetable oil
10 ml (2 tsp) cornflour
30 ml (2 tbsp) dry sherry
15 ml (1 tbsp) soy sauce
15 ml (1 tbsp) hoisin sauce
5 ml (1 tsp) raw cane sugar
75 g (3 oz) unsalted cashew nuts
salt and pepper

/ 1 / Prepare the vegetables. Trim the spring
onions and slice them into thin rings. Trim the
celery and slice finely.

/ 2 / Halve the green pepper, remove the core
and seeds and slice the flesh into thin strips.
Divide the cauliflower florets into tiny sprigs.

/ 3 / Peel the carrots, then grate into thin slivers using the coarse side of a conical or box grater or cut into matchsticks. Wipe the mushrooms and slice them finely.

/ 4 / Skin the chicken and cut into bite-sized
strips about 4 cm (1½ inches) long.

/ 5 / Heat the oil in a wok or deep frying pan,
add the prepared vegetables and stir-fry over
brisk heat for 3 minutes. Remove with a slotted
spoon and set aside.

/ 6 / In a jug, mix the cornflour to a paste with
the sherry, soy sauce and hoisin sauce, then
add the sugar and 150 ml (¼ pint) water.

/ 7 / Add the chicken strips to the pan and stir-
fry over moderate heat until lightly coloured
on all sides. Pour the cornflour mixture into
the pan and bring to the boil, stirring.

/ 8 / Return the vegetables to the pan. Add the
cashew nuts and seasoning to taste, and stir-fry
for a few minutes more. Serve immediately.

MARINATED CHICKEN WITH PEANUT SAUCE

SERVES 4

4 large chicken pieces
75 ml (5 tbsp) soy sauce
30 ml (2 tbsp) sesame or vegetable oil
30 ml (2 tbsp) clear honey
juice of 1 lemon
2.5 ml (½ tsp) chilli powder
1 red pepper
1 green pepper
75 g (3 oz) creamed coconut
150 ml (¼ pint) boiling water
75 ml (5 tbsp) crunchy peanut butter
10 ml (2 tsp) raw cane sugar

/ 1 / Skin the chicken pieces. Cut away the
flesh from the bones with a sharp, pointed
knife and slice the flesh into small cubes.

/ 2 / Put 45 ml (3 tbsp) of the soy sauce in a
bowl with the oil, honey, lemon juice and
chilli powder. Whisk well with a fork.

/ 3 / Add the cubes of chicken to the marinade,
stir well to coat, then cover and leave to marinate for 24 hours, turning occasionally.

/ 4 / When ready to cook, cut the red and green
peppers in half, remove the cores and seeds and
cut the flesh into neat squares.

/ 5 / Thread the chicken cubes and pepper
squares on 4 oiled kebab skewers, place on a
rack in the grill pan and brush liberally with
the marinade.

/ 6 / To make the peanut sauce: grate the
creamed coconut into a heavy-based saucepan.
Add the boiling water and bring slowly back to
the boil, stirring constantly. Simmer, stirring,
until the coconut has dissolved.

/ 7 / Add the peanut butter, remaining soy
sauce and the sugar to the pan and whisk to
combine. Simmer very gently over the lowest
possible heat, stirring until smooth.

/ 8 / Meanwhile, grill the chicken under moderate heat for 15 minutes, turning the skewers
frequently and brushing with the remaining
marinade. Serve hot.

Stir-fried Chicken and Cashew Nuts

QUICK TURKEY CURRY

The subtle blend of spices gives this a medium hot taste, without being too fiery! Chilli powder should be used with caution as it is intensely hot.

Garam Masala is readily available from Indian shops, specialist stores and some supermarkets. However if you want to make your own, you will need about 100 g (4 oz) mixed large and small green cardamoms, 50 g (2 oz) cumin seeds, 15 g (½ oz) each black peppercorns, cloves and stick cinnamon and a little grated nutmeg. Dry-fry the whole spices for a few minutes, then grind together, mix in the nutmeg and store in an airtight container.

VEGETABLE BIRYANI

Indian basmati rice is expensive but worth buying for its unique flavour and fluffy texture. Look for it in Indian shops and specialist supermarkets. Rinse or soak it before cooking, to remove excess starch.

QUICK TURKEY CURRY

SERVES 4 - 6

30 ml (2 tbsp) polyunsaturated oil
3 bay leaves
2 cardamom pods, crushed
1 cinnamon stick, broken into short lengths
1 medium onion, skinned and thinly sliced
1 green pepper, cored, seeded and chopped (optional)
10 ml (2 tsp) paprika
7.5 ml (1½ tsp) garam masala
2.5 ml (½ tsp) ground turmeric
2.5 ml (½ tsp) chilli powder
salt and pepper
50 g (2 oz) unsalted cashew nuts
700 g (1½ lb) turkey fillets, skinned and cut into bite-size pieces
2 medium potatoes, peeled and cut into chunks
4 medium tomatoes, skinned (see page 57) and chopped, or 225 g (8 oz) can tomatoes
bay leaves, to garnish
Boiled Rice (see page 146) and Cucumber Raita (see page 42), to serve (optional)

/ 1 / Heat the oil in a flameproof casserole, add the bay leaves, cardamom and cinnamon and fry over moderate heat for 1-2 minutes. Add the onion and green pepper, if using, with the spices and salt and pepper to taste. Pour in enough water to moisten the mixture, then stir to mix for 1 minute.

/ 2 / Add the cashews and turkey, cover the casserole and simmer for 20 minutes. Turn the turkey occasionally during this time to ensure even cooking.

/ 3 / Add the potatoes and tomatoes and continue cooking for a further 20 minutes until the turkey and potatoes are tender. Garnish with bay leaves. Serve with boiled rice and cucumber raita, if liked.

VEGETABLE BIRYANI

SERVES 4

350 g (12 oz) basmati rice
salt and pepper
50 g (2 oz) ghee or clarified butter
1 large onion, skinned and chopped
2.5 cm (1 inch) piece fresh root ginger, skinned and grated
1-2 garlic cloves, skinned and crushed
5 ml (1 tsp) ground coriander
10 ml (2 tsp) ground cumin
5 ml (1 tsp) ground turmeric
2.5 ml (½ tsp) chilli powder
3 medium carrots, peeled and thinly sliced
225 g (8 oz) fresh or frozen green beans, trimmed and cut in 2 lengthways
225 g (8 oz) cauliflower florets, divided into small sprigs
5 ml (1 tsp) garam masala
juice of 1 lemon
hard-boiled egg slices and coriander sprigs, to garnish

/ 1 / Put the rice in a sieve and hold under cold running water until the water runs clear.

/ 2 / Put the rice in a saucepan with 600 ml (1 pint) water and 5 ml (1 tsp) salt. Bring to the boil, then simmer for 10 minutes until the rice is only just tender.

/ 3 / Meanwhile, melt the ghee or butter in a heavy-based large saucepan, add the onion, ginger and garlic and fry gently for 5 minutes until soft but not coloured. Add the coriander, cumin, turmeric and chilli powder and fry for 2 minutes more, stirring constantly to avoid catching and burning.

/ 4 / Remove the rice from the heat and drain. Add 900 ml (1½ pints) water to the onion and spice mixture with seasoning to taste. Stir well and bring to the boil. Add the carrots and beans and simmer for 15 minutes, then add the cauliflower and simmer for a further 10 minutes. Lastly, add the rice. Fold gently to mix and simmer until reheated.

/ 5 / Stir the garam masala and lemon juice into the biryani and simmer for a few minutes more to reheat and allow the flavours to develop. Taste and adjust the seasoning, then turn into a warmed serving dish. Garnish with egg slices and sprigs of coriander and serve the biryani immediately.

TURKEY WITH CRANBERRY AND COCONUT

SERVES 4

450 g (1 lb) boneless turkey breast
salt and pepper
20 ml (4 tsp) Dijon mustard
60 ml (4 tbsp) cranberry sauce
15 g (½ oz) plain wholemeal flour
1 egg, beaten
15 g (½ oz) desiccated coconut
40 g (1½ oz) fresh wholemeal breadcrumbs
50 g (2 oz) butter or margarine

/ 1 / Thinly slice the turkey breast to make 4 even-sized portions.

/ 2 / Bat out the escalopes between 2 sheets of damp greaseproof paper or cling film. Season with salt and pepper to taste, then spread each portion with mustard and cranberry sauce.

/ 3 / Roll up, starting from the narrow end, and secure with a wooden cocktail stick or toothpick. Dust each portion with flour, then brush with egg. Combine the coconut and breadcrumbs, then dip the escalopes into the mixture until evenly coated.

/ 4 / Melt the butter or margarine in a frying pan, add the escalopes and fry until brown on both sides. Transfer to a baking tin just large enough to take the escalopes in a single layer and baste with some of the fat. Bake in the oven at 180°C (350°F) mark 4 for about 40 minutes until tender.

Vegetable Biryani

RED KIDNEY BEAN HOT POT

SERVES 2

125 g (4 oz) dried red kidney beans, soaked in cold water overnight
30 ml (2 tbsp) polyunsaturated oil
1 medium onion, skinned and chopped
125 g (4 oz) celery, trimmed and sliced
125 g (4 oz) carrots, peeled and sliced
15 ml (1 tbsp) plain wholemeal flour
300 ml (½ pint) vegetable or chicken stock
salt and pepper
125 g (4 oz) French beans, topped and tailed
125 g (4 oz) courgettes, trimmed and sliced
25 g (1 oz) wholemeal breadcrumbs
75 g (3 oz) low-fat Cheddar type cheese, grated
parsley sprigs, to garnish

/ 1 / Drain the soaked kidney beans and rinse well under cold running water. Put in a large saucepan, cover with plenty of fresh cold water and bring slowly to the boil.

/ 2 / Skim off any scum with a slotted spoon, then boil rapidly for 10 minutes. Half cover the pan with a lid and simmer for about 50 minutes, until the beans are tender.

/ 3 / Meanwhile, heat the oil in a large saucepan, add the onion and fry gently for about 5 minutes until softened. Add the celery and carrots. Cover and cook gently for 5 minutes.

/ 4 / Add the flour and cook gently, stirring, for 1-2 minutes. Remove from the heat and gradually blend in the stock. Bring to the boil, stirring constantly, then simmer for 5 minutes. Season with salt and pepper to taste.

/ 5 / Add the French beans and simmer for a further 5 minutes, then add the courgettes. Cook for a further 5-10 minutes, until the vegetables are tender but still with a crisp bite to them.

/ 6 / Drain the kidney beans, add to the vegetables and heat through for about 5 minutes, then turn into a deep flameproof dish.

/ 7 / Mix the breadcrumbs and cheese together. Sprinkle on top of the bean mixture and brown under a preheated grill until crisp and crusty. Garnish with sprigs of parsley and serve hot, straight from the dish.

VEGETABLE LASAGNE

SERVES 4

225 g (8 oz) carrots, peeled and thinly sliced
225 g (8 oz) courgettes, trimmed and thinly sliced
1 medium onion, skinned and thinly sliced
100 g (4 oz) green pepper, cored, seeded and thinly sliced
100 g (4 oz) celery, cleaned and thinly sliced
150 ml (¼ pint) vegetable or chicken stock
30 ml (2 tbsp) polyunsaturated oil
30 ml (2 tbsp) plain wholemeal flour
300 ml (½ pint) semi-skimmed milk
salt and pepper
225 g (8 oz) wholemeal lasagne
175 g (6 oz) low-fat Cheddar type cheese, grated

/ 1 / Put the vegetables in a saucepan with the stock. Bring to the boil, cover and simmer for 10 minutes.

/ 2 / Heat the oil in a saucepan, stir in the flour and cook gently for 1 minute, stirring. Remove the pan from the heat and gradually stir in the milk. Bring to the boil and continue to cook, stirring, until the sauce thickens, then add salt and pepper to taste. If the sauce is too thick, add a little stock from the vegetables.

/ 3 / Meanwhile, cook the lasagne in a saucepan of fast-boiling salted water until tender but not soft. Drain, being careful not to break the lasagne sheets.

/ 4 / Make alternate layers of lasagne, vegetables and 100 g (4 oz) of the cheese in a 1.7 litre (3 pint) shallow ovenproof dish finishing with a layer of lasagne. Top with the sauce, then sprinkle over the remaining cheese.

/ 5 / Bake in the oven at 190°C (375°F) mark 5 for about 30 minutes until golden brown.

RED KIDNEY BEAN HOT POT

Serve this tasty hot pot for a nutritious vegetarian main course, with nutty brown rice or wholemeal bread, and a crisp green salad.

VEGETABLE LASAGNE

Look for the boxes of Italian lasagne with the label 'no pre-cooking required', which are available at most large supermarkets. This type of lasagne will save you both time and energy, because it can be layered in the dish straight from the packet. Ordinary lasagne has to be boiled, then drained before using, and it invariably sticks and tears during this process. When using lasagne straight from the packet, always be sure to use plenty of sauce between the layers, as in this recipe, or the finished dish may be dry.

Picture opposite:
Red Kidney Bean Hot Pot

SPICY VEGETABLE PIE

Roll out the pastry dough on a lightly floured surface. Cut out a thin strip long enough to go around the rim of the pie dish. Moisten the rim with water and place the strip on the rim.

STUFFED AUBERGINES

This recipe can also be used for courgettes. Allow 2-3 medium-sized courgettes per person. Cut them in half lengthways and carefully scoop out the flesh with a sharp-edged teaspoon. Blanch in boiling salted water for 4 minutes only, then drain thoroughly. Chop the scooped out raw courgette flesh and cook for 10 minutes with the tomato mixture. Stand the courgette halves side by side (so that they stand upright) in a well-greased baking tin before stuffing and grilling.

SPICY VEGETABLE PIE

SERVES 4

4 medium carrots, peeled and thinly sliced
4 medium leeks, trimmed and thickly sliced
6 medium courgettes, trimmed and thinly sliced
salt and pepper
120 ml (8 tbsp) polyunsaturated oil
1 medium onion, skinned and sliced
10 ml (2 tsp) ground cumin
150 g (6 oz) plain wholemeal flour
450 ml (¾ pint) semi-skimmed milk plus 30 ml (2 tbsp)
100 g (4 oz) low-fat Cheddar type cheese, grated
1.25 ml (¼ tsp) ground mace
45 ml (3 tbsp) chopped fresh coriander or parsley
2.5 ml (½ tsp) baking powder
50 g (2 oz) butter or margarine
beaten egg, to glaze
10 ml (2 tsp) grated Parmesan cheese
pinch of cayenne pepper or paprika

/ 1 / Make the vegetable filling: blanch the carrots, leeks and courgettes in boiling salted water for 1 minute only. Drain well.

/ 2 / Heat 45 ml (3 tbsp) of the oil in a heavy-based saucepan, add the onion and cumin and fry gently for 5 minutes until soft. Add the carrots, leeks and courgettes and fry for a further 5 minutes, stirring to coat in the onion mixture. Remove from the heat and set aside.

/ 3 / Heat the remaining 75 ml (5 tbsp) oil in a separate pan, sprinkle in 50 g (2 oz) of the flour and cook for 1-2 minutes, stirring, until lightly coloured. Remove from the heat and whisk in 450 ml (¾ pint) milk; return to the heat and simmer for 5 minutes until thick and smooth.

/ 4 / Stir in the Cheddar cheese, mace and salt and pepper to taste. Fold into the vegetables with the chopped coriander and 30 ml (2 tbsp) milk, then turn into a 900 ml (1½ pint) oven-proof pie dish. Leave for 2 hours until cold.

/ 5 / Make the pastry: sift the remaining 100 g (4 oz) flour, baking powder and a pinch of salt into a bowl. Rub in the butter or margarine until the mixture resembles breadcrumbs, then add just enough water to mix to a firm dough. Gather the dough into a ball, knead lightly and wrap in cling film; chill for 30 minutes.

/ 6 / Remove the dough from the refrigerator and roll out on a floured surface. Cut out a thin strip long enough to go around the rim of the pie dish. Moisten the rim with water; place the strip on the rim.

/ 7 / Roll out the remaining dough for a lid, moisten the strip of dough, then place the lid on top and press to seal. Knock up and flute the edge. Decorate with pastry trimmings.

/ 8 / Brush the pastry with beaten egg and dust with Parmesan and cayenne or paprika. Bake in the oven at 190°C (375°F) mark 5 for 20-25 minutes.

STUFFED AUBERGINES

SERVES 4

2 aubergines
25 g (1 oz) butter or margarine
4 small tomatoes, skinned and chopped
10 ml (2 tsp) chopped fresh marjoram or 5 ml (1 tsp) dried
1 shallot, skinned and chopped
1 medium onion, skinned and chopped
50 g (2 oz) wholemeal breadcrumbs
salt and pepper
50 g (2 oz) low-fat Cheddar type cheese, grated
parsley sprigs, to garnish

/ 1 / Cook the whole aubergines in boiling water for about 30 minutes until tender.

/ 2 / Cut the aubergines in half lengthways, scoop out the flesh and chop finely. Reserve the aubergine shells.

/ 3 / Melt the butter or margarine in a saucepan, add the tomatoes, marjoram, shallot and onion and cook gently for 10 minutes. Stir in the aubergine flesh and a few breadcrumbs, then add salt and pepper to taste.

/ 4 / Stuff the aubergine shells with this mixture, sprinkle with the remaining breadcrumbs and then with the grated cheese. Place in a grill pan and grill until golden brown on top. Serve hot, garnished with parsley sprigs.

Stuffed Aubergines

CAULIFLOWER AND
COURGETTE BAKE

This vegetable soufflé mixture is best served with braised chicory or a mixed salad.

ITALIAN COURGETTE AND CHEESE BAKE

Layer the courgettes, tomato sauce and Mozzarella cheese in a shallow ovenproof dish, finishing with a layer of Mozzarella. Sprinkle with the Parmesan cheese.

Italian Courgette and Cheese Bake makes a rich and filling main course served with crusty French bread and a mixed side salad.

CAULIFLOWER AND COURGETTE BAKE

SERVES 4

700 g (1½ lb) cauliflower
salt and pepper
50 g (2 oz) butter or margarine
225 g (8 oz) courgettes, trimmed and thinly sliced
45 ml (3 tbsp) wholemeal flour
150 ml (¼ pint) semi-skimmed milk
3 eggs, separated
15 ml (1 tbsp) grated Parmesan cheese

/ 1 / Divide the cauliflower into small florets, trimming off thick stalks and leaves. Cook in boiling salted water for 10-12 minutes until tender.

/ 2 / Meanwhile, in a separate saucepan, melt 25 g (1 oz) of the butter or margarine, add the courgettes and cook until beginning to soften. Remove from the pan with a slotted spoon and drain on absorbent kitchen paper.

/ 3 / Melt the remaining butter or margarine in the pan, stir in the flour and cook, stirring, for 1-2 minutes. Remove from the heat and add the milk a little at a time, whisking constantly after each addition. Return to the heat and bring to the boil, stirring. Lower the heat and simmer until thickened.

/ 4 / Drain the cauliflower well and place in a blender or food processor with the warm sauce, egg yolks and plenty of seasoning. Blend together until evenly mixed, then turn into a large bowl.

/ 5 / Whisk the egg whites until stiff, then carefully fold into the cauliflower mixture with a large metal spoon until they are evenly distributed throughout the mixture.

/ 6 / Spoon half of the mixture into a 1.6 litre (2 ¾ pint) soufflé dish. Arrange the courgettes on top, reserving a few for garnish, then cover with the remaining cauliflower mixture and reserved drained courgettes.

/ 7 / Sprinkle over the Parmesan cheese and bake in the oven at 190°C (375°F) mark 5 for 35-40 minutes. Serve immediately.

ITALIAN COURGETTE AND CHEESE BAKE

SERVES 4

700 g (1½ lb) courgettes
salt and pepper
about 90 ml (6 tbsp) polyunsaturated oil
1 medium onion, skinned and finely chopped
450 g (1 lb) tomatoes, skinned and chopped
1 large garlic clove, skinned and crushed
30 ml (2 tbsp) tomato purée
15 ml (1 tbsp) chopped fresh marjoram or 5 ml (1 tsp) dried
two 170 g (6 oz) packets Mozzarella cheese, thinly sliced
75 g (3 oz) grated Parmesan cheese

/ 1 / Cut the courgettes into 0.5 cm (¼ inch) thick slices. Sprinkle with salt and leave to dégorge for at least 20 minutes.

/ 2 / Heat 30 ml (2 tbsp) of the oil in a saucepan, add the onion and fry for about 5 minutes until just beginning to brown.

/ 3 / Stir in the tomatoes, garlic, tomato purée and salt and pepper to taste. Simmer for about 10 minutes, stirring with a wooden spoon to break down the tomatoes. Stir in the marjoram and remove from the heat.

/ 4 / Rinse the courgettes and pat dry with absorbent kitchen paper. Fry half at a time in the remaining oil until golden brown. Drain well on kitchen paper.

/ 5 / Layer the courgettes, tomato sauce and Mozzarella cheese in a shallow ovenproof dish, finishing with a layer of cheese. Sprinkle with the Parmesan cheese.

/ 6 / Bake in the oven at 180°C (350°F) mark 4 for about 40 minutes or until brown and bubbling. Serve hot, straight from the dish.

ROOT VEGETABLE HOT POT

SERVES 4 - 6

2 medium leeks
1 onion, skinned and finely chopped
225 g (8 oz) potatoes, peeled and cut into chunks
225 g (8 oz) swede, peeled and cut into chunks
4 medium carrots, peeled and thinly sliced
10 ml (2 tsp) yeast extract
salt and pepper
300 ml (½ pint) vegetable stock
30 ml (2 tbsp) chopped fresh parsley
100 g (4 oz) low-fat Cheddar type cheese, grated

/ 1 / Trim the leeks, cut into thick rings, then place in a colander and rinse thoroughly under cold running water.

/ 2 / Put all the prepared vegetables in a flame-proof casserole with the yeast extract and salt and pepper to taste. Pour in the stock and bring to the boil, stirring thoroughly to mix all the ingredients together.

/ 3 / Cover the casserole and simmer for 30 minutes until the vegetables are tender. Stir in the parsley, then taste and adjust the seasoning, if necessary.

/ 4 / Sprinkle the cheese over the top of the vegetables, then put under a moderate grill for 5 minutes until melted and bubbling. Serve hot, straight from the casserole.

This makes a tasty family vegetarian main course served with chunky slices of wholemeal bread, or on a bed of brown rice.

Root Vegetable Hot Pot

MOONG DAL AND SPINACH

SERVES 4 - 6

225 g (8 oz) moong dal (split, washed moong beans)

900 g (2 lb) fresh spinach, washed and trimmed, or
450 g (1 lb) chopped frozen spinach

75 g (3 oz) ghee or clarified butter

1 medium onion, skinned and finely chopped

15 g (½ oz) fresh root ginger, peeled and finely chopped

1 garlic clove, skinned and crushed

10 ml (2 tsp) ground coriander

5 ml (1 tsp) ground turmeric

2.5 ml (½ tsp) chilli powder

1.25 ml (¼ tsp) asafoetida (optional)

salt and pepper

lemon wedges, to garnish

/ 1 / Rinse the dal under cold running water. Place in a bowl, cover with cold water and leave to soak for about 2 hours. Drain.

/ 2 / Place the fresh spinach in a saucepan with only the water that clings to the leaves. Cover and cook gently for about 5 minutes until tender. Drain well and chop roughly. If using frozen spinach, place in a saucepan and cook for 7-10 minutes to remove as much of the liquid as possible.

/ 3 / Melt the ghee or butter in a large sauté pan, add the onion, ginger and garlic and fry gently for 2-3 minutes until lightly coloured.

/ 4 / Stir in the coriander, turmeric, chilli powder, asafoetida, if using, and the dal. Fry, stirring, for 2-3 minutes.

Moong Dal and Spinach

/ 5 / Pour in 300 ml (½ pint) water, add salt and pepper to taste and bring to the boil. Cover and simmer for about 15 minutes or until the dal is almost tender. Add a little more water if necessary, but the mixture should be almost dry.

/ 6 / Stir in the spinach and cook, stirring, for 2-3 minutes or until heated through. Taste and adjust the seasoning before serving, garnished lemon wedges.

WHOLEWHEAT BRAZIL SALAD

SERVES 4 - 6

75 g (3 oz) dried black-eyed beans, soaked in cold water overnight
100 g (4 oz) wholewheat grain, soaked in cold water overnight
90 ml (6 tbsp) natural low-fat yogurt
30 ml (2 tbsp) olive oil
45 ml (3 tbsp) lemon juice
45 ml (3 tbsp) chopped fresh mint
salt and pepper
½ cucumber, diced
225 g (8 oz) tomatoes, skinned and roughly chopped
100 g (4 oz) low-fat Cheddar type cheese, grated
100 g (4 oz) Brazil nuts, roughly chopped
lettuce leaves, to serve
mint sprigs, to garnish

/ 1 / Drain the beans and place in a saucepan of water. Bring to the boil and simmer gently for 1½ hours or until tender.

/ 2 / Meanwhile, drain the wholewheat and place in a saucepan of water. Bring to the boil and simmer gently for 20-25 minutes or until tender. Drain, rinse well with cold water and cool for 30 minutes. When the beans are cooked, drain and cool for 30 minutes.

/ 3 / Whisk the yogurt and olive oil together with the lemon juice, mint and salt and pepper to taste.

/ 4 / Put the wholewheat, beans, cucumber, tomatoes, cheese and Brazil nuts in a bowl. Pour over the dressing and mix well.

/ 5 / Line a salad bowl with lettuce leaves and pile the wholewheat salad on top. Garnish and chill in the refrigerator.

BEAN, CHEESE AND AVOCADO SALAD

SERVES 4

225 g (8 oz) dried red kidney beans, soaked in cold water overnight
90 ml (6 tbsp) olive oil
finely grated rind and juice of 1 lemon
1.25 ml (¼ tsp) Tabasco sauce
salt and pepper
175 g (6 oz) Edam cheese, rinded and diced
1 small onion, skinned and finely chopped
2 celery sticks, trimmed and finely chopped
2 tomatoes, skinned and chopped
1 ripe avocado
celery leaves, to garnish

/ 1 / Drain the kidney beans and rinse under cold running water. Put in a saucepan, cover with fresh cold water and bring to the boil. Boil rapidly for 10 minutes, then simmer for 1-1½ hours until tender.

/ 2 / Drain the beans and put in a bowl. Add the oil, lemon rind and juice, Tabasco and seasoning. Toss well, then leave until cold.

/ 3 / Add the cheese, onion, celery and tomatoes to the beans and toss again to mix the ingredients together. Cover and chill the salad in the refrigerator.

/ 4 / When ready to serve, peel the avocado, cut in half and remove the stone. Chop the flesh into chunky pieces. Fold the avocado pieces gently into the bean salad and taste and adjust the seasoning. Garnish with celery leaves and serve.

Both these salads can be served with hot wholemeal rolls or jacket-baked potatoes.

WHOLEWHEAT BRAZIL SALAD

All grains contain protein and, when mixed with other second class protein ingredients such as nuts or pulses, will provide good quality protein for healthy growth and repair of body tissue.

STUFFED PLAICE FILLETS

The cottage cheese with prawns used in the stuffing for these plaice fillets is available in cartons from selected supermarkets. Look for a good quality brand which is thick and firm-textured. Some brands of cottage cheese are watery and will not be suitable for this dish. If there is water on the surface of the cheese when you open the carton, be sure to drain it off before use.

Lay the plaice fillets flat with their skinned side facing upwards. Divide the cheese filling equally between them, then roll up and secure with wooden cocktail sticks, if necessary.

Place the stuffed fish rolls close together in a single layer in a lightly oiled ovenproof dish. Sprinkle the mushrooms around the fish, then pour over the wine mixed with the lemon juice and remaining Tabasco. Sprinkle with salt and pepper to taste.

STUFFED PLAICE FILLETS

SERVES 4

4 double plaice fillets
salt and pepper
225 g (8 oz) cottage cheese with prawns
1.25 ml (¼ tsp) Tabasco sauce, or less according to taste
finely grated rind and juice of 1 lemon
225 g (8 oz) button mushrooms, wiped and thinly sliced
90 ml (6 tbsp) dry white wine
5 ml (1 tsp) chopped fresh tarragon or dill or 2.5 ml (½ tsp) dried
8 unshelled prawns and tarragon or dill sprigs, to garnish

/ 1 / Skin the plaice fillets. Lay them flat, skin side down, on a board or work surface. Dip your fingers in salt and grip the tail end, then separate the flesh from the skin at this point with a sharp knife. Work the knife slowly between the skin and flesh using a sawing action until the opposite end of the fillet is reached. Cut each fillet into 2 lengthways.

/ 2 / Drain off any liquid from the cottage cheese, then mash the cheese with half of the Tabasco sauce, the grated lemon rind and salt and pepper to taste.

/ 3 / Lay the plaice fillets flat, with their skinned side facing upwards. Divide the cheese filling equally between them, then roll up and secure the rolls with wooden cocktail sticks, if necessary.

/ 4 / Place the stuffed fish rolls close together in a single layer in a lightly oiled ovenproof dish. Sprinkle the mushrooms around the fish, then pour over the wine mixed with the lemon juice and remaining Tabasco. Sprinkle with seasoning to taste.

/ 5 / Cover the dish with foil and cook in the oven at 180°C (350°F) mark 4 for 20 minutes or until the fish is just tender.

/ 6 / Remove the rolls from the liquid and discard the cocktail sticks. Arrange the fish on a warmed serving dish, cover loosely with foil and keep warm in the oven turned to its lowest setting while making the sauce.

/ 7 / Put the cooked mushrooms in a blender or food processor. Add the tarragon or dill and blend until smooth. Pour into a pan and heat through. Taste and adjust seasoning.

/ 8 / Pour a little sauce over each plaice roll, then top with a prawn and a tarragon or dill sprig. Serve immediately, with any remaining sauce handed separately in a jug.

SEAFOOD STIR-FRY

SERVES 4

2 celery sticks, washed and trimmed
1 medium carrot, peeled
350 g (12 oz) coley, haddock or cod fillet, skinned
350 g (12 oz) Iceberg or Cos lettuce
about 45 ml (3 tbsp) polyunsaturated oil
1 garlic clove, skinned and crushed
100 g (4 oz) peeled prawns
425 g (15 oz) can whole baby sweetcorn, drained
salt and pepper
Boiled Rice (see page 146), to serve (optional)

/ 1 / Slice the celery and carrot into thin matchsticks, 5 cm (2 inch) long. Cut the fish into 2.5 cm (1 inch) chunks. Shred the lettuce finely with a sharp knife, discarding the core and any thick ribs.

/ 2 / Heat 15 ml (1 tbsp) of the oil in a wok or large frying pan until smoking. Add the lettuce and fry for about 30 seconds until lightly cooked. Transfer to a serving dish with a slotted spoon and keep warm.

/ 3 / Heat another 30 ml (2 tbsp) of oil in the pan until smoking. Add the celery, carrot, white fish and garlic and stir-fry over high heat for 2-3 minutes, adding more oil if necessary.

/ 4 / Lower the heat and add the prawns and baby sweetcorn. Toss well together for 2-3 minutes to heat through and coat all the ingredients in the sauce (the fish will flake apart).

/ 5 / Add salt and pepper to taste, spoon on top of the lettuce and serve immediately. Serve with boiled rice, if liked.

Picture opposite:
Stuffed Plaice Fillets

SEAFOOD CURRY

SERVES 4

45 ml (3 tbsp) polyunsaturated oil
2 medium onions, skinned and sliced into rings
25 g (1 oz) desiccated coconut
15 ml (1 tbsp) plain wholemeal flour
5 ml (1 tsp) ground coriander
450 g (1 lb) fresh haddock fillet, skinned and cut into chunks
1 fresh green chilli, halved, seeded and chopped
150 ml (¼ pint) white wine
25 g (1 oz) natural peanuts
125 g (4 oz) frozen prawns, thawed, drained and thoroughly dried
salt and pepper
coriander sprigs and shredded coconut, toasted, to garnish

/ 1 / Heat the oil in a large sauté or frying pan, add the onion rings and fry until browned.

/ 2 / Mix the desiccated coconut, flour and ground coriander together and toss with the haddock and chilli. Add to the pan and fry for 5-10 minutes until golden, stirring.

/ 3 / Pour in the wine, bring to the boil and add the peanuts, prawns and salt and pepper to taste. Cover tightly and simmer for 5-10 minutes or until the fish is tender. Garnish with coriander and coconut.

MONKFISH WITH MUSTARD SEEDS

SERVES 6

45 ml (3 tbsp) black mustard seeds
900 g (2 lb) monkfish fillet, skinned
30 ml (2 tbsp) plain wholemeal flour
60 ml (4 tbsp) mustard oil or polyunsaturated oil
1 medium onion, skinned and thinly sliced
300 ml (½ pint) natural low-fat yogurt
1 garlic clove, skinned and crushed
15 ml (1 tbsp) lemon juice
salt and pepper
whole prawns and fresh coriander, to garnish

/ 1 / Put 30 ml (2 tbsp) of the mustard seeds in a small bowl. Cover with 60 ml (4 tbsp) water and leave to soak for several hours. Grind the remaining seeds in a small electric grinder or blender to a powder.

/ 2 / Cut the monkfish into 2.5 cm (1 inch) cubes and toss in the flour and ground mustard seeds mixed together.

/ 3 / Heat the oil in a large heavy-based frying pan, add the onion and fry for about 5 minutes until golden.

/ 4 / Drain the mustard seeds, then add to the pan with the monkfish. Fry over moderate heat for 3-4 minutes, turning the cubes of monkfish very gently once or twice.

/ 5 / Gradually stir in the yogurt with the crushed garlic, lemon juice and salt and pepper to taste. Bring to the boil, then lower the heat and simmer, uncovered, for 10-15 minutes.

/ 6 / Turn into a warmed serving dish and garnish with the prawns and coriander.

FISH KEBABS

SERVES 4

700 g (1½ lb) monkfish fillets, skinned
60 ml (4 tbsp) sunflower oil
juice of 2 limes or 1 lemon
1 small onion, skinned and roughly chopped
2 garlic cloves, skinned and crushed
2.5 ml (½ tsp) fennel seed
2.5 ml (½ tsp) dried thyme
pepper
1 green pepper, halved, cored and seeded
16 whole cherry tomatoes or 4 small tomatoes, quartered
8 bay leaves

/ 1 / Cut the monkfish into 4 cm (1½ inch) chunks. Place the oil, lime or lemon juice, onion, garlic, fennel, thyme and pepper in a blender or food processor and blend until smooth. Toss the fish in this mixture, cover and marinate for at least 2 hours.

/ 2 / Meanwhile, place the green pepper in a saucepan of cold water and bring to the boil. Drain and cut into 12 pieces.

/ 3 / Thread the fish, green pepper, tomatoes and bay leaves on to 4 oiled skewers. Reserve the marinade for basting.

/ 4 / Cook the kebabs under a pre-heated moderate grill for about 10 minutes, basting with the marinade and turning once.

TANDOORI FISH

Serve on a bed of saffron rice accompanied by a green salad with plenty of chopped fresh coriander sprinkled on the top.

TANDOORI FISH

SERVES 2

350 g (12 oz) thick white fish fillet, such as monkfish, cod or haddock
30 ml (2 tbsp) natural low-fat yogurt
15 ml (1 tbsp) lemon juice
1 small garlic clove, skinned and crushed
1.25 ml (¼ tsp) ground coriander
1.25 ml (¼ tsp) ground cumin
1.25 ml (¼ tsp) ground turmeric
pinch of paprika
a few knobs of butter or margarine
fresh coriander and lime wedges, to garnish

/ 1 / Skin the fish fillet, and then cut into 2 equal portions with a sharp knife.

/ 2 / Make the tandoori marinade: put the yogurt and lemon juice in a bowl with the garlic and spices. Stir well to mix.

/ 3 / Place the fish on a sheet of foil and brush with the marinade. Leave to marinate in a cool place for 30 minutes.

/ 4 / Dot the fish with a few knobs of butter or margarine. Cook under a preheated moderate grill for about 8 minutes, turning once. Serve garnished with fresh coriander and lime.

ITALIAN SQUID STEW

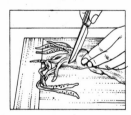

With your hands, carefully peel the skin from the body and the fins of the squid. Cut the tentacles from the head and remove the skin. Reserve 2 ink sacs, being careful not to pierce them. Discard rest of head. Cut the squid bodies into 0.5 cm (¼ inch) rings.

ITALIAN SQUID STEW

SERVES 4

1 kg (2¼ lb) small squid
75 ml (5 tbsp) olive oil
salt and pepper
75 ml (3 fl oz) dry white wine
2 garlic cloves, skinned and crushed
juice of ½ lemon
15 ml (1 tbsp) chopped fresh parsley
Boiled Rice (see page 146) or toasted bread, to serve (optional)

/ 1 / Wash the squid under cold running water. Pull back the edge of the body pouch to expose the transparent quill.

/ 2 / Holding the body pouch firmly with one hand, take hold of the end of the exposed quill with the other, pull it free and discard.

/ 3 / To separate the head and tentacles from the body pouch, hold the body pouch in one hand and pull out the head and tentacles with the other.

/ 4 / Cut through the head, just above the eyes. Discard the eyes and reserve the tentacles and 2 ink sacs, being careful not to pierce them. Wash the tentacles under cold running water, rubbing off the purplish skin.

/ 5 / Rub the purplish skin off the body pouch under cold running water. Carefully cut the triangular fins off the body pouch. Discard the fins.

/ 6 / Cut the squid body into 0.5 cm (¼ inch) rings. Put in a bowl with the tentacles and spoon over 45 ml (3 tbsp) of the oil and season with salt and pepper to taste. Leave for 3 hours.

/ 7 / Pour the squid and marinade into a large frying pan and cook for 5 minutes, turning frequently. Add the wine and garlic and cook for a further 5 minutes. Add the ink sacs, breaking them up with a spoon.

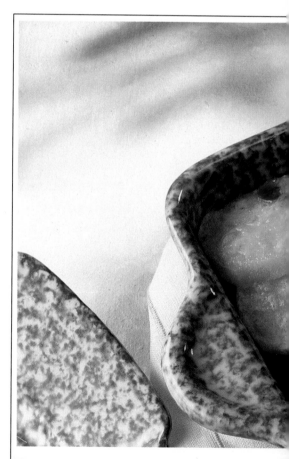

/ 8 / Cover and cook over a low heat for about 40 minutes until the squid is tender.

/ 9 / Add the remaining oil, the lemon juice and parsley. Stir for 3 minutes over a high heat. Serve the stew with boiled rice or toasted bread, if liked.

FISHERMAN'S PIE

SERVES 4

65 g (2½ oz) butter or margarine
100 g (4 oz) red pepper, cored, seeded and thinly sliced
100 g (4 oz) green pepper, cored, seeded and thinly sliced
1 small onion, skinned and sliced
salt and pepper
100 g (4 oz) button mushrooms, wiped and halved
450 ml (¾ pint) tomato juice
550 g (1¼ lb) cod fillet, skinned
450 g (1 lb) potatoes, peeled and thinly sliced
50 g (2 oz) Edam cheese, grated

/ 1 / Melt 25 g (1 oz) of the butter or margarine in a frying pan, add the peppers and onion and fry gently for 10 minutes until soft but not coloured. Transfer to a 2.3 litre (4 pint) oven-proof dish. Season well.

/ 2 / Cook the mushrooms in the remaining fat in the frying pan, stirring frequently, for 3-4 minutes until evenly coloured.

/ 3 / Pour the tomato juice evenly over the pepper and onion mixture in the dish.

/ 4 / Cut the fish into large cubes. Arrange the cubes on top of the tomato juice, pressing them down gently into the juice. Top with the mushrooms. Season again.

/ 5 / Arrange the sliced potatoes on top of the mushrooms. Melt the remaining margarine and brush over the potatoes. Bake in the oven at 190°C (375°F) mark 5 for 25 minutes.

/ 6 / Sprinkle the grated cheese over the pie, return to the oven and bake for a further 15 minutes until melted and bubbling. Serve hot.

Fisherman's Pie

FISH IN SPICY SAUCE WITH TOMATOES

This spiced fish dish makes an excellent family main course dish as it is quick and easy to make. Serve the fish with simple accompaniments, such as Boiled Rice (see page 146) and Cucumber Raita (see page 42).

TIPS FOR MAKING HOT SOUFFLÉS

● Always make sure you use the exact size of soufflé dish specified in the recipe.

● Check your oven temperature carefully and don't be tempted to bake a soufflé at a different temperature from the one specified.

● Preheat oven and baking sheet to required temperature well before baking.

● Fold egg whites in with a large metal spoon in a figure of 8 motion so that the maximum amount of air is incorporated.

● Don't open the oven door during baking.

● Serve immediately – have your guests seated at the table well before the soufflé is due to come out of the oven.

FISH IN SPICY SAUCE WITH TOMATOES

SERVES 4

700 g (1 ½ lb) white fish, such as cod, halibut or haddock, skinned and filleted
60 ml (4 tbsp) ghee or polyunsaturated oil
7.5 ml (1½ tsp) coriander seeds
5 ml (1 tsp) black peppercorns
1 garlic clove, skinned and crushed
5 ml (1 tsp) ground turmeric
1.25 ml (¼ tsp) chilli powder
salt
4 tomatoes, skinned (see page 57) and roughly chopped
2.5 ml (½ tsp) garam masala
chopped fresh coriander, to garnish

/ 1 / Cut the fish into 2.5 cm (1 inch) cubes. Heat the ghee or oil in a heavy-based frying pan. Add the fish a few pieces at a time and fry gently for 2-3 minutes.

/ 2 / Remove the fish carefully from the pan with a slotted spoon and set aside on a plate.

/ 3 / Put the coriander seeds, peppercorns and garlic in a small electric grinder and work to a smooth paste. Add the spice paste to the frying pan with the turmeric, chilli powder and salt to taste and fry gently for 2 minutes.

/ 4 / Stir in the tomatoes and 300 ml (½ pint) water. Bring to the boil, then lower the heat and cook over a medium heat for 5 minutes. Add the fish and simmer, shaking the pan occasionally, for a further 10 minutes, or until the fish is tender. Do not stir or the fish will break up. Remove from the heat.

/ 5 / Sprinkle the garam masala over the fish, cover the pan and let the fish stand for 2 minutes, then turn into a warmed serving dish. Garnish with chopped fresh coriander.

HADDOCK CHEESE SOUFFLÉ

SERVES 4

450 g (1 lb) floury potatoes, such as King Edward
450 g (1 lb) fresh haddock fillets
100 g (4 oz) button mushrooms, thinly sliced
300 ml (½ pint) semi-skimmed milk
1 bay leaf
25 g (1 oz) butter or margarine
25 g (1 oz) plain wholemeal flour
2.5 ml (½ tsp) caraway seeds
125 g (4 oz) low-fat Cheddar type cheese, grated
2 eggs, separated
salt and pepper

/ 1 / Scrub the potatoes, then boil until tender. Drain and peel, then mash the potatoes.

/ 2 / Meanwhile, place the haddock, mushrooms, milk and bay leaf in a small saucepan. Cover and poach for 15-20 minutes until tender. Drain, reserving the milk and mushrooms. Flake the fish, discarding the skin and the bay leaf.

/ 3 / Make the sauce: melt the butter or margarine in a pan, stir in the flour and cook gently for 1 minute, stirring. Remove from the heat, add the caraway seeds and gradually stir in the reserved milk. Bring to the boil, stirring, and simmer for 2-3 minutes until the sauce has thickened and become smooth.

/ 4 / Stir the mashed potato into the sauce with 75 g (3 oz) of the cheese, the egg yolks, fish and mushrooms. Season the mixture with salt and pepper to taste.

/ 5 / Whisk the egg whites until stiff. Fold into the fish mixture. Turn into a 1.6 litre (2¾ pint) greased soufflé dish.

/ 6 / Sprinkle over the remaining grated cheese. Bake in the oven at 190°C (375°F) mark 5 for about 1 hour or until just set and golden brown. Serve at once.

SPANISH COD WITH PEPPERS AND GARLIC

SERVES 4

700 g (1½ lb) cod fillets
1 litre (1¾ pints) mussels or about 450 g (1 lb) weight
30 ml (2 tbsp) polyunsaturated oil
2 medium onions, skinned and sliced
1 red pepper, cored, seeded and sliced
1 green pepper, cored, seeded and sliced
1-2 garlic cloves, skinned and crushed
450 g (1 lb) tomatoes, skinned and chopped or 397 g (14 oz) can tomatoes, drained
300 ml (½ pint) white wine
2.5 ml (½ tsp) Tabasco sauce
1 bay leaf
salt and pepper

/ 1 / Using a sharp knife, skin the cod and cut it into chunks.

/ 2 / Scrub the mussels, discarding any which are open. Place in a saucepan, cover and cook over a high heat for about 8 minutes or until they have opened. Discard any mussels that have not opened.

/ 3 / Shell all but 4 mussels. Heat the oil in a frying pan and cook the onions, peppers and garlic for about 5 minutes until starting to soften. Add the tomatoes and wine, bring to the boil and simmer for 5 minutes, then add the Tabasco.

/ 4 / Layer the fish and vegetables in a casserole and add the bay leaf and salt and pepper to taste. Push the 4 mussels in shells into the top layer. Cover and cook in the oven at 180°C (350°F) mark 4 for 1 hour. Serve hot.

Serve Spanish Cod with Peppers and Garlic with hot French bread, followed by a crisp green salad tossed in an olive oil and lemon juice dressing.

Before preparation in step 2 of the recipe, tap any open mussels against a bowl or work surface – if they do not close they should be thrown away.

Spanish Cod with Peppers and Garlic

Salads and Vegetable Accompaniments

Vegetables should take pride of place in a healthy diet. The different types provide a wide variety of vitamins and minerals and all provide significant amounts of dietary fibre. If a selection are served at each meal, sometimes raw in a salad and sometimes cooked, you will obtain the best possible range of nutrients.

Always buy the freshest vegetables available and store them in a cool, dry place to keep them in the best condition. Do not store them for too long, as their vitamin content starts to diminish as soon as they are picked.

The recipes here are designed to accompany a main course. Pulses and rice dishes make good nutritional accompaniments. Brown rice contains fibre, which makes it a better choice nutritionally, and it has more flavour than white rice.

Cauliflower, Bean and Caper Salad

SPINACH AND MUSHROOM SALAD

SERVES 4

225 g (8 oz) young spinach leaves

225 g (8 oz) button mushrooms

2 oranges

2 thick slices of wholemeal bread

120 ml (8 tbsp) olive oil

1 garlic clove, skinned and crushed

30 ml (2 tbsp) tarragon vinegar

5 ml (1 tsp) tarragon mustard

salt and pepper

2 avocados

/ 1 / Wash the spinach well, discarding any damaged or yellowing leaves. Cut out and discard any thick ribs.

/ 2 / Tear the spinach leaves into a large salad bowl, discarding any thick stalks.

/ 3 / Slice the mushrooms thinly into neat 'T' shapes. Add the mushrooms to the spinach. Using your hands, toss these ingredients together. Peel the oranges using a serrated knife, cutting away all the skin and pith. Cut the oranges into segments, removing the membrane. Discard any pips. Set aside while making the croûtons and dressing.

Spinach and Mushroom Salad

/ 4 / Cut the crusts off the bread and cut the bread into 1 cm (½ inch) cubes. Heat the oil in a frying pan, add the garlic and the cubes of bread and fry until crisp and golden. Remove the croûtons with a slotted spoon and drain well on absorbent kitchen paper.

/ 5 / Add the vinegar to the oil in the pan, with the mustard and salt and pepper to taste. Stir well to combine, then remove from the heat and leave to cool for 5 minutes.

/ 6 / Meanwhile, halve the avocados and re-move the stones. Peel the avocados and chop the flesh into even-sized chunks. Add to the salad with the orange segments and croûtons, then pour over the dressing. Toss well to com-bine and serve immediately.

TOMATO, AVOCADO AND PASTA SALAD

SERVES 4

175 g (6 oz) small wholemeal pasta shells
salt and pepper
105 ml (7 tbsp) olive oil
45 ml (3 tbsp) lemon juice
5 ml (1 tsp) wholegrain mustard
30 ml (2 tbsp) chopped fresh basil
2 ripe avocados
2 red onions, skinned
16 black olives
225 g (8 oz) ripe cherry tomatoes, if available, or small salad tomatoes
fresh basil leaves, to garnish

/ 1 / Cook the pasta in plenty of boiling salted water for about 5 minutes until just tender. Drain in a colander and rinse under cold run-ning water to stop it cooking further. Cool for 20 minutes.

/ 2 / Meanwhile, whisk the oil in a bowl with the lemon juice, mustard, chopped basil and salt and pepper to taste. Halve and stone the avocados, then peel off the skins. Chop the avocado flesh into large pieces and fold gently into the dressing.

/ 3 / Slice the onions thinly into rings. Stone the olives. Halve or quarter the tomatoes and mix with the onion rings, olives and pasta.

/ 4 / Spoon the pasta and tomato mixture on to 4 individual serving plates. Spoon over the avocado and dressing and garnish with fresh basil leaves.

CAULIFLOWER, BEAN AND CAPER SALAD

SERVES 4

175 g (6 oz) dried red kidney beans, soaked in cold water overnight
1 small onion, skinned and finely chopped
1-2 garlic cloves, skinned and crushed
45 ml (3 tbsp) olive oil
15 ml (1 tbsp) red wine vinegar
5 ml (1 tsp) French mustard
salt and pepper
225 g (8 oz) cauliflower
60 ml (4 tbsp) natural low-fat yogurt
60 ml (4 tbsp) Mayonnaise (see page 149)
30 ml (2 tbsp) roughly chopped capers
30 ml (2 tbsp) chopped fresh parsley

/ 1 / Drain and rinse the kidney beans, then place in a saucepan with plenty of water. Bring to the boil and boil rapidly for 10 minutes (this is important – see right). Lower the heat, half cover with a lid and simmer for 1½ hours or until the beans are tender.

/ 2 / Drain the beans, transfer to a bowl and im-mediately add the onion, garlic, olive oil, vinegar, mustard and salt and pepper to taste. Stir well to mix, then cover and leave for at least 4 hours to allow the dressing to flavour the kidney beans.

/ 3 / Divide the cauliflower into small sprigs, cutting away all tough stalks. Wash the florets thoroughly under cold running water, then blanch in boiling water for 1 minute only. Drain thoroughly.

/ 4 / Add the cauliflower florets to the bean salad with the yogurt, mayonnaise, capers and parsley. Mix well and chill in the refrigerator for about 30 minutes before serving.

TOMATO, AVOCADO AND PASTA SALAD

This pretty salad makes a good accompaniment to grilled or barbecued meat. Alternatively, it could be served as a summer starter with chunky slices of wholemeal bread.

CAULIFLOWER, BEAN AND CAPER SALAD

Dried red kidney beans must be boiled fast for the first 10 minutes of their cooking time. This is to make sure you destroy the poisonous enzyme they contain, which can cause stomach upsets. This fast boiling only applies to red kidney beans; other dried pulses can be boiled in the normal way. If you are short of time, you can use canned red kidney beans, but they will not absorb the flavour of the dressing so well.

FENNEL AND TOMATO SALAD

SERVES 6

90 ml (6 tbsp) polyunsaturated oil or half polyunsaturated oil, half walnut oil
45 ml (3 tbsp) lemon juice
salt and pepper
12 black olives, halved and stoned
450 g (1 lb) Florence fennel
450 g (1 lb) ripe tomatoes

/ 1 / In a medium mixing bowl, whisk together the oil(s), lemon juice and salt and pepper to taste. Add the olives to the dressing.

/ 2 / Snip off the feathery ends of the fennel and refrigerate them in a polythene bag until required for garnishing.

/ 3 / Halve each bulb of fennel lengthways, then slice thinly crossways, discarding the roots. Blanch in boiling water for 2-3 minutes, then drain. While warm, stir into the dressing.

Fennel and Tomato Salad

/ 4 / Leave to cool, cover tightly with cling film and refrigerate until required. Meanwhile, skin and slice the tomatoes and refrigerate in a covered bowl.

/ 5 / Just before serving, arrange the tomatoes and fennel mixture on individual serving plates and snip the fennel tops over them.

CRISP ENDIVE WITH ORANGE AND CROÛTONS

SERVES 8

| 1 large head of curly endive |
| ½ bunch of watercress |
| 2 large oranges |
| 2 thick slices of wholemeal bread |
| polyunsaturated oil, for shallow frying |
| 60 ml (4 tbsp) olive oil |
| 60 ml (4 tbsp) white wine vinegar |
| pinch of raw cane sugar |
| salt and pepper |

/ 1 / Remove and discard any coarse or discoloured leaves from the endive. Tear the endive into pieces, wash and dry thoroughly with a clean tea-towel. Wash, trim and dry the watercress. Set aside.

/ 2 / With a small serrated knife and working over a bowl to catch the juices, cut away all the skin and pith from the oranges. Reserve the juices in the bowl.

/ 3 / Cut the orange flesh into segments, leaving the membrane behind. Remove any pips with the tip of the knife.

/ 4 / Arrange the endive, watercress and orange in a serving bowl. Cut the crusts off the bread and cut the bread into 1 cm (½ inch) cubes. Heat the polyunsaturated oil in a frying pan, add the cubes of bread and fry until crisp and golden. Remove the croûtons with a slotted spoon and drain thoroughly on absorbent kitchen paper.

/ 5 / In a jug, whisk the reserved orange juice with the olive oil, vinegar, sugar and salt and pepper to taste. Pour over the salad and add the croûtons just before serving.

CHILLI, AUBERGINE AND PEPPER SALAD

SERVES 4

| 2 red peppers |
| 3 medium aubergines, total weight about 700 g (1½ lb) |
| salt and pepper |
| 90 ml (6 tbsp) olive or polyunsaturated oil |
| 2 medium onions, skinned and roughly chopped |
| 15 ml (1 tbsp) chilli seasoning |
| 150 ml (¼ pint) dry white wine |
| 30 ml (2 tbsp) tomato purée |
| 15 ml (1 tbsp) lemon juice |
| 15 ml (1 tbsp) wine vinegar |
| 2.5 ml (½ tsp) raw cane sugar |
| chopped fresh parsley, to garnish |

/ 1 / Put the red peppers under a preheated moderate grill and cook until the skins char on all sides, turning them frequently. Put the peppers in a bowl.

/ 2 / Trim the aubergines and cut into 2.5 cm (1 inch) cubes. Place in a colander, sprinkling each layer with salt. Cover with a plate, put heavy weights on top and leave to dégorge for 30 minutes.

/ 3 / Meanwhile, hold the peppers under cold running water and rub the skins off with your fingers. Discard the skins, stems, cores and seeds. Cut the pepper flesh into long, thin shreds and set aside.

/ 4 / Rinse the aubergines under cold running water, then pat dry with absorbent kitchen paper. Heat the oil in a heavy-based saucepan. Add the aubergines and onions and fry over moderate heat for 3-4 minutes. Stir in the chilli seasoning. Fry for 1-2 minutes, then add the wine, tomato purée, lemon juice, vinegar, sugar and salt and pepper to taste.

/ 5 / Bring to the boil, cover and simmer for 10-12 minutes or until the aubergine is cooked. Leave to cool for 30 minutes, then turn into a serving bowl.

/ 6 / Stir in the red pepper shreds. Cover and chill in the refrigerator for 1 hour. Sprinkle with plenty of chopped parsley before serving.

CRISP ENDIVE WITH ORANGE AND CROÛTONS

There is always confusion over endive because in the UK it is called endive, yet in France and the US it is called chicory!

The endive used in this recipe is the large, rather wild-looking salad vegetable; it has crinkly or frondy leaves, which vary in colour from dark green on the outside to pale green, almost yellow in the centre.

The flavour of curly endive is rather bitter – like chicory. For this reason it is most successfully used with other ingredients in a mixed salad. The combination of bitter endive with a sweet-tasting fruit such as orange is a good one, as this helps to take the edge off the endive.

CHILLI, AUBERGINE AND PEPPER SALAD

Serve this smoky flavoured salad with plain roast, barbecued or grilled meat. Alternatively, serve as a tasty lunch dish with hot pitta bread.

JAPANESE SALAD

This salad goes well with any oriental dish, or with plain roast or grilled meat.

Look for white radish in large supermarkets by the name *mooli*, or in oriental stores under its Japanese name of *daikon*. It is a long white tapering root vegetable, which can be used raw in salads, or cooked as a hot vegetable accompaniment. It is very crisp in texture, with a distinctive hot 'bite'.

JAPANESE SALAD

SERVES 1

50 g (2 oz) fresh spinach
salt
100 g (4 oz) white radish
1 medium carrot
30 ml (2 tbsp) shoyu
15 ml (1 tbsp) mirin
5 ml (1 tsp) vinegar
2.5 ml (½ tsp) caster sugar
10 ml (2 tsp) sesame seeds

/ 1 / Tie the spinach leaves together around their stems, then plunge into a saucepan of boiling salted water. Bring back to the boil, then drain immediately. Cool, then pat dry with absorbent kitchen paper.

/ 2 / Peel the white radish and carrot, then grate them both coarsely into a bowl.

/ 3 / In a jug, mix together the shoyu, mirin, vinegar, sugar and salt to taste. Pour over the grated radish and carrot in the bowl, then toss well until evenly mixed.

/ 4 / Cut the spinach leaves crossways into shreds, discarding the coarse stalks. Scatter the shreds over the salad. Toss gently to mix the spinach into the other ingredients, then sprinkle with the sesame seeds. Serve the salad immediately.

TABOULEH

TABOULEH

This salad is Lebanese in origin, and there are numerous different versions. All are based on burghul or cracked wheat and all contain masses of parsley and mint, with a dressing of olive oil and lemon juice, although the proportion of these ingredients varies.

SERVES 6 - 8

225 g (8 oz) burghul (cracked wheat)
4 spring onions, washed and trimmed
1 large bunch fresh parsley, total weight about 100 g (4 oz)
3 large mint sprigs
60 ml (4 tbsp) olive oil
rind and juice of 1½ lemons
salt and pepper
a few vine or Cos lettuce leaves
lemon wedges and fresh mint sprigs, to garnish

/ 1 / Put the burghul in a bowl and add cold water to cover by about 2.5 cm (1 inch). Soak for 30 minutes. Drain well in a sieve, then spread it out on a tea-towel and leave to dry.

/ 2 / Meanwhile, finely chop the spring onions. Then, using a blender or food processor, chop the parsley and mint.

144

Tabouleh

/ 3 / Mix the burghul, spring onions, parsley and mint together in a bowl, add the olive oil, lemon rind and juice and salt and pepper.

/ 4 / To serve, place the salad on a serving dish lined with lettuce or vine leaves. Garnish with lemon wedges and mint sprigs.

145

Long-grain varieties of rice are generally the best in salads as round-grain rice tends to be rather too sticky and glutinous. Brown rice has a nuttier flavour than white, and is better for you as it contains more fibre.

RICE SALAD

This nutty brown rice salad has a tangy orange dressing, which makes it the perfect accompaniment to rich meat dishes such as pork and duck. Alternatively, it can be served with other vegetable salads for a vegetarian meal – it goes particularly well with green salad ingredients such as chicory, endive, lettuce and watercress.

BOILED RICE

SERVES 4

225 g (8 oz) long-grain brown rice

salt

Method One

/ 1 / Put 3.4 litres (6 pints) water in a large saucepan and bring to a fast boil. Add the rice and salt to taste.

/ 2 / Stir once to loosen the grains at the base of the pan, then cook, uncovered, for 35 minutes until tender.

/ 3 / Drain well, rinse with hot water and drain again. Pour into a warmed serving dish and separate the grains with a fork.

Method Two

An alternative method is to use an exact amount of water which is completely absorbed by the rice. For this method allow 600 ml (1 pint) water to 225 g (8 oz) brown rice.

/ 1 / Put the rice, salt to taste and water in a heavy-based pan and bring quickly to the boil, stir well and cover with a tightly fitting lid. Reduce the heat and simmer very gently for about 35 minutes or until the rice is tender and the water has been absorbed.

/ 2 / Remove from the heat and separate the grains with a fork before serving.

——————— V A R I A T I O N S ———————

HERBY RICE
Add a pinch of dried herbs, such as sage, marjoram, thyme, mixed herbs, with the cooking liquid.

SAFFRON RICE
Add a pinch of ground saffron to the cooking water to give the rice a delicate yellow colour.
   Soak a good pinch of saffron strands in a little boiling water for 15 minutes, then add to the rice before cooking.

TURMERIC RICE
Also used to give rice a yellow colour, but add only a pinch of turmeric to the cooking water as it has a more pronounced colour than saffron.

RICE SALAD

SERVES 4

275g (10 oz) long-grain brown rice

salt and pepper

1 small fennel bulb

1 red pepper

175 g (6 oz) beansprouts

75 g (3 oz) cashew nuts

90 ml (6 tbsp) polyunsaturated oil

finely grated rind and juice of 1 large orange

few orange segments, to garnish

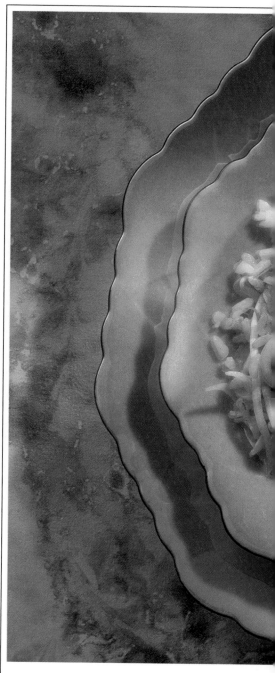

/ 1 / Cook the brown rice in plenty of boiling salted water for 35 minutes until tender but firm to the bite.

/ 2 / Meanwhile, prepare the remaining ingredients. Trim the fennel, reserving a few feathery tops for the garnish. Cut the stalk off the red pepper and remove the core and seeds. Chop the fennel bulb and the red pepper into fine dice.

/ 3 / Wash the beansprouts and drain well. Chop the cashew nuts roughly.

/ 4 / In a jug, whisk the oil, orange rind and juice together, with salt and pepper to taste.

/ 5 / Drain the rice thoroughly, then turn into a bowl. Add the dressing while the rice is still hot and toss well to combine. Leave to stand for about 1 hour or until cold.

/ 6 / Add the prepared vegetables and nuts to the rice and toss well to mix. Turn the salad into a serving bowl and garnish with the reserved fennel tops and the orange segments. Serve at room temperature.

Rice Salad

LEMONY BEAN SALAD

SERVES 4

Green flageolet beans are a very pretty, delicate light green in colour. They are haricot beans which have been removed from their pods when very young and tender, and they get their name from the French word for flute, which they are said to resemble in shape. Most large supermarkets stock green flageolets, but health food shops probably have the fastest turnover.

100 g (4 oz) green flageolet beans, soaked in cold water overnight
90 ml (6 tbsp) olive oil
finely grated rind and juice of 1 lemon
1-2 garlic cloves, skinned and crushed
salt and pepper
50 g (2 oz) black olives
30 ml (2 tbsp) chopped mixed fresh herbs, such as basil, marjoram, lemon balm, chives
4 large firm tomatoes
about 1.25 ml (¼ tsp) raw cane sugar

/ 1 / Drain and rinse the beans, then place in a saucepan with plenty of water. Bring to the boil, then lower the heat, half cover with a lid and simmer for about 1 hour until tender.

/ 2 / Drain the beans, transfer to a bowl and immediately add the oil, lemon rind and juice, garlic and salt and pepper to taste. Stir well to mix, then cover and leave for at least 4 hours to allow the dressing to flavour the beans.

/ 3 / Stone the olives, then chop roughly. Add to the salad with the herbs.

/ 4 / Skin the tomatoes: put them in a bowl, pour over boiling water and leave for 2 minutes. Drain, then plunge into a bowl of cold water. Remove the tomatoes one at a time and peel off the skin with your fingers.

/ 5 / Slice the tomatoes thinly, then arrange on 4 serving plates. Sprinkle with the sugar and salt and pepper to taste. Pile the bean salad on top of each plate.. Serve chilled.

Lemony Bean Salad

M A Y O N N A I S E

M A K E S 1 5 0 M L (¹/₄ P I N T)

1 egg yolk
2.5 ml (½ tsp) mustard powder or 5 ml (1 tsp) Dijon mustard
salt and pepper
pinch of raw cane sugar
15 ml (1 tbsp) white wine vinegar or lemon juice
about 150 ml (¼ pint) polyunsaturated oil

/ 1 / Put the egg yolk into a bowl with the mustard, salt and pepper to taste, sugar and 5 ml (1 tsp) of the vinegar or lemon juice.

/ 2 / To keep the bowl firmly in position and prevent it from slipping, twist a damp cloth tightly around the base. Mix thoroughly, then add the oil drop by drop, stirring briskly with a wooden spoon the whole time, or whisking constantly, until the sauce is thick and smooth. If it becomes too thick, add a little more of the vinegar or lemon juice.

/ 3 / When all the oil has been added, add the remaining vinegar or lemon juice gradually and mix thoroughly. The dressing can be stored for 2-3 weeks in a screw-topped jar in the refrigerator.

—————— V A R I A T I O N S ——————

These variations are made by adding the ingredients to 150 ml (¼ pint) mayonnaise.

CAPER MAYONNAISE
Add 10 ml (2 tsp) chopped capers, 5 ml (1 tsp) chopped pimento and 2.5 ml (½ tsp) tarragon vinegar. Caper mayonnaise makes an ideal accompaniment for fish.

CELERY MAYONNAISE
Add 15 ml (1 tbsp) chopped celery and 15 ml (1 tbsp) snipped fresh chives.

CUCUMBER MAYONNAISE
Add 30 ml (2 tbsp) finely chopped cucumber. This mayonnaise goes well with fish salads, especially crab, lobster or salmon salads.

CURRY MAYONNAISE
Add 5 ml (1 tsp) curry powder to the egg yolk mixture before adding the oil.

GREEN MAYONNAISE
Blanch 3 large spinach leaves quickly in boiling water, drain and chop finely. Add to the mayonnaise with 15 ml (1 tsp) chopped fresh parsley and 30 ml (2 tbsp) snipped fresh chives.

HERB MAYONNAISE
Add 30 ml (2 tbsp) snipped fresh chives and 15 ml (1 tbsp) chopped fresh parsley.

HORSERADISH MAYONNAISE
Add 15 ml (1 tbsp) horseradish sauce.

LEMON MAYONNAISE
Add the finely grated rind of 1 lemon and use lemon juice instead of vinegar.

PIQUANT MAYONNAISE
Add 5 ml (1 tsp) tomato ketchup, 5 ml (1 tsp) chopped stuffed olives and a pinch of paprika.

TOMATO MAYONNAISE
Add ½ a tomato, skinned and diced, 1 spring onion, finely chopped and 5 ml (1 tsp) white wine vinegar or lemon juice.

WATERCRESS MAYONNAISE
Add ¼ of a bunch of watercress, very finely chopped, to 150 ml (¼ pint) lemon mayonnaise.

F R E N C H D R E S S I N G

Sauce Vinaigrette

M A K E S 1 2 0 M L (8 T B S P)

90 ml (6 tbsp) olive oil
30 ml (2 tbsp) wine or herb vinegar or lemon juice
2.5 ml (½ tsp) raw cane sugar
2.5 ml (½ tsp) mustard (wholegrain, Dijon, French, or mustard powder)
salt and pepper

/ 1 / Place all the ingredients in a small bowl or screw-topped jar and whisk or shake together until well blended. The oil separates out on standing, so whisk or shake the dressing again if necessary immediately before use.

/ 2 / The dressing can be stored in a bottle or screw-topped jar for up to a year in the refrigerator, but shake it up vigorously just before serving as it will separate.

—————— V A R I A T I O N S ——————

The following variations are made by adding the ingredients to the above basic French dressing. Shake or whisk well to combine.

FRESH HERB VINAIGRETTE
Add 15 ml (1 tbsp) chopped fresh parsley or 15 ml (1 tbsp) chopped fresh mint or 10 ml (2 tsp) snipped fresh chives, or a mixture of all three.

MUSTARD VINAIGRETTE
Add an extra 15 ml (1 tbsp) wholegrain mustard.

BOMBAY DRESSING
Add a large pinch of curry powder, 1 finely chopped hard-boiled egg and 10 ml (2 tsp) chopped onion.

GARLIC VINAIGRETTE
Add 2 garlic cloves, skinned and crushed.

MAYONNAISE

Put the egg yolk into a bowl with the mustard, salt and pepper to taste, sugar and 5 ml (1 tsp) of the vinegar or lemon juice.

Mix thoroughly, then add the oil, drop by drop, stirring briskly with a wooden spoon the whole time, or whisking constantly, until the sauce is thick and smooth.

HOW TO RESCUE CURDLED MAYONNAISE

If your mayonnaise curdles during – or after – making, don't panic and don't throw it away. There are several ways to rescue it so that you need not waste the ingredients. Beat the curdled mayonnaise into one of the following:

5 ml (1 tsp) hot water
5 ml (1 tsp) Dijon mustard
5 ml (1 tsp) vinegar or lemon juice
1 egg yolk
30 ml (2 tbsp) bottled mayonnaise

Add the curdled mayonnaise a little at a time, beating vigorously after each addition to make sure it is incorporated. When the mixture is smooth, continue adding the oil, a drop at a time.

MEXICAN RE-FRIED
BEANS

Mash the beans in a bowl
with a potato masher or
the end of a rolling pin.

Serve this dish as an
accompaniment to any
Mexican main course.
Alternatively, serve as a
filling for tortillas (Mexican
pancakes). For a vegetarian
meal, the beans taste
particularly good topped
with grated low fat
Cheddar type cheese and
served with Boiled Rice
(see page 146) and a mixed
salad.

Re-fried beans, or *frijoles
refritos*, are a popular
vegetable accompaniment
in Mexico. They can be re-
fried again and again, with
the addition of a little more
water each time.

BUTTERMILK
DRESSING

MAKES 300 ML (¹/₂ PINT)

300 ml (½ pint) buttermilk
30 ml (2 tbsp) polyunsaturated oil
salt and pepper
30 ml (2 tbsp) chopped spring onions

/ 1 / Mix all the ingredients together. Add any
of the ingredients used in variations for French
dressing (see below) to add extra flavour, if
liked. The dressing can be stored for up to 4
days in a screw-topped jar in the refrigerator.

YOGURT
DRESSING

MAKES 150 ML (¹/₄ PINT)

150 ml (¼ pint) natural low-fat yogurt
15 ml (1 tbsp) polyunsaturated oil
5-10 ml (1-2 tsp) white wine vinegar
5 ml (1 tsp) wholegrain mustard

/ 1 / Mix all the ingredients well together and
chill. The dressing can be stored for up to a
week in a screw-topped jar in the refrigerator.

TOMATO AND
YOGURT
DRESSING

MAKES 600 ML (1 PINT)

60 ml (4 tbsp) olive oil
5 ml (1 tsp) raw cane sugar
30 ml (2 tbsp) white wine vinegar
300 ml (½ pint) tomato juice
salt and pepper
150 ml (¼ pint) natural low-fat yogurt
10 ml (2 tsp) grated onion
30 ml (2 tbsp) horseradish sauce

/ 1 / Put the oil, sugar, vinegar, tomato juice
and salt to taste in a bowl and whisk well together. Whisk in the yogurt, followed by the
onion and horseradish. Season with pepper.

/ 2 / The dressing can be stored for up to a week
in a screw-topped jar in the refrigerator.

ROUILLE

MAKES ABOUT 200 ML
(¹/₃ PINT)

2 garlic cloves, skinned
2 red peppers, halved, seeded and chopped
2 slices wholemeal bread, crusts removed
30 ml (2 tbsp) olive oil
200 ml (⅓ pint) fish stock

/ 1 / Purée the garlic and peppers together in a
blender or food processor until they are completely smooth.

/ 2 / Soak the bread in 150 ml (¼ pint) of water
and squeeze dry. Add to the pepper mixture
and blend until smooth.

/ 3 / Slowly add the olive oil, mixing well, then
enough of the fish stock to give a consistency
similar to mayonnaise. The dressing can be
stored in the refrigerator for up to a week.

MEXICAN
RE-FRIED BEANS

SERVES 4 - 6

30 ml (2 tbsp) polyunsaturated oil
1 medium onion, skinned and finely chopped
1 garlic clove, skinned and crushed
1 green chilli, seeded and finely chopped
450 g (1 lb) cooked red kidney or pinto beans, or two 425 g (15 oz) cans red kidney or pinto beans, drained
low-fat Cheddar type cheese, to serve (optional)

/ 1 / Heat the oil in a large frying pan, add the
onion and fry gently for about 5 minutes until
soft and lightly coloured. Stir in the garlic and
chilli and continue cooking for 1-2 minutes.
Remove from the heat.

/ 2 / Mash the beans in a bowl with a potato
masher or the end of a rolling pin. Add to the
frying pan with 150 ml (¼ pint) water and stir
well to mix.

/ 3 / Return the pan to the heat and fry for
about 5 minutes, stirring constantly until the
beans resemble porridge, adding more water if
necessary. Take care that the beans do not
catch and burn. Serve hot, topped with grated
low-fat Cheddar type cheese, if liked.

Picture opposite:
Mexican Re-fried Beans

Summer Vegetable Fricassée

S U M M E R V E G E T A B L E F R I C A S S É E

S E R V E S   4 - 6

4 medium courgettes, trimmed
225 g (8 oz) French beans, topped and tailed and cut into 5 cm (2 inch) lengths
salt and pepper
45 ml (3 tbsp) olive oil
1 medium onion, skinned and sliced
2 garlic cloves, skinned and crushed
5 ml (1 tsp) crushed coriander seeds
3 peppers (red, yellow, green), cored, seeded and sliced
150 ml (¼ pint) dry white wine
10 ml (2 tsp) tomato purée
2.5 ml (½ tsp) raw cane sugar

/ 1 / Cut the courgettes crossways into thirds, then cut them lengthways into slices about 0.5 cm (¼ inch) thick.

/ 2 / Blanch the courgettes and beans in boiling salted water for 5 minutes only. Drain well.

/ 3 / Heat the oil in a flameproof casserole, add the onion, garlic and coriander seeds and fry gently for 5 minutes until the onion is soft.

/ 4 / Add the pepper slices and fry gently for a further 5 minutes, stirring constantly. Stir in the wine, tomato purée and sugar, with salt and pepper to taste. Bring to the boil, then simmer for a few minutes, stirring all the time until the liquid begins to reduce.

/ 5 / Add the courgettes and beans to the pan and stir gently to combine with the sauce. Heat through, taking care not to overcook the vegetables. Serve piping hot, straight from the casserole.

F E N N E L   A U G R A T I N

S E R V E S   4 - 6

4 small fennel bulbs, trimmed
salt and pepper
90 ml (6 tbsp) olive oil
50 g (2 oz) Fontina, Gruyère or Emmental cheese, grated
45 ml (3 tbsp) grated Parmesan cheese

/ 1 / Using a sharp knife, carefully cut each bulb of fennel into quarters lengthways.

/ 2 / Cook the fennel quarters in a large saucepan of boiling salted water for 20 minutes until just tender. Drain thoroughly.

/ 3 / Heat the oil in a flameproof gratin dish. Add the fennel and toss to coat.

/ 4 / Turn the fennel quarters cut side up in the dish. Sprinkle with the 2 cheeses and season with salt and pepper to taste.

/ 5 / Grill under a preheated hot grill for 5 minutes or until both the cheeses have melted and are bubbling.

C O L C A N N O N

Irish Mashed Potatoes with Kale and Leeks

S E R V E S   6

450 g (1 lb) potatoes, peeled and quartered
salt and pepper
450 g (1 lb) kale or cabbage, cored and shredded
2 small leeks, sliced and washed
150 ml (¼ pint) semi-skimmed milk
50 g (2 oz) butter or margarine
melted butter, to serve

/ 1 / Cook the potatoes in boiling salted water for 15-20 minutes until tender. Meanwhile, cook the kale or cabbage in a separate saucepan of boiling salted water for 5-10 minutes until tender. Drain both the cooked potatoes and the kale or cabbage.

/ 2 / Put the leeks and milk in a saucepan and simmer gently for 10-15 minutes until soft.

/ 3 / Put the leeks in a large bowl, add the potatoes, then the kale or cabbage, butter or margarine and salt and pepper to taste. Beat together over gentle heat until the mixture is thoroughly blended.

/ 4 / Mound the mixture on a warmed serving dish and make a hollow in the top. Pour a little melted butter into the hollow, to be mixed in at the last minute.

COLCANNON

Serve Colcannon for a mid-week family meal with chops or sausages.

In Ireland, Colcannon is traditionally eaten on All Hallows' Day, which is Hallowe'en, 31 October. Older recipes were made with kale, which was cooked with bacon to make it really tasty, but nowadays cabbage is often used or a mixture of kale and cabbage. Minced onion can be substituted for the leeks, if leeks are not available.

There is a superstition surrounding Colcannon in Ireland, much the same as the one associated with plum pudding in Britain. Years ago, Irish cooks are said to have hidden gold wedding rings in the mixture, and it was believed that the finders would be married within the year. If the cook hid a thimble, however, this would mean the finder would remain unmarried.

COURGETTES STUFFED WITH RICOTTA

Score the courgettes lengthways with the prongs of a fork, then cut them in half lengthways.

Spoon the ricotta filling into the blanched and drained courgette shells, dividing it equally between them.

Serve Courgettes Stuffed with Ricotta with a plain main course dish. Alternatively it could be served as a starter for a dinner party.

POTATO AND CARROT CASSEROLE

This vegetable casserole is the perfect dish to cook in the oven while you are roasting meat or cooking a meat or poultry casserole for a main course.

COURGETTES STUFFED WITH RICOTTA

SERVES 4

8 even-sized medium courgettes

30 ml (2 tbsp) olive oil

1 medium onion, skinned and finely chopped

1 garlic clove, skinned and crushed

175 g (6 oz) ricotta cheese

20 ml (4 tsp) chopped fresh basil or 10 ml (2 tsp) dried

45 ml (3 tbsp) dried wholemeal breadcrumbs

fresh basil sprigs, to garnish

TOMATO SAUCE

397 g (14 oz) can tomatoes, with their juice

1 small onion, skinned and roughly chopped

1 garlic clove, skinned and chopped

1 celery stick, sliced

1 bay leaf

parsley sprig

2.5 ml (½ tsp) raw cane sugar

salt and pepper

/ 1 / First make the tomato sauce. Put all the ingredients in a saucepan, bring to the boil and simmer, uncovered, for 30 minutes until thickened. Stir occasionally to prevent the sauce sticking to the bottom of the pan.

/ 2 / Remove the bay leaf and purée the mixture in a blender or food processor until smooth, or push through a sieve using a wooden spoon.

/ 3 / Meanwhile, score the courgettes lengthways with the prongs of a fork, then cut them in half lengthways.

/ 4 / Scoop out the flesh from the courgette halves with a sharp-edged teaspoon. Leave a thin margin of flesh next to the skin and make sure not to scoop out all the flesh from the bottoms or the skin may break.

/ 5 / Blanch the courgette shells in boiling salted water for 10 minutes. Drain, then stand skin side up on absorbent paper.

/ 6 / Heat the oil in a frying pan, add the onion, garlic and scooped-out flesh from the courgettes. Fry gently for about 5 minutes until soft and lightly coloured, then turn into a bowl and add the ricotta, basil and salt and pepper to taste. Stir well.

/ 7 / Spoon the ricotta filling into the drained courgette shells, dividing it equally between the 16 shells.

/ 8 / Pour the tomato sauce into the bottom of a shallow ovenproof dish large enough to hold the courgettes in a single layer. Place the filled courgettes in the dish side by side. Sprinkle with the breadcrumbs.

/ 9 / Bake in the oven at 200°C (400°F) mark 6 for 20 minutes. Serve hot, garnished with plenty of fresh basil sprigs.

POTATO AND CARROT CASSEROLE

SERVES 2

25 g (1 oz) butter or margarine

15 ml (1 tbsp) polyunsaturated oil

15 ml (1 tbsp) raw cane demerara sugar

225 g (8 oz) carrots, peeled and thickly sliced

225 g (8 oz) small onions, skinned

450 g (1 lb) small new potatoes, scrubbed and cut in half

125 g (4 oz) button mushrooms

15 ml (1 tbsp) plain flour

150 ml (¼ pint) red wine

10 ml (2 tsp) tomato purée

150 ml (¼ pint) vegetable stock

1 bay leaf

salt and pepper

chopped fresh parsley, to garnish

/ 1 / Heat the butter or margarine and oil together in a flameproof casserole. Add the sugar, carrots, onions and potatoes. Cook, stirring, over high heat for 5 minutes until the vegetables colour.

/ 2 / Add the mushrooms and cook for a further minute. Stir in the flour, scraping any sediment from the bottom of the pan, then add the red wine, tomato purée, stock, bay leaf and salt and pepper to taste.

/ 3 / Cover the casserole tightly, then bake in the oven at 190°C (375°F) mark 5 for about 1 hour or until the vegetables are tender.

/ 4 / Remove the bay leaf. Taste and adjust the seasoning and sprinkle with chopped parsley. Serve immediately.

Potato and Carrot Casserole

Lentils come in so many shapes and sizes (see page 92) that it is very easy to become confused about the correct ones to use for a particular recipe. This warming winter hot pot calls for green lentils. They are whole, with quite a pronounced 'earthy' flavour.

The beauty of this type of lentil is that it keeps its shape during cooking, unlike the split red and yellow varieties which quickly disintegrate to a mush.

LENTIL HOT POT

SERVES 2

175 g (6 oz) green lentils
salt and pepper
25 g (1 oz) butter or margarine
1 medium onion, skinned and chopped
2.5 ml (½ tsp) curry powder
125 g (4 oz) celery, trimmed and sliced
125 g (4 oz) carrots, peeled and sliced
15 ml (1 tbsp) plain flour
1 chicken stock cube
125 g (4 oz) French beans, topped and tailed
125 g (4 oz) courgettes, sliced
25 g (1 oz) fresh breadcrumbs
75 g (3 oz) low-fat Cheddar type cheese, grated

/ 1 / Cook the lentils in boiling salted water for 20 minutes or until tender. Drain well.

/ 2 / Meanwhile, melt the butter or margarine in a large saucepan, add the onion and fry for about 5 minutes until soft but not coloured. Add the curry powder, celery and carrots, cover and cook gently for 5 minutes.

/ 3 / Stir in the flour, stock cube and 300 ml (½ pint) water. Bring to the boil, stirring. Season with salt and pepper to taste and simmer for 5 minutes.

/ 4 / Add the French beans and simmer for a further 5 minutes, then add the courgettes. Continue cooking for about 10 minutes or until the vegetables are tender, but still have bite.

/ 5 / Drain the lentils and add to the vegetables. Heat through for 2-3 minutes. Taste and adjust seasoning, then turn into a deep oven-proof dish.

Hot Beetroot with Horseradish

/ 6 / Mix the breadcrumbs and cheese together and sprinkle on top. Put under a preheated hot grill until crisp and golden brown. Serve hot.

HOT BEETROOT WITH HORSERADISH

SERVES 4 - 6

450 g (1 lb) cooked beetroot
15 ml (1 tbsp) caster sugar
60 ml (4 tbsp) red wine vinegar
30 ml (2 tbsp) freshly grated horseradish
salt and pepper
15 ml (1 tbsp) cornflour

/ 1 / Rub the skin off the beetroot carefully, using your fingers. Slice the beetroot neatly into rounds.

/ 2 / Put the beetroot in a large heavy-based pan, then sprinkle with the sugar. Pour in the wine vinegar and add the horseradish with salt and pepper to taste.

/ 3 / Bring to the boil, without stirring, then cover and simmer gently for 10 minutes.

/ 4 / Transfer the beetroot slices carefully with a slotted spoon to a warmed serving dish. Mix the cornflour to a paste with a little cold water, then stir into the cooking liquid in the pan. Boil for 1-2 minutes, stirring vigorously until the liquid thickens. Adjust seasoning, then pour over the beetroot. Serve immediately.

TURNIPS IN CURRY CREAM SAUCE

SERVES 4

700 g (1½ lb) small turnips
salt and pepper
50 g (2 oz) butter or margarine
1 medium onion, skinned and finely chopped
100 g (4 oz) cooking apple
50 g (2 oz) sultanas
5 ml (1 tsp) mild curry powder
5 ml (1 tsp) plain flour
150 ml (¼ pint) dry cider
150 ml (¼ pint) single cream
10 ml (2 tsp) lemon juice

/ 1 / Peel the turnips, boil in salted water for 10-15 minutes until just tender. Meanwhile, make the sauce. Melt the butter or margarine, add the onion, cover and cook gently for 10 minutes until soft and tinged with colour. Peel and finely chop the apple and add to the onion, together with the sultanas, curry powder and flour. Cook, stirring, for 3-4 minutes.

/ 2 / Pour the cider into the pan, bring to the boil, bubble gently for 2 minutes, stirring. Off the heat stir in the cream, lemon juice and seasoning. Keep warm without boiling.

/ 3 / Drain the turnips in a colander. To serve, place in a heated dish and pour over the curry cream sauce. Serve immediately.

HOT BEETROOT WITH HORSERADISH

Rub the skin off the cooked beetroot carefully, using your fingers.

Horseradish, which is related to mustard, is a perennial plant, of which the long, tapering, creamy coloured root is used. Lift the roots in autumn, scrub and grate them and preserve them in jars, covered with wine vinegar.

TURNIPS IN CURRY CREAM SAUCE

Use sweet, tender early turnips for this recipe. They have green and white skins and a slightly mustard flavour.

This vegetable casserole has a tangy fruit flavour, which makes it the ideal accompaniment for rich meats. It is especially good with roast pork, duck, pheasant and partridge, and would also go well with the festive turkey at Christmas.

Casseroles of cabbage like this one are popular in northern France, particularly in Ardennes, which borders on Belgium. Both white and red cabbage are used, but with white cabbage dry white wine is usually preferred to the red used here. A spoonful of redcurrant jelly is sometimes added to red cabbage casseroles. Substitute this for the port if liked, plus a few crushed juniper berries, which are a favourite flavouring ingredient in northern Europe.

RED CABBAGE AND APPLE CASSEROLE

SERVES 4 - 6

700 g (1½ lb) red cabbage
2 cooking apples
1 large Spanish onion, skinned
50 g (2 oz) raisins
salt and pepper
30 ml (2 tbsp) raw cane sugar
60 ml (4 tbsp) white wine or wine vinegar
30 ml (2 tbsp) port (optional)

/ 1 / Shred the cabbage finely, discarding the thick central stalk. Peel and core the apples and slice thinly. Slice the onion thinly.

/ 2 / Grease a large ovenproof dish. Put a layer of shredded cabbage in the bottom and cover with a layer of sliced apple and onion. Sprinkle over a few of the raisins and season with salt and pepper to taste.

/ 3 / In a small jug, mix the sugar with the wine or vinegar and the port, if using. Sprinkle a little of this mixture over the layered ingredients in the dish.

/ 4 / Continue layering the ingredients in the dish until they are all used up. Cover the dish and bake in the oven at 150°C (300°F) mark 2 for 3 hours. Turn into a warmed serving dish and serve hot, as an accompaniment to turkey, pheasant or partridge, if liked.

SAG ALOO

Curried Spinach and Potatoes

SERVES 4 - 6

two 225 g (8 oz) packets frozen leaf spinach, thawed and drained
50 g (2 oz) ghee or vegetable oil
1 medium onion, skinned and thinly sliced
2 garlic cloves, skinned and crushed
10 ml (2 tsp) ground coriander
5 ml (1 tsp) mustard seeds
2.5 ml (½ tsp) ground turmeric
1.25-2.5 ml (¼-½ tsp) chilli powder, according to taste
salt and pepper
450 g (1 lb) potatoes, peeled and cut roughly into cubes

/ 1 / Put the spinach in a heavy-based pan and place over very gentle heat for about 5 minutes to drive off as much liquid as possible.

/ 2 / Meanwhile, melt the ghee or heat the oil in a separate heavy-based pan. Add the onion, garlic, spices and salt to taste and fry gently for about 5 minutes, stirring frequently.

/ 3 / Add the potatoes and fold gently into the spice mixture, then pour in 150 ml (¼ pint) water. Bring to the boil, then lower the heat and simmer, uncovered, for 10 minutes. Stir occasionally during this time and add a few more spoonfuls of water if necessary.

/ 4 / Fold the spinach gently into the potato mixture. Simmer for a further 5-10 minutes until the potatoes are just tender. To serve, taste and adjust seasoning, then turn into a warmed serving dish. Serve hot.

VEGETABLE PILAU

SERVES 6

1 small cauliflower, washed
225 g (8 oz) leeks
50 g (2 oz) butter or margarine
450 g (1 lb) carrots, peeled and thinly sliced
350 g (12 oz) long-grain rice
5 ml (1 tsp) ground cardamom
5 ml (1 tsp) paprika
2.5 ml (½ tsp) ground cloves
2.5 ml (½ tsp) ground cinnamon
1 litre (1¾ pints) chicken stock
salt and pepper
1 green pepper, cored, seeded and diced
lime twist, to garnish

/ 1 / With a sharp knife, divide the cauliflower into small florets, discarding any thick stems.

/ 2 / Cut the leeks into 1 cm (½ inch) slices, discarding any coarse leaves; wash and drain.

/ 3 / Heat the butter or margarine in a large flameproof casserole. Fry the sliced carrots, cauliflower and leeks for 5 minutes.

/ 4 / Stir in the rice with the cardamom, paprika, cloves and cinnamon and cook for 1 minute, stirring.

This Indian vegetable accompaniment (*sag* meaning spinach and *aloo* potatoes) goes particularly well with curries. As an alternative to spinach you could use cauliflower florets to make *Aloo Gobi*: blanch 450 g (1 lb) cauliflower florets in boiling water in step 1, then add to the potatoes in step 4.

Sag Aloo (top); Vegetable Pilau (bottom)

/ 5 / Pour in the stock, season well and bring to the boil. Cover and cook in the oven at 180°C (350°F) mark 4 for 15 minutes.

/ 6 / Stir the diced pepper into the pilau. Return covered casserole to the oven for a further 10 minutes. Garnish with a twist of lime.

159

FRENCH BEANS WITH
WATER CHESTNUTS

It is possible to buy fresh water chestnuts from oriental specialist stores in some large cities, but canned water chestnuts are available in most supermarkets and make a perfectly acceptable substitute. They do not have much flavour, but are very crisp and crunchy, providing a good contrast to the tenderness of the beans. Water chestnuts are in fact a sweet root vegetable, and do not belong to the chestnut family at all.

Serve French Beans with Water Chestnuts with an oriental-style main course, or to add interest to plain roast or grilled meat.

FRENCH BEANS WITH WATER CHESTNUTS

SERVES 1

| 100 g (4 oz) French beans |
| salt and pepper |
| 3 canned water chestnuts, drained |
| 25 g (1 oz) butter or margarine |

/ 1 / Top and tail the French beans. Cook in boiling salted water for about 3 minutes. Drain the beans and plunge into a bowl of cold water to set the colour and prevent further cooking.

/ 2 / Meanwhile, slice the water chestnuts and set aside. Drain the beans. Melt the butter or margarine in a frying pan, add the French beans and cook, stirring, for 1-2 minutes. Stir in the water chestnuts and cook for a further minute, tossing the vegetables continuously. Season and serve immediately.

/ 3 / To serve 2: double the quantity of ingredients and follow the recipe above.

COURGETTES AND ALMONDS

SERVES 1

| 2 medium courgettes |
| 25 g (1 oz) butter or margarine |
| finely grated rind and juice of ½ lemon |
| salt and pepper |
| 25 g (1 oz) flaked almonds |

/ 1 / Slice the courgettes in 3 horizontally. Halve the slices and cut into fingers.

/ 2 / Melt the butter or margarine in a frying pan, add the courgettes, lemon rind and juice, and salt and pepper to taste. Cook over moderate heat, stirring from time to time, for about 5 minutes or until the courgette fingers turn opaque. Remove from the heat.

/ 3 / Spread the flaked almonds on a baking sheet and toast under a preheated hot grill until golden. Add the almonds to the courgettes, return to the heat and cook, stirring, for a further minute. Serve immediately.

COURGETTES AND ALMONDS

If liked, you can dégorge the courgettes to make them less watery. Sprinkle them with salt at the end of step I, drain for 30 minutes, rinse and pat dry.

/ 4 / To serve 2: double the quantity of ingredients and follow the recipe above.

TRIO OF VEGETABLE PURÉES

SERVES 4

| 450 g (1 lb) carrots, scrubbed or peeled and roughly chopped |
| 450 g (1 lb) parsnips or turnips, peeled and roughly chopped |
| salt and pepper |
| 350 g (12 oz) frozen peas |
| a few mint sprigs |
| 5 ml (1 tsp) lemon juice |
| pinch of granulated sugar |
| 40 g (1½ oz) butter or margarine |
| 45 ml (3 tbsp) single cream |
| 1.25 ml (¼ tsp) ground coriander |
| good pinch of freshly grated nutmeg |

/ 1 / Cook the carrots and parsnips or turnips in separate pans of boiling salted water for about 20 minutes or until tender. At the same time, cook the frozen peas in boiling salted water according to packet instructions, with the mint sprigs, lemon juice and sugar.

/ 2 / Drain the vegetables, keeping them separate. Put the peas and mint in a blender or food processor with one-third of the butter or margarine and 15 ml (1 tbsp) of the cream. Work to a smooth purée, then season with salt and pepper to taste.

/ 3 / Rinse out the machine, then add the carrots, another third of the butter or margarine, 15 ml (1 tbsp) cream and the coriander. Work to a smooth purée, then season with salt and pepper to taste.

/ 4 / Repeat puréeing with the parsnips or turnips, the remaining butter or margarine and cream and the nutmeg. Season with salt and pepper to taste.

/ 5 / Return all 3 purées to individual pans and reheat gently, stirring all the time. Spoon into 3 warmed serving bowls or in 3 or more sections in 1 large bowl. Serve immediately.

French Beans with Water Chestnuts (top); Courgettes and Almonds

CHAKCHOUKA

Chakchouka is a spicy, Moroccan version of the well-known French vegetable dish ratatouille. Like ratatouille, it keeps extremely well and seems to taste even better if stored in the refrigerator for 2-3 days before eating. In this recipe, it is served hot as a vegetable accompaniment, but it tastes just as good served chilled as a starter, with crusty French bread.

Although it is time-consuming to have to dégorge the aubergine, try not to skimp on this part of the preparation. Salting the aubergine flesh draws out the bitter juices from the vegetable; if these are not extracted the finished dish may be spoilt.

Grilling peppers until charred, wrapping them in kitchen paper until cold, and then peeling them, gives them a wonderful smoky flavour and soft, juicy texture. It is a favourite way of preparing peppers on the continent and in the Middle East and Africa. In summertime they can be charred on the barbecue, in which case they will taste even better.

CHINESE VEGETABLE STIR-FRY

The beauty of the Chinese stir-frying technique is that it is so quick and easy – perfect for entertaining when you want to be with your guests as much as possible. With stir-frying, everything can be prepared ahead of time so that all you have to do is quickly cook the ingredients at the last moment.

CHAKCHOUKA

Moroccan Vegetable Stew

SERVES 2

1 small aubergine
salt and pepper
1 red pepper
1 green pepper
225 g (8 oz) tomatoes
1 fresh green chilli or 2.5 ml (½ tsp) chilli powder
60 ml (4 tbsp) olive oil
1 medium onion, skinned and thinly sliced
1 garlic clove, skinned and crushed

/1/ Slice the aubergine thinly, then place in a colander, sprinkling each layer with salt. Cover with a plate, put heavy weights on top and leave to dégorge for 20-30 minutes while preparing the other vegetables.

/2/ Put the peppers under a preheated moderate grill and cook until the skins char on all sides, turning them frequently.

/3/ Remove the peppers from the grill and wrap immediately in absorbent kitchen paper. Leave to cool.

/4/ Skin the tomatoes: plunge them into boiling water, then into cold. Peel off the skins and chop the flesh roughly. Halve the chilli, if using, remove the seeds under cold running water, then chop the flesh finely.

/5/ Rinse the aubergine slices under cold running water, then pat dry with absorbent kitchen paper. Heat the oil in a heavy-based saucepan, add the onion, garlic and fresh chilli, if using, and fry gently for about 5 minutes until soft but not coloured.

/6/ Add the aubergine slices, the chopped tomato, chilli powder, if using, and salt and pepper to taste. Cook for 20 minutes, stirring frequently to prevent sticking.

/7/ Meanwhile, unwrap the peppers and peel off the skins by rubbing with your fingers under cold running water. Discard the cores and seeds, then pat the flesh dry with absorbent kitchen paper. Cut into thin strips.

/8/ Add the pepper strips to the pan and heat through for about 5 minutes. Taste and adjust seasoning before serving.

CHINESE VEGETABLE STIR-FRY

SERVES 4

1 turnip, peeled
4 small carrots, peeled
4 celery sticks
2 young leeks, washed and trimmed
30 ml (2 tbsp) sesame oil
15 ml (1 tbsp) polyunsaturated oil
100 g (4 oz) beansprouts, washed and drained
10 ml (2 tsp) soy sauce
5 ml (1 tsp) white wine vinegar
5 ml (1 tsp) raw cane sugar
5 ml (1 tsp) five-spice powder
salt

/1/ Using a sharp knife, cut the turnip and the peeled carrots into matchstick strips. Slice the celery and leeks finely.

/2/ Heat the oils in a wok, then add the prepared vegetables with the beansprouts. Stir-fry over moderate heat for 3-4 minutes, then sprinkle in the soy sauce, wine vinegar, sugar, five-spice powder and salt to taste. Stir-fry for 1 further minute. Serve at once, while hot.

CABBAGE WITH CARAWAY

SERVES 6

1.4 kg (3 lb) green cabbage
salt
50 g (2 oz) butter or margarine
5 ml (1 tsp) caraway seeds
pepper

/1/ Shred the cabbage finely, discarding any core or tough outer leaves. Wash well under cold running water.

/2/ Cook in a large saucepan of boiling salted water for 2 minutes only – the cabbage should retain its crispness and texture. Drain well.

/3/ Melt the butter or margarine in the pan; add the drained cabbage with the caraway seeds and salt and pepper to taste. Stir over a moderate heat for 2-3 minutes until hot. Adjust seasoning and serve immediately.

CELERIAC WITH TOMATO SAUCE

SERVES 4

2 heads of celeriac, total weight about 900 g (2 lb)
5 ml (1 tsp) lemon juice
50 g (2 oz) dried brown or white breadcrumbs
50 g (2 oz) Parmesan cheese, freshly grated
SPICY TOMATO SAUCE
60 ml (4 tbsp) olive oil
1 large onion, skinned and finely chopped
3 garlic cloves, skinned and crushed
350 g (12 oz) ripe tomatoes, skinned and finely chopped
15 ml (1 tbsp) tomato purée
30 ml (2 tbsp) red wine or red wine vinegar
60 ml (4 tbsp) chopped fresh parsley
5 ml (1 tsp) ground cinnamon
1 bay leaf
salt and pepper
450 ml (¾ pint) hot water

/ 1 / First, make the tomato sauce. Heat the oil in a heavy-based saucepan, add the onion and garlic and fry gently for about 10 minutes until very soft and lightly coloured.

/ 2 / Add the tomatoes, tomato purée, wine or vinegar, parsley, cinnamon, bay leaf and salt and pepper to taste. Add the hot water and bring to the boil, stirring with a wooden spoon to break up the tomatoes.

/ 3 / Lower the heat, cover and simmer the sauce for 30 minutes, stirring occasionally.

/ 4 / Meanwhile, peel the celeriac, then cut into chunky pieces. As you prepare the celeriac, place the pieces in a bowl of water to which the lemon juice has been added.

/ 5 / Drain the celeriac, then plunge quickly into a large pan of boiling salted water. Return to the boil and blanch for 10 minutes.

/ 6 / Drain the celeriac well, the put in an ovenproof dish. Pour over the tomato sauce (discarding the bay leaf), then sprinkle the breadcrumbs and cheese evenly over the top.

/ 7 / Bake the celeriac in the oven at 190°C (375°F) mark 5 for 30 minutes, until the celeriac is tender when pierced with a skewer and the topping is golden brown. Serve hot, straight from the dish.

With its strongly flavoured tomato sauce, this gratin of celeriac tastes good with plain roast or grilled meat and poultry. It also makes a tasty vegetarian dish on its own.

Chakchouka

HOT POTATOES WITH DILL

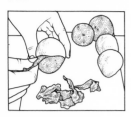

Put the potatoes in cold salted water, bring to the boil and cook for 12-15 minutes until tender. Drain the potatoes, leave until just cool enough to handle, then remove the skins.

PIPERANA

SERVES 4 - 6

5 peppers (red, green and yellow)

2 large garlic cloves, skinned and crushed

5 ml (1 tsp) grated onion

75 ml (5 tbsp) olive oil

30 ml (2 tbsp) lemon juice

30 ml (2 tbsp) chopped fresh herbs, such as marjoram, thyme, parsley

salt and pepper

/ 1 / Put the peppers under a preheated moderate grill and cook until the skins char on all sides, turning them frequently.

/ 2 / Hold the peppers under cold running water and rub the skins off with your fingers. Discard the skins, stems, cores and seeds. Cut the pepper flesh into long, thin shreds.

/ 3 / Put the garlic in a screw-topped jar with the grated onion, oil and lemon juice. Add the herbs and salt and pepper to taste. Shake well to mix.

/ 4 / Arrange the peppers decoratively on a plate. Pour over the dressing, then leave to stand for at least 10 minutes before serving.

HOT POTATOES WITH DILL

SERVES 6

900 g (2 lb) potatoes

salt and pepper

4 spring onions, washed and finely chopped

15 ml (1 tbsp) chopped fresh dill and a sprig, to garnish

142 ml (5 fl oz) soured cream

Hot Potatoes with Dill

/ 1 / Place the potatoes in cold salted water, bring to the boil and cook for 12-15 minutes until tender.

/ 2 / Drain the potatoes, leave until just cool enough to handle, then remove the skins.

/ 3 / Cut the potatoes into small dice and place in a bowl. Add the chopped onions to the potatoes with the dill and season with salt and pepper to taste.

/ 4 / Thin the soured cream, if necessary, with a little boiling water or milk. Stir it into the potatoes and toss gently.

/ 5 / Leave to stand for a few minutes so that the flavours can blend. To serve, garnish with a sprig of dill.

AUBERGINE AU GRATIN

SERVES 4

450 g (1 lb) aubergines
salt and pepper
about 120 ml (8 tbsp) olive or polyunsaturated oil
25 g (1 oz) plain wholemeal flour
300 ml (½ pint) semi-skimmed milk
60 ml (4 tbsp) grated Parmesan cheese
1.25 ml (¼ tsp) freshly grated nutmeg
350 g (12 oz) tomatoes, skinned and sliced
2 garlic cloves, skinned and roughly chopped
2 eggs, beaten

/ 1 / Slice the aubergines thinly, then place in a colander, sprinkling each layer with salt. Cover with a plate, place heavy weights on top and leave to dégorge for 30 minutes.

/ 2 / Meanwhile, heat 30 ml (2 tbsp) of the oil in a saucepan, add the flour and cook gently, stirring, for 1-2 minutes. Remove from the heat and gradually blend in the milk. Bring to the boil, stirring constantly, then simmer for 3 minutes until thick and smooth. Add half of the cheese, the nutmeg and salt and pepper to taste, stir well to mix, then remove from the heat and set aside.

/ 3 / Rinse the aubergine slices under cold running water, then pat dry with absorbent kitchen paper.

/ 4 / Pour enough oil into a heavy-based frying pan to cover the base. Heat until very hot, then add a layer of aubergine slices. Fry over moderate heat until golden brown on both sides, turning once. Remove with a slotted spoon and drain on absorbent kitchen paper. Repeat with more oil and aubergines.

/ 5 / Arrange alternate layers of aubergines and tomatoes in an oiled gratin or baking dish. Sprinkle each layer with garlic, a little salt and plenty of pepper.

/ 6 / Beat the eggs into the sauce, then pour slowly into the dish. Sprinkle the remaining cheese evenly over the top. Bake in the oven at 200°C (400°F) mark 6 for 20 minutes or until golden brown and bubbling. Serve hot, straight from the dish.

AUBERGINE AU GRATIN

Pour enough oil into a heavy-based frying pan to cover the base. Heat until very hot, then add a layer of aubergine slices. Fry over moderate heat until golden brown on both sides, turning once. Remove with a slotted spoon and drain on absorbent kitchen paper. Repeat with more oil and aubergines.

This substantial, creamy vegetable dish is excellent served with roast lamb or grilled chops. It also makes a tasty vegetarian dinner with potatoes and a salad.

LENTIL AND CELERY
PEPPERS

Serve these stuffed peppers for a tasty family main course, accompanied by warm wholemeal bread and a tomato salad.

SOUFFLÉED
CAULIFLOWER

This delicious cauliflower dish can be served as an accompaniment to a grilled chop, chicken portion or steak. It would also make a good light lunch or supper dish, with wholemeal French-style bread.

The French Dijon mustard specified in this recipe is a smooth, mild-flavoured mustard which will not override the other, delicate flavours of this dish. Made in the town of Dijon in the region of Burgundy, *moutarde à la Dijon* is unique in that it is made from mustard grains mixed with verjuice (the juice of sour Burgundy grapes), plus herbs and flavourings. Most other mustards are made with vinegar which is why they are sharper in flavour than Dijon.

PEPPERED CARROTS

SERVES 4

50 g (2 oz) butter or margarine

5 ml (1 tsp) sugar

450 g (1 lb) carrots, peeled or scrubbed and thinly sliced

3 spring onions, washed and trimmed

1.25 ml (¼ tsp) cayenne pepper or to taste

45 ml (3 tbsp) soured cream

salt and pepper

/ 1 / Melt the butter or margarine with the sugar in a deep sauté pan which has a tightly fitting lid. Add the carrots to the pan, cover tightly and cook gently for 10-15 minutes until the carrots are tender.

/ 2 / Remove the lid from the pan and snip in the spring onions with a pair of sharp kitchen scissors. Transfer carrots and onions with a slotted spoon to a serving dish and keep warm.

/ 3 / Stir the cayenne pepper and soured cream into the pan. Taste and adjust seasoning, then warm through for 1-2 minutes. Pour over the carrots and serve.

LENTIL AND CELERY PEPPERS

SERVES 2

125 g (4 oz) red lentils

salt and pepper

2 green peppers, about 175 g (6 oz) each

25 g (1 oz) butter or margarine

1 medium onion, skinned and finely chopped

75 g (3 oz) celery, trimmed and finely chopped

75 g (3 oz) low-fat soft cheese

1 egg

/ 1 / Cook the lentils in boiling salted water for 12-15 minutes until just tender.

/ 2 / Meanwhile, halve the peppers and remove the cores and seeds. Place on a steamer and steam, covered, for about 15 minutes or until soft.

/ 3 / Melt the butter or margarine in a frying pan, add the onion and celery and fry gently for 2-3 minutes.

/ 4 / Drain the lentils and add to the onion and celery. Cook, stirring, for 1-2 minutes until heated through.

/ 5 / Remove the pan from the heat and beat in the cheese and egg and season with salt and pepper to taste.

/ 6 / Remove the peppers from the steamer and fill with the mixture. Place under a hot grill for about 5 minutes or until golden brown. Serve the peppers piping hot.

SOUFFLÉED CAULIFLOWER

SERVES 1

175 g (6 oz) cauliflower florets

salt and pepper

75 ml (5 tbsp) thick mayonnaise

5 ml (1 tsp) Dijon mustard

finely grated rind of ½ lemon

2 eggs, separated

50 g (2 oz) low-fat Cheddar type cheese, grated

parsley sprig, to garnish

/ 1 / Cook the cauliflower florets in boiling salted water for about 5 minutes – they should still be crisp. Drain well.

/ 2 / Butter a small, shallow ovenproof dish and place the cauliflower in the bottom.

/ 3 / Put the mayonnaise, mustard and lemon rind in a medium bowl, stir in the egg yolks and 25 g (1 oz) of the grated cheese. Season with salt and pepper to taste.

/ 4 / Put the egg whites in a separate bowl and whisk until stiff. Fold the egg whites carefully into the mayonnaise mixture.

/ 5 / Spoon this mixture over the cauliflower, sprinkle with the remaining cheese and bake in the oven at 190°C (375°F) mark 5 for about 25 minutes or until risen and golden. Serve immediately, garnished with a sprig of parsley.

/ 6 / To serve 2: double the quantity of ingredients, but use 3 eggs and 75 g (3 oz) Cheddar cheese. Follow the recipe above.

Soufléed Cauliflower

Desserts and Puddings

Fresh fruit and low-fat yogurt are the natural choice for the end of a healthy meal, but there is no need to cut out puddings altogether.

The recipes in this chapter use wholefood ingredients – wholemeal flour, raw cane sugar, honey and yogurt, and make the most of the natural sweetness of both fresh and dried fruits.

Low-fat natural yogurt can be used in many recipes instead of cream and its tangy light flavour provides a pleasant contrast when served with puddings.

Summer Fruit Salad

ALMOND AND MANGO ICE CREAM

This ice cream is made with tofu and is much healthier than ordinary ice cream. Tofu is a very low-fat source of protein, and further protein is contributed in this dish by the milk and almonds.

SUGAR-FREE CHRISTMAS PUDDING

The combination of grated carrot and fruit in this pudding is quite sweet enough without additional sugar, and the absence of suet also helps to make it a healthy recipe.

Picture opposite: Sugar-free Christmas Pudding

ALMOND AND MANGO ICE CREAM

SERVES 8

2 medium ripe mangoes
275 g (10 oz) silken tofu
300 ml (½ pint) semi-skimmed milk
finely grated rind and juice of 1½ limes
50 g (2 oz) blanched almonds, toasted and chopped
lime slices and toasted flaked almonds, to decorate

/ 1 / Cut a chunk off each side of the mangoes lengthways to expose the stone. Ease off the flesh. Remove the outer skin and coarsely chop the flesh. Put half the mango in a blender or food processor with the tofu, milk and lime rind and juice. Blend well until smooth.

/ 2 / Pour the mixture into a shallow freezer container and freeze for about 2 hours or until ice crystals form around the edges.

/ 3 / Turn into a large, chilled bowl and mash the ice crystals with a fork. Fold in the remaining mango and the chopped almonds. Return to the freezer for 3-4 hours or until firm.

/ 4 / About 30 minutes before serving, remove from the freezer and leave the ice cream to soften at room temperature. Serve decorated with lime slices and toasted flaked almonds.

CHARENTAIS GRANITA

SERVES 4

1.6 kg (3½ lb) Charentais melon
15 ml (1 tbsp) clear light honey, such as Acacia
finely grated rind and juice of 1 small orange
finely grated rind and juice of 1 lemon
mint sprigs, to decorate

/ 1 / Cut the melon in half, then scoop out and discard the seeds. Cut the flesh into chunks. Purée the melon in a blender or food processor, then put in a bowl with the honey, orange and lemon rind and juices and mix well.

/ 2 / Transfer to a freezer container and freeze for 3 hours or until the mixture is partly frozen and setting around the edges.

/ 3 / Turn the mixture into a bowl and whisk well to break up the ice crystals. Return to the container and freeze for about 4 hours or until frozen. Before serving, soften in the refrigerator for about 45 minutes. Spoon into chilled glasses or dishes and decorate with mint sprigs.

SUGAR-FREE CHRISTMAS PUDDING

SERVES 6

225 g (8 oz) mixed dried fruit
juice of 2 oranges
150 ml (¼ pint) brandy
1 large carrot, grated
1 large apple, grated
50 g (2 oz) plain wholemeal flour
50 g (2 oz) fresh wholemeal breadcrumbs
25 g (1 oz) blanched almonds, chopped
5 ml (1 tsp) freshly grated nutmeg
5 ml (1 tsp) ground cinnamon
2 eggs, beaten
holly sprig, to decorate

/ 1 / Put the mixed dried fruit in a large bowl. Stir in the orange juice and the brandy. Cover and leave overnight. Add all the remaining ingredients and mix well together.

/ 2 / Grease a 900 ml (1½ pint) pudding basin and fill with the mixture. Cover with a piece of pleated greaseproof paper and then foil. Secure tightly with string, making a handle for easy lifting in and out of the saucepan.

/ 3 / Place the basin in a steamer or on a trivet or upturned saucer in a saucepan filled with boiling water to come halfway up the sides of the basin. Steam for about 4 hours, topping up with boiling water as necessary.

/ 4 / When cooked, remove the pudding from the pan and leave to cool for at least 2 hours. Unwrap, then rewrap in fresh greaseproof paper and foil.

/ 5 / Store in a cool, dry place to mature for at least 1 month. To serve, steam for a further 2 hours. Turn out on to a warmed plate and decorate with holly.

RHUBARB BROWN BETTY

SERVES 4

450 g (1 lb) rhubarb

225 g (8 oz) fresh wholemeal breadcrumbs

50 g (2 oz) raw cane sugar

2.5 ml (½ tsp) ground ginger

50 ml (2 fl oz) fresh orange juice

300 ml (½ pint) natural low-fat yogurt, to serve

/ 1 / Trim the rhubarb and cut the stalks into short lengths. Put in a greased 900 ml (1½ pint) ovenproof dish.

/ 2 / Mix the breadcrumbs, sugar and ground ginger together and sprinkle over the fruit. Spoon the orange juice over the crumbs.

/ 3 / Bake in the oven at 170°C (325°F) mark 3 for 40 minutes or until the fruit is soft and the topping browned. Serve hot or cold, with the natural low-fat yogurt.

Rhubarb Brown Betty

DATE AND FIG PUDDING

SERVES 4

finely grated rind and juice of 1 orange
100 g (4 oz) dried stoned dates, chopped
100 g (4 oz) dried figs, coarsely chopped
50 g (2 oz) fresh root ginger, peeled and finely shredded
25 g (1 oz) margarine
25 g (1 oz) plain wholemeal flour
25 g (1 oz) plain white flour
5 ml (1 tsp) baking powder
2 eggs, beaten
150 g (5 oz) fresh wholemeal breadcrumbs

/ 1 / Lightly grease a 900 ml (1½ pint) pudding basin. Mix the orange rind and juice with the dates, figs and ginger. Set aside for 1 hour, stirring occasionally.

/ 2 / Add the margarine, flours, baking powder, eggs and breadcrumbs to the fruit mixture. Spoon into the basin and level the surface. Tie a pleated double thickness of greaseproof paper over the top and steam for 1½ hours or until well risen. Turn out and serve.

MINTED STRAWBERRY CUSTARDS

SERVES 6

450 ml (¾ pint) semi-skimmed milk
4 large mint sprigs
1 whole egg
2 egg yolks
45 ml (3 tbsp) raw cane sugar
20 ml (4 tsp) gelatine
700 g (1½ lb) strawberries
15 ml (1 tbsp) icing sugar
a few strawberries, to decorate

/ 1 / Place the milk and mint sprigs in a saucepan. Bring slowly to the boil, then remove from the heat, cover and leave to infuse for about 30 minutes. Strain.

/ 2 / Whisk the whole egg and the yolks with the sugar and strain into the milk. Return to the pan and cook gently, stirring, until the custard just coats the back of the spoon. Do *not* boil. Leave to cool.

/ 3 / Sprinkle the gelatine over 45 ml (3 tbsp) cold water in a heatproof bowl and leave to soften for 1 minute. Place over a saucepan of gently simmering water and stir until the gelatine has dissolved. Cool slightly, then stir into the custard.

/ 4 / Purée the strawberries in a blender or food processor, then press through a sieve. Whisk about two-thirds of the puréed strawberries into the cold, but not set, custard.

/ 5 / Oil six 150 ml (¼ pint) ramekin dishes. Pour in the custard and chill for about 3 hours or until set.

/ 6 / Meanwhile, whisk the icing sugar into the remaining strawberry purée and chill.

/ 7 / To serve, turn out the custards and surround with the strawberry sauce. Decorate with strawberries.

RASPBERRY BOMBE

SERVES 4

225 g (8 oz) raspberries, thawed if frozen
25 ml (1½ tbsp) raw cane sugar
10 ml (2 tsp) Crème de Cassis (blackcurrant liqueur)
225 g (8 oz) natural low-fat set yogurt
1 egg white, size 2

/ 1 / Put 175 g (6 oz) raspberries in a blender or food processor with half the sugar and the liqueur and blend to a purée. Pour into a freezerproof bowl and fold in the yogurt. Freeze for 1 hour or until ice crystals begin to form around the edge.

/ 2 / Whisk the egg white until stiff, then whisk in the remaining sugar. Remove the raspberry purée from the freezer and fold in the egg white. Pour into a 900 ml (1½ pint) decorative freezerproof mould and freeze for at least 6 hours or until frozen. Stir at least once during this time.

/ 3 / To serve, turn the bombe out of the bowl on to a serving plate and decorate with the remaining raspberries. Cut into slices.

DATE AND FIG PUDDING
This deliciously gingered pudding provides a whole selection of nutrients as well as plenty of fibre.

RASPBERRY BOMBE
This stunning dessert proves that healthy desserts are not dull and dreary.

Put the dried fruit in a saucepan, then strain in the tea and spice liquid. Add the wine and sugar and heat gently until the sugar has dissolved.

SPICED FRUIT COMPOTE

SERVES 4

15 ml (1 tbsp) jasmine tea
2.5 ml (½ tsp) ground cinnamon
1.25 ml (¼ tsp) ground cloves
300 ml (½ pint) boiling water
100 g (4 oz) dried apricots, soaked overnight, drained
100 g (4 oz) dried prunes, soaked overnight, drained and stoned
100 g (4 oz) dried apple rings
150 ml (¼ pint) dry white wine
50 g (2 oz) raw cane sugar
toasted flaked almonds, to decorate

/ 1 / Put the tea, cinnamon and cloves in a bowl and pour in the boiling water. Leave for 20 minutes.

/ 2 / Put the dried fruit in a saucepan, then strain in the tea and spice liquid. Add the wine and sugar and heat gently until the sugar has completely dissolved.

/ 3 / Simmer for 20 minutes until the fruit is tender, then cover and leave in a cool place for 1-2 hours until cold.

/ 4 / Turn the compote into a serving bowl and chill for at least 2 hours. Sprinkle with almonds just before serving.

Spiced Fruit Compote

Crunchy Pears in Cinnamon and Honey Wine

CRUNCHY PEARS IN CINNAMON AND HONEY WINE

SERVES 4 - 6

60 ml (4 tbsp) white wine, vermouth or sherry
60 ml (4 tbsp) clear honey
5 ml (1 tsp) ground cinnamon
50 g (2 oz) butter or margarine
100 g (4 oz) wholemeal breadcrumbs (made from a day-old loaf)
50 g (2 oz) raw cane demerara sugar
4 ripe dessert pears

/ 1 / In a jug, mix together the wine, vermouth or sherry, honey and half of the cinnamon. Set aside while preparing the topping and pears.

/ 2 / Melt the butter or margarine in a small saucepan, add the breadcrumbs, sugar and remaining cinnamon and stir together until evenly mixed. Set aside.

/ 3 / Peel and halve the pears. Remove the cores. Arrange the pear halves, cut side down, in a greased ovenproof dish and pour over the white wine mixture.

/ 4 / Sprinkle the pears evenly with the breadcrumb mixture and bake in the oven at 190°C (375°F) mark 5 for 40 minutes. Serve hot.

For this recipe you can use Comice dessert pears, but be careful that they are not too ripe – Comice pears very quickly become overripe and bruised and cannot be stored for any length of time. Buy them on the day you intend to cook them and check they are perfect and only just ripe before purchase. Conference pears are a dual-purpose pear; they are ideal for cooking and eating, so these too can be used for this recipe.

A luscious dessert for a special occasion, Lemon Muesli Cheesecake is made with healthier ingredients than other cheesecakes.

If you are buying muesli specially to make the base for this cheesecake, select a sugar-free variety, or at least one that is low in sugar. Health food shops sell muesli loose by the kg (lb), and most stock a sugar-free one. Recipes for muesli vary considerably from one brand to another and most health food shops mix their own, but the majority of muesli mixtures contain rolled oats, barley or wholewheat flakes and some dried fruit such as sultanas or raisins. You can, of course, make up your own muesli to suit yourself. The addition of chopped hazelnuts gives extra nutritional value, and would be especially good in the base of this cheesecake.

LEMON MUESLI CHEESECAKE

SERVES 6

175 g (6 oz) muesli
75 g (3 oz) butter or margarine, melted
3 lemons
15 ml (1 tbsp) gelatine
225 (8 oz) low-fat soft cheese
150 ml (¼ pint) natural low-fat yogurt
60 ml (4 tbsp) clear honey
2 egg whites

/ 1 / Mix the muesli and melted butter or margarine together. With the back of a metal spoon, press the mixture over the base of a greased 20.5 cm (8 inch) springform cake tin. Chill in the refrigerator to set while making the filling.

/ 2 / Finely grate the rind of 2 of the lemons. Set aside. Squeeze the juice from the 2 lemons and make up to 150 ml (¼ pint) with water. Pour into a heatproof bowl.

/ 3 / Sprinkle the gelatine over the lemon juice and leave to stand for 5 minutes until spongy. Stand the bowl in a saucepan of hot water and heat gently, stirring occasionally, until dissolved. Remove the bowl from the water and set aside to cool slightly.

/ 4 / Whisk the cheese, yogurt and honey together in a separate bowl. Stir in the grated lemon rind and cooled gelatine until they are both evenly incorporated.

/ 5 / Whisk the egg whites until stiff. Fold into the cheesecake mixture until evenly incorporated. Spoon the mixture into the springform tin and level the surface. Chill in the refrigerator for at least 4 hours until set.

/ 6 / Coarsely grate the rind from the remaining lemon over the centre of the cheesecake, to decorate. Alternatively, slice the lemon thinly and arrange on top of the cheesecake.

/ 7 / To serve, remove the cheesecake from the tin and place on a serving plate. Serve chilled.

STRAWBERRY CREAM

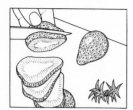

Hull the strawberries and slice finely, reserving 6 whole ones to decorate.

Strawberry Cream is rich and creamy in flavour yet surprisingly low in calories. Serve it as a special summertime dessert.

STRAWBERRY CREAM

SERVES 6

| 100 g (4 oz) cottage cheese |
| 150 ml (¼ pint) natural low-fat yogurt |
| clear honey, to taste |
| 700 g (1½ lb) fresh strawberries |
| wholemeal shortbread biscuits, to serve (optional) |

/ 1 / Purée the cottage cheese in a blender or food processor until smooth. Alternatively, work it through a fine wire sieve.

/ 2 / In a bowl, beat the cheese and yogurt together with honey to taste. Set aside.

/ 3 / Hull the strawberries, reserve 6 whole ones to decorate, and thinly slice the remainder with a sharp knife.

/ 4 / Divide the sliced strawberries equally between 6 individual glass dishes.

/ 5 / Pour the cheese mixture over the strawberries and chill in the refrigerator for about 1 hour. Serve chilled, decorated with the reserved whole strawberries. Accompany with wholemeal shortbread biscuits, if liked.

APPLE AND LEMON SORBET

The eating apples and no-soak dried apricots eliminate the need for added sugar in this dessert.

APPLE AND LEMON SORBET

SERVES 4

| 3 red eating apples, peeled, cored and sliced |
| 75 g (3 oz) no-soak dried apricots, rinsed and chopped |
| grated rind and juice of ½ lemon |
| 300 ml (½ pint) unsweetened apple juice |
| 2 egg whites |

/ 1 / Place the apples in a blender or food processor with the apricots, lemon rind and juice and apple juice and purée until smooth.

/ 2 / Pour into a shallow freezer bowl and freeze for 45-60 minutes or until ice crystals begin to form around the edge.

/ 3 / Tip the semi-set sorbet into a bowl and beat until smooth. Whisk the egg whites until stiff but not dry, then fold into the sorbet. Return to the container and freeze for 3-4 hours.

Picture opposite:
Strawberry Cream

Fruit and Nut Crumble

FRUIT AND NUT CRUMBLE

SERVES 4

100 g (4 oz) plain wholemeal flour
pinch of salt
50 g (2 oz) butter or margarine, cut into pieces
100 g (4 oz) raw cane demerara sugar
25 g (1 oz) walnuts, finely chopped
3 cooking pears
1 large cooking apple
30 ml (2 tbsp) redcurrant jelly
finely grated rind and juice of 1 lemon

/ 1 / Mix the flour and salt in a bowl. Add the butter or margarine and rub in until the mixture resembles fine breadcrumbs. Stir in half of the sugar and the walnuts. Set aside.

/ 2 / Peel and quarter the pears and apple. Remove the cores, then slice the flesh thinly.

/ 3 / In a bowl, mix the redcurrant jelly and the lemon rind and juice with the remaining sugar. Add the sliced fruit and fold gently to mix.

/ 4 / Turn the fruit into an ovenproof dish and sprinkle the crumble mixture over the top.

/ 5 / Bake in the oven at 180°C (350°F) mark 4 for 40 minutes or until the fruit feels soft when pierced with a skewer and the crumble topping is crisp and golden. Serve hot.

FRUIT JELLY

SERVES 4

225 g (8 oz) no-soak prunes
thinly pared rind of 1 orange
150 ml (¼ pint) unsweetened orange juice
15 g (½ oz) gelatine
3 large oranges, peeled and segmented

/ 1 / Put the prunes, orange rind and 450 ml (¾ pint) water in a saucepan. Cook gently for 10-15 minutes or until the prunes are tender. Drain, reserving the cooking liquid, and discard the rind. Halve the prunes and remove the stones.

/ 2 / Add the orange juice and enough cold water to the prune cooking liquid to make it up to 600 ml (1 pint).

/ 3 / Sprinkle the gelatine over 45 ml (3 tbsp) cold water in a heatproof bowl and leave to soften for 1 minute. Place over a saucepan of gently simmering water and stir until the gelatine has dissolved. Leave to cool, then mix into the fruit juices.

/ 4 / Place a 1.1 litre (2 pint) jelly mould or dish in a large mixing bowl containing ice cubes. Pour a little of the jelly mixture into the mould to a depth of 2.5 cm (1 inch) and allow to set.

/ 5 / Arrange either a layer of halved prunes or orange segments on top of the jelly. Cover with a little jelly and allow to set. Add more jelly, then more fruit, allowing each layer to set before starting the next. Continue until all the jelly and fruit have been used. Chill for 3 hours or until set.

EXOTIC FRUIT SALAD

SERVES 10

1 medium pineapple
1 mango
1 papaya (optional)
3 nectarines
100 g (4 oz) black or green grapes
1 ogen melon, halved and seeded
juice of 3 large oranges
juice of 1 lemon
45 ml (3 tbsp) orange liqueur
fresh mint sprigs, to decorate

/ 1 / Cut the pineapple into 1 cm (½ inch) slices. Remove the skin and cut the flesh into cubes. Place in a serving dish.

/ 2 / Cut a chunk off each side of the mango lengthways to expose the stone. Ease off the flesh. Remove the outer skin and slice the flesh thinly. Add to dish. Repeat with papaya.

/ 3 / Wash the nectarines and slice the flesh away from the stone. Add to the dish with the halved and seeded grapes.

/ 4 / With a melon baller, scoop out the melon flesh into the dish. Scrape out the remaining flesh, chop and add to dish. Mix together the fruit juices and liqueur. Pour over the fruit and chill 2-3 hours. Decorate with mint.

FRUIT AND NUT CRUMBLE

This nutty pear and apple crumble is a filling family pudding. Serve it with natural low-fat yogurt.

EXOTIC FRUIT SALAD

Cut the pineapple into 1 cm (½ inch) slices. Remove the skin and cut the flesh into cubes.

Cut a chunk off each side of the mango lengthways to expose the stone. Ease off the flesh. Remove the outer skin and slice the flesh thinly.

SWEET INDIAN SAFFRON RICE

SERVES 4 - 6

10-12 large strands of saffron
600 ml (1 pint) cold water, plus 30 ml (2 tbsp) boiling water
225 g (8 oz) basmati rice
75 g (3 oz) sugar
pinch of freshly grated nutmeg
30 ml (2 tbsp) ghee or polyunsaturated oil
seeds from 6 green cardamom pods, crushed
4 cloves
2.5 cm (1 inch) stick of cinnamon
100 g (4 oz) blanched almonds, sliced or chopped
50 g (2 oz) unsalted pistachio nuts, sliced or chopped
25 g (1 oz) raisins
15 ml (1 tbsp) lemon juice

/ 1 / Let the saffron infuse in the 30 ml (2 tbsp) boiling water for 30 minutes. Put the rice in a sieve and then wash thoroughly under a running cold tap until the water runs clear; soak it in cold water for 15 minutes.

/ 2 / Drain the rice and place in a heavy-based saucepan with 300 ml (½ pint) water. Strain in the saffron water. Bring to the boil, stir once, then cover with a tight-fitting lid. Reduce heat and cook for 12-15 minutes until the water is absorbed and the rice is parboiled.

/ 3 / In a separate pan, dissolve the sugar in the remaining water. Add the nutmeg and bring to the boil. Continue boiling for 2-3 minutes, then remove from the heat.

/ 4 / Heat the ghee or oil in a large heavy-based pan, add the crushed cardamom seeds, cloves and the cinnamon. Stirring all the time, fry these for 2-3 minutes. Stand well back, in case of spattering, and pour in the syrup. Bring to the boil, then reduce heat to low.

/ 5 / Add the parboiled rice, with the sliced or chopped almonds, pistachio nuts, raisins and the lemon juice. Stir just once, cover with a tight-fitting lid and cook for a further 10 minutes until the syrup is completely absorbed. The rice should be light and fluffy and a delicate yellow colour.

Put the rice in a sieve and wash thoroughly under a running cold tap until the water runs clear, then soak it in cold water for 15 minutes.

Although ordinary long-grain rice can be used to make this Indian dessert, basmati rice will give the dish authenticity. Basmati rice comes from the foothills of the Himalayas; it is expensive, but well worth using for all Indian dishes – sweet and savoury.

Strawberries with Raspberry Sauce

STRAWBERRIES WITH RASPBERRY SAUCE

SERVES 6

900 g (2 lb) small strawberries
450 g (1 lb) raspberries
50 g (2 oz) icing sugar

/ 1 / Hull the strawberries and place them in individual serving dishes.

/ 2 / Purée the raspberries in a blender or food processor until just smooth, then work through a nylon sieve into a bowl to remove the pips.

/ 3 / Sift the icing sugar over the bowl of raspberry purée, then whisk in until evenly incorporated. Pour over the strawberries. Chill in the refrigerator for 30 minutes before serving.

CAROB AND BANANA CHEESECAKE

SERVES 6

175 g (6 oz) muesli
75 g (3 oz) butter or margarine, melted
10 ml (2 tsp) lemon juice
15 ml (1 tbsp) gelatine
225 g (8 oz) low-fat soft cheese
150 ml (¼ pint) natural low-fat yogurt
30 ml (2 tbsp) carob powder
1 large ripe banana
15 ml (1 tbsp) clear honey
1 egg white
grated plain carob, to decorate

/ 1 / Mix the muesli and melted butter or margarine together. Press the mixture into the base of a greased 20.5 cm (8 inch) springform cake tin. Chill while making the filling.

/ 2 / Put the lemon juice and 150 ml (¼ pint) water in a small heatproof bowl. Sprinkle the gelatine over the top and leave to stand for 5 minutes until spongy. Stand the bowl in a saucepan of hot water and heat gently, stirring occasionally, until dissolved. Remove the bowl from the water and cool slightly.

/ 3 / Whisk together the cheese, yogurt and carob powder. Mash the banana and stir into the cheese mixture with the honey. Stir in the cooled gelatine mixture until evenly incorporated into the cheese and banana.

/ 4 / Whisk the egg white until stiff and fold into the cheese mixture. Spoon into the tin and level the surface. Chill in the refrigerator for at least 4 hours until set. To serve, remove from the tin and place on a serving plate. Sprinkle with grated carob.

GINGER FRUIT SALAD

SERVES 4

2 apricots
2 eating apples
1 orange
241 ml (8½ fl oz) bottle low-calorie ginger ale
50 g (2 oz) green grapes
2 bananas
30 ml (2 tbsp) lemon juice
natural low-fat yogurt, to serve (optional)

/ 1 / Plunge the apricots into a bowl of boiling water for 30 seconds. Drain and peel off the skin with your fingers.

/ 2 / Halve the apricots, remove the stones and dice the flesh. Core and dice the apples, but do not peel them. Peel the orange and divide into segments, discarding all white pith.

/ 3 / Put the prepared fruits in a serving bowl with the ginger ale. Stir lightly, then cover and leave to macerate for 1 hour.

/ 4 / Cut the grapes in half, then remove the seeds by flicking them out with the point of a sharp knife.

/ 5 / Peel and slice the bananas and mix them with the lemon juice to prevent discoloration.

/ 6 / Add the grapes and bananas to the macerated fruits. Serve in individual glasses topped with yogurt, if liked.

STRAWBERRIES WITH RASPBERRY SAUCE

Freshly picked raspberries freeze successfully (unlike strawberries which tend to lose texture and shape due to their high water content). If you have raspberries which are slightly overripe or misshapen, the best way to freeze them is as a purée; this takes up less space in the freezer and is immensely useful for making quick desserts and sauces. For this recipe, you can freeze the purée up to 12 months in advance, then it will only take a few minutes to put the dessert together after the purée has thawed. The purée can be frozen with or without the icing sugar.

CAROB AND BANANA CHEESECAKE

Carob powder is produced from the carob bean (also known as the locust bean) and is naturally sweet. It contains vitamins A and D, some B vitamins and minerals such as calcium and magnesium. It also includes protein and a small amount of fibre. Carob powder contains less fat and sodium than cocoa, fewer calories and no caffeine. Because of its sweet flavour, you need less sugar or other sweetener.

GINGER FRUIT SALAD

If you wish to make this salad in wintertime you can use dried apricots instead of fresh ones. Take a good look at the wide choice of dried apricots at your local health food shop. The kind sold in packets in supermarkets are invariably bright orange in colour, which means that they may not be naturally dried – their colour may come from edible dye, so check the ingredients on the label before buying. Dried apricots sold loose in health food shops are a much better buy, especially the *hunza* variety, which are sun-dried.

KIWI FRUIT SORBET

Halve the kiwi fruit and peel thinly or pull away the skins without damaging the flesh.

KIWI FRUIT SORBET

SERVES 6

50 g (2 oz) sugar
150 ml (¼ pint) water
6 kiwi fruit
2 egg whites
slices of kiwi fruit, to decorate
orange-flavoured liqueur and wafers, to serve

/ 1 / Place the sugar in a saucepan with the water. Heat gently until dissolved, then simmer for 2 minutes. Cool for 30 minutes.

/ 2 / Halve the kiwi fruit and peel thinly or pull away the skins without damaging the flesh.

/ 3 / Place the fruit in a blender or food processor with the cool syrup. Work to a smooth purée, then pass through a nylon sieve to remove the pips. Pour into a chilled shallow freezer container. Freeze for 2 hours.

/ 4 / Beat the mixture with a fork to break down any ice crystals. Whisk the egg whites until stiff, then fold through the fruit mixture until evenly blended. Freeze for 4 hours.

/ 5 / Scoop into individual glass dishes, decorate with slices of kiwi fruit and spoon over some liqueur. Serve with wafers.

FLAMBÉ BANANAS

SERVES 4

25 g (1 oz) butter or margarine
grated rind and juice of 1 large orange
2.5 ml (½ tsp) ground cinnamon
4 large bananas, peeled
50 g (2 oz) raw cane demerara sugar
60 ml (4 tbsp) dark rum
orange shreds and slices, to decorate

/ 1 / Melt the butter or margarine in a frying pan and add the orange rind and juice. Stir in the cinnamon, then add the bananas and cook for a few minutes, until softened.

/ 2 / Add the sugar and stir until dissolved. Add the rum, set alight and stir gently to mix. Decorate with orange shreds and slices.

Kiwi Fruit Sorbet

The wholemeal flour and
fresh fruit in this tart
contribute different forms
of dietary fibre – insoluble
cereal fibre and soluble
pectin found in fruit.

BAKED APPLE COCONUT PUDDING

SERVES 6

100 g (4 oz) raw cane sugar

100 g (4 oz) margarine

finely grated rind of 1 lemon

2 eggs, separated

100 g (4 oz) plain wholemeal flour

7.5 ml (1½ tsp) baking powder

25 g (1 oz) desiccated coconut

6 medium eating apples, each weighing about 100 g (4 oz)

60 ml (4 tbsp) lemon juice

60 ml (4 tbsp) reduced-sugar apricot jam

toasted shredded coconut, to decorate

/ 1 / Beat together the sugar and the margarine until well blended. Add the lemon rind, then beat in the egg yolks one at a time. Fold in the flour, baking powder and desiccated coconut.

/ 2 / Peel and core the apples, keeping them whole, and brush them with 45 ml (3 tbsp) of the lemon juice.

/ 3 / Whisk the egg whites until stiff but not dry and fold into the creamed ingredients. Spoon into a lightly greased 24-25.5 cm (9½-10 inch) fluted flan dish. Press the apples into the mixture, spooning a little of the remaining lemon juice over them.

/ 4 / Stand the dish on a baking sheet and bake at 170°C (325°F) mark 3 for 1-1¼ hours or until well browned and firm to the touch, covering lightly if necessary. Leave to cool in the dish for about 15 minutes.

/ 5 / Put the jam and remaining lemon juice in a small saucepan and heat gently, stirring, until the jam softens. Bring to the boil and simmer for 1 minute. Brush the dessert with the apricot glaze and scatter over the shredded coconut. Serve warm.

GOOSEBERRY AND PLUM TART

MAKES 8 SLICES

100 g (4 oz) plain wholemeal flour

2.5 ml (½ tsp) cream of tartar

1.25 ml (¼ tsp) bicarbonate of soda

50 g (2 oz) margarine

45 ml (3 tbsp) raw cane sugar

1 egg yolk

15 ml (1 tbsp) semi-skimmed milk

700 g (1½ lb) ripe plums, halved, stoned and quartered

175 g (6 oz) ripe gooseberries, topped and tailed

30 ml (2 tbsp) ginger wine

5 ml (1 tsp) gelatine

/ 1 / Lightly grease a 23 cm (9 inch) fluted loose-based flan tin or ring and set aside. Sift the flour, cream of tartar and bicarbonate of soda into a bowl.

/ 2 / Add the margarine and rub in lightly, then stir in 15 ml (1 tbsp) of the sugar. Add the egg yolk and milk and mix to a smooth dough. Press the dough into the prepared tin, shaping it up the sides to form a rim. Chill in the refrigerator for 30 minutes.

/ 3 / Arrange the plum quarters, skin side up, in the flan case. Sprinkle with 15 ml (1 tbsp) sugar. Bake at 190°C (375°F) mark 5 for 30 minutes. Leave to cool.

/ 4 / Meanwhile, put the gooseberries, wine and remaining sugar in a saucepan with 45 ml (3 tbsp) water. Simmer for 5 minutes, then cool and sieve.

/ 5 / Sprinkle the gelatine over 30 ml (2 tbsp) cold water and leave to soften for 1 minute. Place over a saucepan of gently simmering water and stir until the gelatine has dissolved. Cool slightly, then stir into the gooseberry mixture. Spoon the gooseberry glaze evenly over the plums and leave to chill for about 2 hours before serving.

RUM AND COFFEE JUNKET

SERVES 4

586 ml (1 pint) plus 60 ml (4 tbsp) milk – not UHT, long-life or sterilized
30 ml (2 tbsp) caster sugar
10 ml (2 tsp) essence of rennet
10 ml (2 tsp) rum
150 ml (¼ pint) soured cream
10 ml (2 tsp) coffee and chicory essence
plain and white chocolate, to decorate

/ 1 / Put the 586 ml (1 pint) milk in a saucepan and heat until just warm to the finger.

/ 2 / Add the sugar, rennet and rum and stir until the sugar has dissolved.

/ 3 / Pour the mixture at once into 4 individual dishes or a 900 ml (1½ pint) shallow, edged serving dish. Put in a warm place, undisturbed, for 4 hours to set.

/ 4 / Lightly whisk the soured cream. Gradually add the 60 ml (4 tbsp) milk and the coffee essence, whisking until smooth.

/ 5 / Carefully flood the top of the junket with the coffee cream, taking care not to disturb the junket. Decorate with pared or coarsely grated chocolate. Refrigerate for 1 hour.

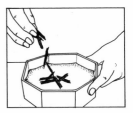

Carefully flood the top of the junket with the coffee cream, taking care not to disturb the junket. Decorate with pared or coarsely grated chocolate.

Rum and Coffee Junket

PINEAPPLE AND BANANA FLAMBÉ

SERVES 6 - 8

1 medium pineapple
900 g (2 lb) firm bananas
100 g (4 oz) dried figs
50 g (2 oz) butter or margarine
100 (4 oz) raw cane demerara sugar
45 ml (3 tbsp) lemon juice
2.5 ml (½ tsp) ground mixed spice
60 ml (4 tbsp) dark rum

/ 1 / Slice the pineapple into 1 cm (½ inch) pieces. Snip off the skin and cut the flesh into chunks, discarding the core.

/ 2 / Peel and thickly slice the bananas into the bottom of a shallow ovenproof dish; spoon the pineapple on top.

/ 3 / Cut the figs into coarse shreds and scatter over the fruit. Put the butter or margarine, sugar, strained lemon juice and spice together in a saucepan and heat until well blended, then pour the mixture over the prepared fruit.

/ 4 / Cover tightly and bake in the oven at 200°C (400°F) mark 6 for 25 minutes.

/ 5 / Heat the rum gently in a small saucepan, remove from the heat and ignite with a match. Pour immediately over the fruit and bring the dish to the table while still flaming.

Pineapple and Banana Flambé

SUMMER FRUIT SALAD

SERVES 4 - 6

100 g (4 oz) sugar
a few fresh mint sprigs
1 strip of orange peel
225 g (8 oz) fresh strawberries
225 g (8 oz) fresh raspberries
1 small Ogen melon
30 ml (2 tbsp) orange-flavoured liqueur
30 ml (2 tbsp) finely chopped fresh mint
a few whole fresh mint leaves, to decorate

/ 1 / Put the sugar in a heavy-based pan, add 200 ml (7 fl oz) water and heat gently for 5-10 minutes until the sugar has dissolved, stirring occasionally with a wooden spoon.

/ 2 / Add the mint sprigs and orange peel, then boil the syrup rapidly for 5 minutes, without stirring. Remove from the heat and leave for about 1 hour until completely cold.

/ 3 / Meanwhile, prepare the fruit. Hull the strawberries, then slice them lengthways.

/ 4 / Leave the raspberries whole. Cut the melon in half, then scoop out and discard the seeds.

/ 5 / Cut the flesh into balls using a melon baller. Remove the mint sprigs and orange peel from the cold syrup, then stir in the liqueur and chopped mint.

/ 6 / Put the fruit in a serving bowl, pour over the syrup, then carefully fold together. Chill in the refrigerator for at least 30 minutes. Serve the salad chilled, decorated with a few whole fresh mint leaves.

WALNUT PEAR SLICE

SERVES 4

50 g (2 oz) plain white flour
50 g (2 oz) plain wholemeal flour
2.5 ml (½ tsp) ground cinnamon
25 g (1 oz) ground walnuts
finely grated rind and juice of ½ lemon
1 egg
50 g (2 oz) raw cane sugar
50 g (2 oz) margarine
45 ml (3 tbsp) fresh wholemeal breadcrumbs
3 ripe dessert pears
natural low-fat yogurt, to serve

/ 1 / Sift the flours with the cinnamon on to a clean dry work surface, adding any bran remaining in the sieve. Sprinkle the walnuts and lemon rind over the flour.

/ 2 / Make a well in the centre and break in the egg. Add the sugar and margarine. With the fingertips of one hand only, pinch the ingredients from the well together until evenly blended. Draw in the flour gradually, with the help of a palette knife, and knead to a smooth dough. Wrap and chill for about 30 minutes.

/ 3 / Roll out the pastry on a lightly floured surface to an oblong about 30.5×10 cm (12×4 inches). Lift the pastry on to a baking sheet and sprinkle over the breadcrumbs.

/ 4 / Peel, quarter and core the pears. Slice each quarter into 4 or 5 pieces and toss gently in the lemon juice. Drain and arrange in overlapping lines across the dough.

/ 5 / Bake at 190°C (375°F) mark 5 for about 30 minutes or until the pastry is well browned and crisp around the edges. Allow to cool slightly. Cut into slices and serve with yogurt.

SUMMER FRUIT SALAD

The Ogen melon specified in this fruit salad is available most of the year from specialist greengrocers and markets. The name Ogen comes from the kibbutz in Israel where these melons were first grown.

Ogen melons are well worth looking for, because their flesh is very sweet – perfect for summer fruit salads, and also for winter desserts when other fresh fruits are scarce. Ogen melons are easily identified by their yellowy green, stripy skins and their almost perfectly round shape.

Ogen melons are ideal for making into melon baskets – a pretty way to serve a fruit salad. If you buy small Ogens, make individual baskets for each place setting; large Ogens make spectacular table centre-pieces.

TO MAKE A MELON BASKET

Level the base of the melon so that it will stand upright. With the tip of a knife score round the centre of the melon, keeping the line as straight as possible. Cut down from the top of the melon to the scored line, working about 1 cm (½ inch) to one side of the centre.

Cut through the scored line on one side so that a wedge-shaped piece of melon is removed. Repeat so that both sides are removed. Scrape away the melon flesh inside the 'handle' left in the centre. Scoop out and discard the seeds, then remove the flesh in the bottom half of the basket with a melon baller or sharp knife.

BANANA WHIPS

This quickly made dessert will appeal to children of all ages.

BANANA WHIPS

SERVES 4

2 egg whites
300 ml (½ pint) natural low-fat set yogurt
finely grated rind and juice of ½ orange
60 ml (4 tbsp) raw cane sugar
2 bananas
50 g (2 oz) crunchy breakfast cereal

/ 1 / Whisk the egg whites until standing in stiff peaks. Put the yogurt in a bowl and stir until smooth. Fold in the egg whites until evenly incorporated into the yogurt.

/ 2 / In a separate bowl, mix together the orange rind and juice and the sugar. Peel the bananas and slice thinly into the juice mixture. Fold gently to mix.

/ 3 / Put a layer of the yogurt mixture in the bottom of 4 individual glasses. Cover with a layer of cereal, then with a layer of the banana mixture. Repeat these 3 layers once more. Serve immediately.

PEARS WITH BLACKCURRANT SAUCE

This makes a particularly healthy dessert when soft summer fruits are not available. Blackcurrants are renowned for their vitamin C content, and ensuring a good vitamin C intake when you have a cold reduces the severity of the symptoms.

PEARS WITH BLACKCURRANT SAUCE

SERVES 4

4 cooking pears, peeled, but with stalks left intact
225 g (8 oz) frozen blackcurrants
50 g (2 oz) raw cane sugar

/ 1 / Place the pears, blackcurrants, sugar and 100 ml (4 fl oz) water in a saucepan and bring slowly to the boil.

/ 2 / Lower the heat, cover and simmer for about 25 minutes, turning once, until the pears are soft but not mushy. Gently remove the pears and place them on individual plates.

/ 3 / Increase the heat and boil the blackcurrants rapidly for 3-4 minutes or until the liquid has reduced slightly. Press through a fine sieve and pour a little sauce over each pear. Serve at once or chill.

Banana Whips

Baking

Many of the breads and cakes in this chapter use wholemeal flour instead of white flour. Wholemeal flour is a healthier choice as it contains more vitamins and is high in fibre. It does give a slightly denser texture to cakes and pastries so try using half white flour: half wholemeal flour until you get used to the different texture.

Wholemeal bread is not difficult to make at home and it has far more flavour than white bread. Cakes, too, can just as easily be made with wholemeal flour but they will probably need more raising agent and a little more liquid too. If you sift the flour, always tip the bran left in the sieve back into the flour.

The natural sugar in fruit and moderate amounts of honey and raw cane sugar are used to sweeten cakes and biscuits in this chapter.

A selection of brown bread loaves and rolls

Bran Flowerpots

BRAN FLOWERPOTS

MAKES 3 LOAVES

25 g (1 oz) fresh yeast or 15 ml (1 tbsp) dried yeast and a pinch of raw cane sugar
600 ml (1 pint) tepid water
700 g (1½ lb) plain wholemeal flour
7.5 ml (1½ tsp) salt
40 g (1½ oz) bran
milk or water, to glaze
cracked wheat, to finish

/ 1 / Choose 3 clean, new clay 10-12.5 cm (4-5 inch) flowerpots (see right).

/ 2 / Blend the fresh yeast with the water. If using dried yeast, sprinkle it into the water with the sugar and leave in a warm place for about 15 minutes until frothy.

/ 3 / Mix the flour and salt in a bowl. Stir in the bran. Make a well in the centre.

/ 4 / Pour in the yeast liquid and mix to a soft dough that leaves the bowl clean. Turn the dough on to a lightly floured surface and knead thoroughly for about 10 minutes until smooth and elastic.

/ 5 / Return the dough to the bowl, cover with a clean tea-towel and leave to rise in a warm place for about 45 minutes or until the dough has doubled in size.

/ 6 / Turn the dough on to a floured surface again and knead for 10 minutes.

/ 7 / Divide and shape into the 3 greased flowerpots. Cover with a clean cloth and leave to prove for 30-45 minutes until the dough has risen to the top of the flowerpots.

/ 8 / Brush the tops lightly with milk or water and sprinkle with cracked wheat. Bake in the oven at 230°C (450°F) mark 8 for 15 minutes, then reduce the oven temperature to 200°C (400°F) mark 6 and bake for a further 30-40 minutes until well risen and firm. Turn out of the flowerpots and leave to cool on a wire rack for about 1 hour.

QUICK WHOLEMEAL BREAD

MAKES 2 LOAVES

15 g (½ oz) fresh yeast or 7.5 ml (1½ tsp) dried yeast and a pinch of raw cane sugar
300 ml (½ pint) tepid water
450 g (1 lb) strong wholemeal flour or 225 g (8 oz) strong wholemeal flour and 225 g (8 oz) strong white flour
5 ml (1 tsp) raw cane sugar
5 ml (1 tsp) salt
25 g (1 oz) butter or margarine, cut into pieces

/ 1 / Grease 2 baking sheets. Blend the fresh yeast with the water. If using dried yeast, sprinkle it into the water with the pinch of sugar and leave in a warm place for 15 minutes until frothy. Mix together the flour, sugar and salt, then rub in the butter or margarine until the mixture resembles breadcrumbs. Add the yeast liquid and mix to give a fairly soft dough, adding a little more water if necessary.

/ 2 / Turn on to a floured surface and knead for about 10 minutes until the dough feels firm and elastic and no longer sticky. Divide into 2, shape the dough into rounds and place on the 2 baking sheets.

/ 3 / Cover with a clean tea-towel and leave until the dough has doubled in size. Bake in the oven at 230°C (450°F) make 8 for about 15 minutes, then reduce the oven temperature to 200°C (400°F) mark 6 and bake for a further 20-30 minutes. Cool on a wire rack.

VARIATION

To make wholemeal bread rolls, divide it into about 12 pieces and roll each into a ball. Place on greased baking sheets and cover with a clean tea-towel. Leave to rise until doubled in size. Bake in the oven at 230°C (450°F) mark 8 for 15-20 minutes until risen and firm. Cool on a wire rack.

BRAN FLOWERPOTS

Divide the dough and shape into the 3 greased flowerpots. Cover with a clean cloth and leave to prove for 30-40 minutes until the dough has risen to the top of the flowerpots.

Brush the tops lightly with milk or water and sprinkle with cracked wheat.

Before using clay flowerpots for the first time, grease them well and bake in a hot oven for about 30 minutes. This stops the flowerpots cracking and the loaves sticking. Leave to cool, then grease again.

Bran Flowerpots, with their attractive shape, will appeal particularly to children. Spread lightly buttered slices with a low-sugar jam or a savoury spread such as peanut butter.

POPPY SEED GRANARY ROUND

Using a sharp knife, divide the dough into 8 equal pieces and shape into neat, even-sized rolls with your hands.

Arrange in the tin, cover with a clean cloth and leave to prove in a warm place for about 30 minutes until doubled in size.

Picture opposite:
Poppy Seed Granary Round
(top); Herby Cheese Loaf
(bottom)

GRANARY BREAD

MAKES 2 LOAVES

900 g (2 lb) granary flour
12.5 ml (2½ tsp) salt
25 g (1 oz) butter or margarine, cut into pieces
25 g (1 oz) fresh yeast or 15 ml (1 tbsp) dried yeast and a pinch of raw cane sugar
15 ml (1 tbsp) malt extract
600 ml (1 pint) tepid water

/ 1 / Grease two 450 g (1 lb) loaf tins. Mix together the flour and salt in a bowl, then rub in the butter or margarine until the mixture resembles breadcrumbs. Cream the fresh yeast with the malt extract and water and add to the flour. If using dried yeast, sprinkle it into the water with the sugar and leave in a warm place for 15 minutes, until frothy. Add to the flour mixture with the malt extract.

/ 2 / Mix to a stiff dough. Turn on to a lightly floured surface and knead for 10 minutes until the dough feels firm and elastic and not sticky. Transfer to a bowl.

/ 3 / Cover with a clean tea-towel and leave to rise in a warm place until the dough has doubled in size. Turn on to a lightly floured surface and knead for 2-3 minutes.

/ 4 / Divide the dough into 2 pieces and place in the loaf tins. Cover and leave to prove until the dough is 1 cm (½ inch) above the top of the 2 loaf tins.

/ 5 / Bake in the oven at 230°C (450°F) mark 8 for 30-35 minutes. Turn out of the tins and leave to cool on a wire rack.

POPPY SEED GRANARY ROUND

MAKES 8 ROLLS

15 g (½ oz) fresh yeast or 7.5 g (¼ oz) dried yeast and 2.5 ml (½ tsp) sugar
300 ml (½ pint) warm water
450 g (1 lb) granary bread flour
5 ml (1 tsp) salt
50 g (2 oz) butter
50 g (2 oz) low-fat Cheddar type cheese, grated
25 g (1 oz) poppy seeds

/ 1 / Grease a 20.5 cm (8 inch) sandwich tin. In a bowl, crumble the fresh yeast into the water and stir until dissolved. If using dried yeast, sprinkle it into water mixed with the sugar. Leave in a warm place for 15 minutes.

/ 2 / Put the flour and salt in a large bowl and rub in the butter until the mixture resembles breadcrumbs. Add the cheese and the poppy seeds, reserving 5 ml (1 tsp) to garnish. Stir in the yeast liquid and mix to a stiff dough.

/ 3 / Turn on to a lightly floured surface and knead for 10 minutes until smooth. Place in a bowl, cover with a cloth and leave to rise in a warm place for about 1 hour until doubled.

/ 4 / Turn on to a lightly floured surface and knead for 2-3 minutes until smooth.

/ 5 / Using a sharp knife, divide the dough into 8 equal pieces and shape into neat rolls.

/ 6 / Arrange in the tin, cover with a clean cloth and leave to prove in a warm place for about 30 minutes until doubled in size.

/ 7 / Sprinkle with the reserved poppy seeds. Bake in the oven at 200°C (400°F) mark 6 for about 25 minutes until golden and sounds hollow when bottom of the bread is tapped.

HERBY CHEESE LOAF

MAKES 1 LOAF

225 g (8 oz) self-raising flour
7.5 ml (1½ tsp) salt
5 ml (1 tsp) mustard powder
5 ml (1 tsp) snipped fresh chives
15 ml (1 tbsp) chopped fresh parsley
75 g (3 oz) low-fat Cheddar type cheese, grated
1 egg, beaten
25 g (1 oz) butter or block margarine, melted

/ 1 / Grease a 450 g (1 lb) loaf tin. Sift the flour, salt and mustard into a bowl and stir in the herbs and cheese. Add the egg, 150 ml (¼ pint) water and melted butter or margarine.

/ 2 / Spoon into the loaf tin and bake in the oven at 190°C (375°F) mark 5 for about 45 minutes. Turn out and cool on a wire rack for about 1 hour. Serve sliced while warm.

ZIGZAG BATON

With a pair of sharp scissors held at a 30° angle, make V-shaped cuts about three-quarters of the way through the dough at 5 cm (2 inch) intervals.

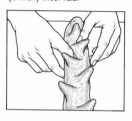

Pull each section of dough out to alternate sides to give a 'zigzag' appearance.

Serve this unusual shaped loaf just as you would ordinary bread. Made with half wholemeal and half white flour, it has an interesting texture and flavour.

Picture opposite:
Zigzag Baton

WHOLEMEAL BREAD

MAKES 2 LARGE OR 4 SMALL LOAVES

40 g (1½ oz) fresh yeast or 22.5 ml (4½ tsp) dried yeast and 5 ml (1 tsp) raw cane sugar
900 ml (1½ pints) tepid water
1.4 kg (3 lb) strong wholemeal flour
30 ml (2 tbsp) raw cane sugar
20 ml (4 tsp) salt
25 g (1 oz) butter or margarine, cut into pieces
cracked wheat, to finish

/ 1 / Grease two 900 g (2 lb) or four 450 g (1 lb) loaf tins. Blend the fresh yeast with 300 ml (½ pint) of the water. If using dried yeast, sprinkle it into the water with the 5 ml (1 tsp) sugar and leave in a warm place for 15 minutes until the mixture is frothy.

/ 2 / Mix the flour, sugar and salt together in a large bowl. Rub in the butter or margarine until the mixture resembles breadcrumbs. Stir in the yeast liquid, adding enough of the remaining water to make a firm dough that leaves the bowl clean.

/ 3 / Turn out on to a lightly floured surface and knead the dough until firm, elastic and no longer sticky. Shape into a ball, cover with a clean tea-towel and leave to rise in a warm place for about 1 hour until the dough has doubled in size.

/ 4 / Turn the dough on to a floured surface and knead again until firm. Divide into 2 or 4 pieces and flatten firmly with the knuckles to knock out any air bubbles. Knead well until the dough is firm.

/ 5 / Shape the dough into the tins. Brush with salted water and sprinkle with cracked wheat. Cover with a cloth and leave to prove for 1 hour at room temperature until the dough rises to the tops of the tins.

/ 6 / Bake in the oven at 230°C (450°F) mark 8 for 30-40 minutes for the large loaves, 20-25 minutes for the small, until well risen and firm. Turn out and cool on a wire rack.

ZIGZAG BATON

MAKES 1 LOAF

about 300 ml (½ pint) milk and water, mixed
5 ml (1 tsp) sugar
7.5 ml (1½ tsp) dried yeast
225 g (8 oz) plain wholemeal flour
225 g (8 oz) strong plain white flour
10 ml (2 tsp) salt
25 g (1 oz) butter
beaten egg, to glaze
poppy seeds, to decorate

/ 1 / Warm milk mixture to lukewarm. Pour half into a bowl; stir in sugar until dissolved.

/ 2 / Sprinkle in the yeast, whisk with a fork, then leave to stand in a warm place for 10-15 minutes until frothy.

/ 3 / Mix the flours and salt in a warmed large bowl. Rub in the butter with the fingertips.

/ 4 / Make a well in the centre, add the yeast and the remaining milk and water and mix with a wooden spoon. If too dry, add a little more lukewarm water.

/ 5 / Turn the dough on to a floured surface and knead for 10 minutes until smooth and elastic. Place in a lightly oiled polythene bag and leave to rise in the refrigerator for 24 hours.

/ 6 / Remove the risen dough from the refrigerator and allow to come to room temperature for 1 hour. Turn on to a floured surface and knead for 2-3 minutes.

/ 7 / Using both hands, roll the dough into a sausage shape, about 40.5 cm (16 inches) long. Place on a greased baking sheet.

/ 8 / With a pair of sharp scissors held at a 30° angle to the top surface of the dough, make V-shaped cuts about three-quarters of the way through it at 5 cm (2 inch) intervals.

/ 9 / Pull each section of dough out to alternate sides to give a 'zigzag' appearance. Leave to prove in a warm place until doubled in bulk.

/ 10 / Brush the dough with beaten egg, then sprinkle with poppy seeds. Bake in the oven at 230°C (450°F) mark 8 for 30 minutes until golden. Cool on a wire rack before serving.

BROWN SODA BREAD

Soda bread is the ideal bread to make when you are short of time for baking. The raising agent in soda bread is bicarbonate of soda mixed with an acid, which releases the carbon dioxide necessary to make the bread light. In this recipe, fresh milk is made sour (acid) with cream of tartar, but you can use bicarbonate of soda on its own with sour milk or buttermilk, which will provide enough acid without the cream of tartar. The end result is much the same whichever ingredients you use, although bread made with buttermilk does tend to have a softer texture.

Soda bread is best eaten really fresh – on the day of baking. Serve with cheese, tomatoes and spring onions for a home-made 'ploughman's lunch'.

BROWN SODA BREAD

SERVES 6

550 g (1¼ lb) plain wholemeal flour
350 g (12 oz) plain white flour
10 ml (2 tsp) bicarbonate of soda
20 ml (4 tsp) cream of tartar
10 ml (2 tsp) salt
900 ml (1½ pints) milk and water, mixed

/ 1 / Grease a baking sheet. Sift the flours, bicarbonate of soda, cream of tartar and salt into a bowl. Stir in the bran left in the bottom of the sieve. Add enough milk and water to mix to a soft dough.

/ 2 / Turn the dough on to a floured surface and knead lightly until smooth and soft.

/ 3 / Shape the dough into a round. Score into quarters with a sharp knife and place on the greased baking sheet.

/ 4 / Bake in the oven at 220°C (425°F) mark 7 for 25-30 minutes until the bottom of the bread sounds hollow when tapped with the knuckles of your hand. Cool on a wire rack.

PITTA BREAD

MAKES 6

450 g (1 lb) plain wholemeal flour
7.5 ml (1½ tsp) baking powder
5 ml (1 tsp) salt
1 egg, beaten
30 ml (2 tbsp) polyunsaturated oil
225 ml (8 fl oz) natural low-fat yogurt
about 100 ml (4 fl oz) semi-skimmed milk

/ 1 / Sift the flour, baking powder and salt into a bowl. Stir in the bran left in the bottom of the sieve. Make a well in the centre and stir in the egg, oil, yogurt and enough of the milk to form a soft dough.

/ 2 / Turn on to a lightly floured surface and knead well for 2-3 minutes until smooth. Divide into 6 equal pieces and roll out each piece into an oval shape about 20.5 cm (8 inches) long.

/ 3 / Preheat a grill. Place 2 pitta breads at a time on a baking sheet and brush each with a little water. Grill under a moderate heat for 2-3 minutes on each side until golden brown. Serve while still warm.

Brown Soda Bread

PARATHAS

Fried Unleavened Wholemeal Bread

MAKES 8

225 g (8 oz) plain wholemeal flour

ghee or melted margarine, for brushing

/ 1 / Put the flour in a bowl and mix in 150-200 ml (5-7 fl oz) water to form a stiff dough.

/ 2 / Turn on to a lightly floured surface and with floured hands knead thoroughly for 6-8 minutes until smooth and elastic.

/ 3 / Return the dough to the bowl, cover with a damp cloth and leave for 15 minutes.

/ 4 / Divide the dough into 8 pieces. With floured hands, take a piece of dough and shape into a smooth ball. Dip in flour to coat, then roll out on a floured surface into any of the shapes below.

TRIANGULAR PARATHAS

Roll out the piece of dough to a round about 12.5 cm (5 inches) in diameter. Brush a little melted ghee or margarine on top. Fold the round in half, brush the top with ghee or margarine and fold in half again to make a triangle. Press the layers together and, using a little extra flour, roll out thinly into a large triangle, the sides measuring about 18 cm (7 inches).

ROUND PARATHAS

Roll out the piece of dough to a round about 15 cm (6 inches) in diameter. Brush a little melted ghee or margarine on top. Roll the round into a tube shape, hold the tube upright and place one end in the centre of your hand. Carefully wind the rest of the roll around the centre point to form a disc. Press lightly together and, using a little extra flour, roll out thinly into a round about 15 cm (6 inches) in diameter.

SQUARE PARATHAS

Roll out the piece of dough to a round about 12.5 cm (5 inches) in diameter. Brush a little melted ghee or margarine on top. Fold one side of the round into the centre and fold in the opposite side to meet the first to form a rectangle. Brush the top with ghee or margarine and repeat the folding to form a square. Using a little extra flour, roll out thinly into a square about 15 cm (6 inches).

/ 5 / Cover with a damp cloth and roll out the remaining dough to make 8 parathas.

/ 6 / Heat a *tava* (flat Indian frying pan), a heavy frying pan or griddle over a low flame. Place 1 paratha in the hot pan and cook until small bubbles appear on the surface. Turn the paratha over and brush the top with melted ghee or margarine. Cook until the underside is golden brown, turn again and brush with ghee or margarine. Press down the edges and cook the other side until golden brown.

/ 7 / Brush with ghee or margarine and serve at once or keep warm wrapped in foil. Continue cooking the remaining parathas.

CHAPPATIS

Unleavened Wholemeal Bread

MAKES 8-10

225 g (8 oz) plain wholemeal flour

melted ghee or margarine, for brushing

/ 1 / Put the flour in a bowl and mix in 150-200 ml (5-7 fl oz) water to form a stiff dough.

/ 2 / Turn on to a lightly floured surface and, with floured hands, knead thoroughly for 6-8 minutes until smooth and elastic.

/ 3 / Return the dough to the bowl, cover with a damp cloth and leave for 15 minutes.

/ 4 / Set a *tava* (flat Indian frying pan), a heavy frying pan or griddle to heat over a low flame. Divide the dough into 8-10 pieces. With floured hands, take a piece of dough and shape into a smooth ball. Dip in flour to coat, then put on to a floured surface and roll out to a round about 12.5 cm (5 inches) in diameter and 1 cm (½ inch) thick.

/ 5 / Slap the chappati on to the hot pan or griddle. As soon as brown specks appear on the underside, turn it over and repeat on the other side. Turn it over again and with a clean tea-towel, press down the edges of the chappati to circulate the steam and make the chappati puff up. Cook until the underside is golden brown, and then cook the other side in the same way. Brush with the melted ghee or margarine. Serve at once or keep warm wrapped in foil. Continue cooking the remaining chappatis.

PARATHAS

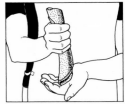

To make round parathas: roll out the piece of dough to a round about 15 cm (6 inches) in diameter. Brush a little melted ghee or margarine on top. Roll the round into a tube shape, hold the tube upright and place one end in the centre of your hand.

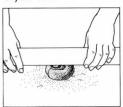

Carefully wind the rest of the roll around the centre point to form a disc. Press lightly together and, using a little extra flour, roll out thinly into a round about 15 cm (6 inches) in diameter.

A teabread mixture is usually less rich than a cake, but no less delicious for that. Serve it sliced and thinly spread with butter or margarine, like good fresh bread. It is excellent served with afternoon tea or mid-morning coffee or try it occasionally as a lunchtime pudding. A fruity teabread like this one improves as it matures, the flavour and moisture from the fruit penetrating the cake and mellowing it over a number of days.

In continental Europe it is traditional to serve sweet breads for breakfast, with either butter or cheese. Try thin slices of Edam or Gouda cheese or spread with curd cheese instead of butter.

PRUNE AND NUT TEABREAD

SERVES 8 - 10

275 g (10 oz) self-raising flour
pinch of salt
7.5 ml (1½ tsp) ground cinnamon
75 g (3 oz) butter or block margarine, cut into pieces
75 g (3 oz) raw cane demerara sugar
1 egg, beaten
100 ml (4 fl oz) milk
50 g (2 oz) shelled walnuts, chopped
100 g (4 oz) stoned no-soak prunes
15 ml (1 tbsp) clear honey

/ 1 / Grease a 2 litre (3½ pint) loaf tin. Base-line the loaf tin with greaseproof paper and grease the paper.

/ 2 / Sift the flour and salt into a bowl and add the cinnamon. Rub in the butter or margarine until the mixture resembles fine breadcrumbs.

/ 3 / Stir in the sugar, and make a well in the centre. Add the egg and milk and gradually draw in the dry ingredients to form a smooth dough using a wooden spoon.

/ 4 / Using floured hands shape the mixture into 16 even-sized rounds. Place 8 in the base of the tin. Sprinkle over half the nuts.

/ 5 / Snip the prunes and sprinkle on top of the nuts. Place the remaining dough rounds on top and sprinkle over the remaining walnuts.

/ 6 / Bake in the oven at 190°C (375°F) mark 5 for about 50 minutes or until firm to the touch. Check near the end of cooking time and cover with a piece of greaseproof paper if the tea-bread is overbrowning.

/ 7 / Turn out on to a wire rack to cool for 1 hour. When cold, brush with the honey to glaze. Wrap and store for 1-2 days in an airtight tin before slicing and buttering.

Prune and Nut Teabread

Mixed Fruit Teabread

MIXED FRUIT TEABREAD

SERVES 8 - 10

175 g (6 oz) raisins
100 g (4 oz) sultanas
50 g (2 oz) currants
175 g (6 oz) raw cane sugar
300 ml (½ pint) strained cold tea
1 egg, beaten
225 g (8 oz) plain wholemeal flour
7.5 ml (1½ tsp) baking powder
2.5 ml (½ tsp) ground mixed spice

/ 1 / Place the dried fruit and the sugar in a bowl. Pour over the tea; soak overnight.

/ 2 / The next day, grease and base-line a 900 g (2 lb) loaf tin. Add the egg, flour, baking powder and mixed spice to the fruit and tea mixture. Beat thoroughly with a wooden spoon until all the ingredients are combined.

/ 3 / Spoon the mixture into the prepared tin. Level the surface.

/ 4 / Bake in the oven at 180°C (350°F) mark 4 for about 1¼ hours until well risen and a skewer inserted in the centre comes out clean.

/ 5 / Turn the teabread out of the tin and leave on a wire rack until completely cold. Wrap in cling film and store in an airtight container for 1-2 days before slicing and eating.

Serve this moist, fruity teabread sliced and buttered at teatime.

205

WHOLEMEAL DATE AND BANANA BREAD

SERVES 10-12

225 g (8 oz) stoned dates, roughly chopped

5 ml (1 tsp) bicarbonate of soda

300 ml (½ pint) semi-skimmed milk

275 g (10 oz) self-raising wholemeal flour

100 g (4 oz) butter or margarine, cut into pieces

75 g (3 oz) shelled hazelnuts, chopped

2 ripe medium bananas

1 egg, beaten

30 ml (2 tbsp) clear honey

/ 1 / Grease and base line a 1 kg (2 lb) loaf tin. Put the dates in a saucepan with the bicarbonate of soda and milk. Bring slowly to boiling point, stirring, then remove the saucepan from the heat and leave until the chopped dates and milk are cold.

This lovely moist bread, more like a dense cake in texture, can be served un-buttered at teatime. It can be made entirely without sugar because of the high proportion of dates used. Dates have the highest natural sugar content of all dried fruit and if used in breads such as this one there is no need to add extra sugar.

/ 2 / Put the flour in a large bowl and rub in the butter or margarine until the mixture resembles breadcrumbs. Stir in the hazelnuts, reserving 30 ml (2 tbsp) for decorating.

/ 3 / Peel and mash the bananas, then add to the flour mixture with the dates and the egg. Beat well to mix.

/ 4 / Spoon the mixture into the prepared tin. Bake in the oven at 180°C (350°F) mark 4 for 1-1¼ hours until a skewer inserted in the centre comes out clean.

/ 5 / Leave the loaf to cool in the tin for about 5 minutes. Turn out, peel off the lining paper and place the right way up on a rack.

/ 6 / Heat the honey gently, then brush over the top of the loaf. Sprinkle the reserved hazelnuts on to the honey and leave until cold. Store in an airtight tin if not eating the tea-bread immediately.

Oat Crunchies; Wholemeal Date and Banana Bread

SPICED WALNUT SCONES

MAKES 16

225 g (8 oz) plain wholemeal flour
15 ml (1 tbsp) baking powder
2.5 ml (½ tsp) ground mixed spice
pinch of salt
50 g (2 oz) butter or margarine, cut into pieces
15 ml (1 tbsp) raw cane sugar
75 g (3 oz) walnut pieces, roughly chopped
10 ml (2 tsp) lemon juice
200 ml (7 fl oz) semi-skimmed milk
clear honey, to decorate

/ 1 / Sift the flour into a bowl with the baking powder, mixed spice and salt. Stir in the bran left in the bottom of the sieve. Rub in the butter or margarine until the mixture resembles breadcrumbs. Stir in the sugar and two-thirds of the walnuts.

/ 2 / Mix the lemon juice with 170 ml (6 fl oz) of the milk and stir into the dry ingredients until evenly mixed.

/ 3 / Turn the dough on to a floured surface and knead lightly until smooth and soft.

/ 4 / Roll out the dough to a 20.5 cm (8 inch) square and place on a baking sheet. Mark the surface into 16 squares, cutting the dough through to a depth of 0.3 cm (⅛ inch). Lightly brush the dough with the remaining milk.

/ 5 / Bake in the oven at 220°C (425°F) mark 7 for about 18 minutes or until well risen, golden brown and firm to the touch. Cut into squares. Brush with honey and sprinkle with the remaining chopped walnut pieces. Serve warm.

OAT CRUNCHES

MAKES 12

75 g (3 oz) plain wholemeal flour
75 g (3 oz) rolled (porridge) oats
75 g (3 oz) raw cane demerara sugar
100 g (4 oz) butter or margarine
100 g (4 oz) dried apricots, soaked in cold water overnight

/ 1 / Lightly grease a shallow oblong tin measuring 28×18×3.5 cm (11×7×1½ inches).

/ 2 / Mix together the flour, oats and sugar in a bowl. Rub in the butter or margarine until the mixture resembles breadcrumbs.

/ 3 / Spread half the mixture over the base of the tin, pressing it down. Drain and chop the apricots. Spread them over the oat mixture.

/ 4 / Sprinkle over the remaining crumb mixture and press down well. Bake in the oven at 180°C (350°F) mark 4 for 25 minutes until golden brown. Leave in the tin for about 1 hour until cold. Cut into bars to serve.

WHEATMEAL RINGS

MAKES ABOUT 20

175 g (6 oz) plain wholemeal flour
1.25 ml (¼ tsp) bicarbonate of soda
1.25 ml (¼ tsp) salt
50 g (2 oz) raw cane sugar
75 g (3 oz) butter or margarine, cut into pieces
100 g (4 oz) currants
50 g (2 oz) rolled (porridge) oats
1 egg, beaten

/ 1 / Grease 2 baking sheets. Sift the flour, bicarbonate of soda, salt and sugar into a bowl. Rub in the butter or margarine until the mixture resembles breadcrumbs.

/ 2 / Stir in the currants and oats, then stir in the beaten egg and just enough water (about 15 ml/1 tbsp) to bind the mixture together. Knead in the bowl until smooth. Cover and refrigerate for 20 minutes.

/ 3 / On a lightly floured surface, roll the dough out to about 0.5 cm (¼ inch) thickness. Cut into rounds with a 6.5 cm (2½ inch) fluted cutter and remove the centres with a 2.5 cm (1 inch) cutter.

/ 4 / Carefully transfer the rings to the prepared baking sheets. Re-roll the trimmings as necessary. Refrigerate for at least 20 minutes.

/ 5 / Bake in the oven at 190°C (375°F) mark 5 for about 15 minutes until firm. Transfer to a wire rack to cool for 30 minutes.

SPICED WALNUT SCONES

Roll out the dough to a 20.5 cm (8 inch) square and place on a baking sheet. Mark the surface into 16 squares, cutting the dough through to a depth of 0.3 cm (⅛ inch). Lightly brush the dough with the remaining milk.

Quick to make from store cupboard ingredients, these scones can be served plain or buttered, whichever you prefer.

CAROB AND NUT CAKE

SERVES 6 - 8

175 g (6 oz) butter or margarine
100 g (4 oz) raw cane sugar
4 eggs, separated
75 g (3 oz) plain wholemeal flour
25 g (1 oz) carob powder
pinch of salt
finely grated rind and juice of 1 orange
two 75 g (2.65 oz) orange-flavoured or plain carob bars
75 g (3 oz) shelled walnuts, chopped

Break the carob bars into small pieces and add to the juice, then heat gently until melted. Stir to combine, then remove from the heat and beat in the remaining butter or margarine. Leave to cool for about 10 minutes, stirring occasionally.

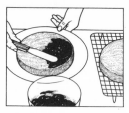

Spread half of the melted carob mixture over 1 of the cakes and sprinkle with half of the walnuts. Top with the remaining cake and swirl the remaining melted carob over the top. Sprinkle the remaining nuts around the edge to decorate.

Carob gives this teatime cake a delicious chocolate flavour. Both carob powder and carob bars are obtainable from health food shops.

/ 1 / Grease and base-line two 18 cm (7 inch) sandwich tins. Put 125 g (4 oz) of the butter or margarine in a bowl with the sugar and beat together until light and fluffy. Beat in the egg yolks one at a time.

/ 2 / Sift together the flour, carob powder and salt, stirring in any bran left in the sieve. Fold into the creamed mixture with the orange rind and 15 ml (1 tbsp) of the orange juice.

/ 3 / Whisk the egg whites until standing in stiff peaks, then fold into the cake mixture until evenly incorporated.

/ 4 / Divide the mixture equally between the prepared tins. Level the surface of the mixture, then bake in the oven at 180°C (350°F) mark 4 for 20 minutes or until risen and firm.

/ 5 / Leave to cool in the tins for 1-2 minutes, then turn out on to a wire rack and peel off the lining papers. Turn the cakes the right way up and leave to cool completely.

/ 6 / Make the filling and topping. Pour the remaining orange juice into a heatproof bowl standing over a pan of simmering water.

/ 7 / Break the carob bars into small pieces and add to the juice, then heat gently until melted. Stir to combine, then remove from the heat and beat in the remaining butter or margarine. Cool for 10 minutes, stirring occasionally.

/ 8 / Spread half of the melted carob mixture over 1 of the cakes and sprinkle with half of the walnuts. Top with the remaining cake and swirl the remaining melted carob over the top. Sprinkle the remaining nuts around the edge to decorate.

GUERNSEY APPLE CAKE

SERVES 8

225 g (8 oz) plain wholemeal flour

10 ml (2 tsp) freshly grated nutmeg

5 ml (1 tsp) ground cinnamon

10 ml (2 tsp) baking powder

225 g (8 oz) cooking apples, peeled, cored and chopped

100 g (4 oz) butter

225 g (8 oz) raw cane sugar

2 eggs, beaten

15 ml (1 tbsp) clear honey

15 ml (1 tbsp) raw cane demerara sugar

/ 1 / Grease an 18 cm (7 inch) deep round loose-bottomed cake tin. Line with grease-proof paper and grease the paper.

/ 2 / Sift together the flour, nutmeg, cinnamon and baking powder, stirring in any bran left in the sieve. Mix in the chopped cooking apples and stir well to combine.

/ 3 / Put the butter and raw cane sugar into a bowl and beat until pale and fluffy. Add the eggs, a little at a time, and continue to beat with a wooden spoon.

/ 4 / Fold the flour and spice mixture into the creamed mixture.

/ 5 / Turn the mixture into the prepared tin. Bake in the oven at 170°C (325°F) mark 3 for about 1½ hours. Turn out on to a wire rack to cool for 1-2 hours. Brush with honey and sprinkle with the demerara sugar to decorate. Eat within 1-2 days.

Guernsey Apple Cake

Lemon Cake

L E M O N   C A K E

S E R V E S   8

25 g (1 oz) butter or margarine
30 ml (2 tbsp) semi-skimmed milk
3 eggs
75 g (3 oz) raw cane sugar
50 g (2 oz) plain wholemeal flour
25 g (1 oz) bran
5 ml (1 tsp) baking powder
finely grated rind of 1 lemon
175 g (6 oz) quark or low-fat soft cheese
20 ml (4 tsp) lemon juice
30 ml (2 tbsp) clear honey

/ 1 / Grease and base-line two 18 cm (7 inch) sandwich tins. Grease the lining papers. Put the butter or margarine and milk in a saucepan. Warm until the fat melts. Cool slightly.

/ 2 / Put the eggs and sugar in a large bowl. Using an electric whisk, beat the mixture until very thick and light.

/ 3 / Fold in the flour, bran, baking powder and lemon rind. Gently stir in the cooled fat until evenly incorporated.

/ 4 / Divide the mixture between the prepared tins. Bake in the oven at 190°C (375°F) mark 5 for about 25 minutes until firm to the touch. Leave to cool for a few minutes in the tins, then turn out on to a wire rack. Remove the lining paper and leave to cool for about 1 hour.

/ 5 / Put the quark, lemon juice and honey in a bowl and beat together until evenly mixed. Use half to sandwich the cakes together and swirl the remaining half on top to decorate. Keep in a cool place until serving time.

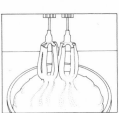

Put the eggs and sugar in a large bowl. Using an electric whisk, beat the mixture until very thick and light.

Ring the changes of the flavouring by substituting all or half the lemon rind and juice with orange.

211

MENU SUGGESTIONS

WEEKEND BREAKFAST

DRIED FRUIT COMPOTE
(see page 12)

SMOKED FISH KEDGEREE
(see page 17)

BRAN MUFFINS
(see page 12) served with honey

LIGHT LUNCH

ICED SWEET PEPPER SOUP
(see page 20)

FETTUCINE WITH CLAM SAUCE
(see page 49)

CAULIFLOWER, BEAN AND CAPER SALAD
(see page 141)

GINGER FRUIT SALAD
(see page 185)

INDIAN-STYLE LUNCH

BUTTERFLY PRAWNS
(see page 35)

MOONG DAL AND SPINACH
(see page 128)

CHAPPATIS
(see page 203)

CHILLI, AUBERGINE AND PEPPER SALAD
(see page 143)

ALMOND AND MANGO ICE CREAM,
HALF QUANTITY
(see page 170)

VEGETARIAN LUNCH

MARINATED MUSHROOMS
(see page 38)

SPICY VEGETABLE PIE
(see page 124)

APPLE AND LEMON SORBET
(see page 178)

INFORMAL SUMMER LUNCH

Mussels with Garlic and Parsley
(see page 37)

Mushroom Flan
(see page 47)

Summer Vegetable Fricassée
(see page 153)

Summer Fruit Salad
(see page 191)

SUMMER BUFFET FOR TWELVE

Hors d'oeuvres variés,
DOUBLE QUANTITY
(see page 35)

Smoked Fish Timbale,
DOUBLE QUANTITY
(see page 59)

Vegetable Terrine
(see page 55)

Cheese and Pineapple Salad,
DOUBLE QUANTITY
(see page 74)

Rice Salad,
DOUBLE QUANTITY
(see page 146)

Minted Strawberry Custards
(see page 173)

Lemon Muesli Cheesecake
(see page 176)

Exotic Fruit Salad
(see page 181)

MEDITERRANEAN MEAL

Spanish Summer Soup
(see page 27)

Italian Chicken with Rosemary
(see page 108)

Crisp Endive with Orange and Croûtons,
HALF QUANTITY
(see page 143)

Charentais Granita
(see page 170)

MID-WEEK DINNER PARTY

Chilled Cucumber Soup
(see page 20)

Quick Chicken and Mussel Paella
(see page 114)

Tomato, Avocado and Pasta Salad
(see page 141)

Flambé Bananas
(see page 186)

WINTER DINNER PARTY FOR SIX

Smoked Mackerel with Apple
(see page 39)

Lamb with Rosemary
(see page 88)

Potato and Carrot Casserole,
TREBLE QUANTITY
(see page 154)

Pears with Blackcurrant Sauce
(see page 192)

VEGETARIAN DINNER PARTY

Avocado Ramekins
(see page 32)

Stuffed Aubergines
(see page 124)

Tomato Sauce
(see page 154)

Boiled Rice
(see page 146)

Spinach and Mushroom Salad
(see page 140)

Pineapple and Banana Flambé,
HALF QUANTITY
(see page 190)

SUMMER DINNER PARTY

Artichoke Hearts à la Grécque
(see page 30)

Stuffed Plaice Fillets
(see page 130)

New potatoes cooked in their skins

Fennel and Tomato Salad
(see page 142)

Raspberry Bombe
(see page 173)

SLIMMERS' SUPPER

Tomato Ice with Vegetable Julienne
(see page 28)

Slimmers' Moussaka
(see page 104)

Greek Salad
(see page 43)

Strawberry Cream,
TWO-THIRDS QUANTITY
(see page 178)

INDEX

Lamb burgers with cucumber, minted 92
Lamb cutlets with lemon and garlic 85
Lamb grill, minted 79
Lamb in tomato sauce 79
Lamb kebabs, marinated 83
Lamb kebabs, spicy 80
Lamb korma 79
Lamb meatballs, minted 92
Lamb with courgettes and mushrooms 74
Lamb with rosemary 88
Lamb with spinach, spiced 82
Lemon cake 211
Lemon mayonnaise 149
Lemon muesli cheesecake 176
Lentil and celery peppers 166
Lentil croquettes 61
Lentil hot pot 156-7
Lettuce and mushroom cocotte 38
Lettuce soup 20
Liver and tomato, pan-fried 90
Liver goujons with orange sauce 88
Liver with vermouth 82

M
Mayonnaise 149
Mayonnaise, piquant 149
Meat loaf 98
Melon and prawn salad 41
Mexican re-fried beans 150
Mixed fruit teabread 205
Monkfish with mustard seeds 132
Moong dal and spinach 128-9
Moussaka, slimmers' 104
Mozzarella, avocado and tomato salad 43
Muesli 11
Mushroom flan 47
Mushrooms, marinated 38
Mussels with garlic and parsley 37
Mustard vinaigrette 149

N
Navarin d'agneau 80
Nut burgers, curried 70-1

O
Oat crunchies 207

P
Paprika beef 103
Parathas 203
Pasta, prawn and apple salad 50
Pears in cinnamon and honey wine, crunchy 175
Pears with blackcurrant sauce 192
Pepper and tomato omelette 71
Peppercorn burgers 58
Pineapple and banana flambé 190

Piperana 164
Pitta bread 202
Plaice fillets, stuffed 131
Poppy seed granary round 198
Pork chops, crumb-topped 96
Potato and carrot casserole 154
Potatoes with dill, hot 164-5
Potato skins, crunchy baked 55
Potted chicken with tarragon 38
Prawn risotto 49
Prune and nut teabread 204

R
Rabbit with cider and mustard 96
Raspberry bombe 173
Ratatouille, chilled 40
Red cabbage and apple casserole 158
Red kidney bean hot pot 123
Rhubarb brown betty 172
Rice, boiled 146
Rice salad 146-7
Rogan josh 94
Root vegetable hot pot 127
Rouille 150
Rum and coffee junket 189

S
Saffron rice, sweet Indian 182
Sag aloo 158
Salad, Japanese 144
Seafood curry 132
Seafood stir-fry 130
Shami kebabs 42
Smoked fish kedgeree 17
Smoked fish timbale 59
Smoked mackerel with apple 39
Smoked salmon pâté 28
Smoked trout with tomatoes and mushrooms 31
Soda bread, brown 202
Southern baked beans 56
Spaghetti with ratatouille sauce 57
Spanish cod with peppers and garlic 137
Spanish summer soup 27
Spinach and mushroom salad 140-1
Spinach pancakes 74-5
Spinach roulade 51
Spinach soup 23
Squid stew, Italian 134-5
Strawberries with raspberry sauce 185
Strawberry cream, 178
Strawberry custards, minted 173
Summer fruit salad 191
Summer soup, Spanish 27
Summer vegetable fricassée 153
Sweet pepper soup, iced 20

T
Tabouleh 144-5
Tagliatelle with cheese and nut sauce 67
Tandoori chicken 106
Tandoori chicken kebabs 108
Tandoori fish 134
Taramasalata 30-1
Tofu burgers with tomato sauce 57
Tomato and yogurt dressing 150
Tomato, avocado and pasta salad 141
Tomato ice with vegetable julienne 28
Tomato mayonnaise 149
Trout with yogurt dressing, chilled 47
Tuna and pasta in soured cream 67
Turkey curry, quick 120
Turkey escalopes en papillote 114
Turkey groundnut stew 117
Turkey in spiced yogurt 115
Turkey with cranberry and coconut 121
Turnips in curry cream sauce 157

V
Veal with peppers, spiced 98
Vegetable and oatmeal broth 27
Vegetable biryani 120
Vegetable fricassée, summer 153
Vegetable lasagne 123
Vegetable pie, spicy 124
Vegetable pilau 158-9
Vegetable purées, trio of 160
Vegetable soup 23
Vegetable stir-fry, Chinese 162
Vegetable terrine 55
Vegetable vitality drink 11

W
Walnut pear slice 191
Walnut scones, spiced 207
Watercress mayonnaise 149
Wheatmeal rings 207
Wholemeal bread 200
Wholemeal bread, quick 197
Wholemeal date and banana bread 206
Wholewheat apricot and nut salad 71
Wholewheat brazil salad 129
Wholewheat macaroni bake 62

Y
Yogurt dressing 150
Yogurt vitality drink 11

Z
Zigzag baton 200